A Vision of Vygotsky

Joan Wink

California State University, Stanislaus

LeAnn G. Putney

University of Nevada, Las Vegas

Allyn and Bacon

Boston ■ London ■ Toronto ■ Sydney ■ Tokyo ■ Singapore

Series Editor: *Arnis E. Burvikovs*
Editorial Assistant: *Matthew Forster*
Editorial-Production Administrator: *Kathy Smith*
Editorial-Production Service: *Chestnut Hill Enterprises, Inc.*
Composition and Prepress Buyer: *Linda Cox*
Manufacturing Buyer: *Suzanne Lareau*
Cover Administrator: *Kristina Mose-Libon*
Electronic Composition: *Omegatype Typography, Inc.*

Between the time Website information is gathered and then published, it is not unusual for some sites to have closed. Also, the transcription of URLs can result in unintended typographical errors. The publisher would appreciate notification where these occur so that they may be corrected in subsequent editions. Thank you.

Library of Congress Cataloging-in-Publication Data
Wink, Joan.
  A vision of Vygotsky / Joan Wink, LeAnn Putney.
    p. cm.
  Includes bibliographical references and index.
  ISBN 0-321-08240-0
    1. Vygotskiæ, L. S. (Lev Semenovich), 1896–1934. 2. Psychology—Soviet Union—History. I. Putney, LeAnn. II. Title.

  BF109.V95 W56 2001
  150'.92–dc21   2001040179

Printed in the United States of America
10 9 8 7 6 5 4 3 2   06 05 04 03 02

CONTENTS

DEDICATION

To Lev Vygotsky, our distant mentor.

This book is the culmination of our learning, teaching, researching, and living in and out of our educational spaces with others too numerous to list individually. We have taught and learned about Vygotsky in the courses we have taken and the courses we have taught. We have learned from our readings and discussions with others, and from our own experiences. We made meaning with others, and then we made sense for ourselves. The journey of this book has been a Vygotskian adventure, which we have written in and between the nooks and crannies of our complex lives.

Along the way we have encountered colleagues, mentors, classroom students and teachers, administrators, and preservice teachers who have shared ideas in class, in informal chats with us, as well as in our research endeavors. Many times their experiences were far more compelling than any we could conceive; thus, their histories appear in this book. We thank those participants, educators all, because we have learned much from our educational journeys with them.

We are indebted to Dawn for sharing the *grit and grace* of her life with us as we journeyed through this book. The insightful and critical comments from Judith illuminated specific pebbles in our path.

We honor all of the teachers/learners who have taught/learned with us along the way. Each of you has contributed immensely to our learning and developing. As we have continued to write this book with your help, we salute you for your daily work to right the world. We specifically acknowledge the contributions of Andrea from Tracey, Beth from Santa Barbara, Chris from Turlock, Chris from Las Vegas, Debbie from Las Vegas, Elaine from the Sierras, Juanita from Las Vegas, Nancy from Las Vegas, Pam from Modesto, Sharon from Modesto, Sherry from Israel, and Yvette from Las Vegas. Denise of Accent on Words was a helpful surprise who made the trip easier. Many students in our classes were willing to read, comment, and critically question. Thank you. We hope you know how you are woven throughout this book.

Although many have contributed, we are responsible for the interpretations of their sharing. It is not what people say, it is what people mean. Many times, we felt we heard the words of Horton and Freire (1990): We make this path by walking.

The editorial support for this journey has had some unexpected turns in the road. In the days when Longman's was Longman's, this book was originally discussed with Ginny Blanford. When Longman's became Addison Wesley Longman's, Art Pomponio joined in the discussion and encouraged us to focus on this specific project. Eventually, Amy Cronin guided us for part of the journey. Priscilla McGeehon jumped in to support us during various sharp curves in the road. When we were nearing the end of the road, a new home, Allyn & Bacon, suddenly emerged and beckoned us. Arnis Burvikovs and Matthew Forster took over and guided this project through to its final form. We especially appreciate the careful and detailed work of the copy editors. To all of these editors and the encompassing support of Pearson Publishing, we are indebted. We appreciate their support and encouragement even as the publishing world continued to transform itself throughout the process.

We wish to thank the following reviewers whose reading helped our writing: Edward E. Coates, Abilene Christian University; William E. Herman, SUNY, Potsdam; Hermine H. Marshall, San Francisco State University; Stacey Neubarth-Pritchett, the University of Georgia; and Barba Patton, University of Houston–Victoria. We appreciate their thorough, critical, and timely comments. To our colleagues at California State University, Stanislaus and University of Nevada, Las Vegas who support us and make us glad to be where we are, we thank you.

In some cases, the learning and writing continued because of the support of those outside of education and academia, yet who are central to our lives. Betty from Turlock has followed our journey since it began, and kept encouraging us throughout the process. Tom offered steadfast technical assistance as our *alpha-geek;* he provided his unwavering love and support as spouse of LeAnn. Dean continued his ongoing love and good humor, both as our *alpha-rancher,* and as supportive spouse of Joan. During this process, we were blessed with the addition of Wynn, who joined her brothers, Wyatt and Luke, in giving us just one more book to read, as we wrote. Bo and Lisa joined other family members and friends who offered encouragement, listened to us talk Vygotsky, offered suggestions and questions, made us think more, and made space for us to "Lev-itate." We are thankful for having had the opportunity to accomplish this journey.

PREFACE

Education is just as meaningless outside the real world as is a fire without oxygen, or as is breathing in a vacuum. The teacher's educational work, therefore, must inevitably be connected with his creative, social, and life work.
(Vygotsky, 1997, p. 345)

This is a book about Vygotsky: the man and a vision of his pedagogy. Our purpose is to introduce students of education and psychology to Vygotskian theories of teaching, learning, and development as described in the legacy of his written documents. The complexity of the sociocultural context of our time raises new questions and calls each of us to reexamine, rethink, and regenerate principles and practices that inform the pedagogical context of today. Our own search for new understandings of teaching, learning, and development has led us to Vygotsky, the educator/psychologist from the past who offers hope for the future.

Vygotsky was a Russian psychologist who continues to influence educational thought decades after his death. John-Steiner and Meehan (2000, p. 37) describe Vygotsky as a "distant teacher" whose work continues to inspire us to think and rethink his constructs as well as our own educational processes. In pre- and post-revolutionary Russia, he generated enthusiasm and excitement in his continuing search to comprehend and articulate the processes of learning. The fact that we are able to know even parts of his life is a tribute to the power of his ideas as very little was written about him while he was still living. His legacy does not include an autobiography, nor a complete biography; rather, it leaves us with ideas that are relevant for our own time.

The Vygotskian Metaphor: Water

One of the greatest influences on Vygotsky was his early study of the work of the philosopher, Hegel. In his own work, Vygotsky tried to apply the Hegelian theory of dialectics: the combination of two seemingly opposite elements into one distinct entity. This new synthesis of elements contains the properties of both, yet the distinct properties are changed by the very process of combining them. Vygotsky (1986) used the metaphor of water to explain his perceptions of teaching, learning, and development within the sociocultural context. Water, when separated into its parts, is qualitatively changed. The separate atoms of two parts hydrogen and one part oxygen are not water; it is their union that creates water. If we want to understand the properties of water that extinguish fire, we cannot do so by studying the separated elements because hydrogen (H_2) burns and oxygen (O) sustains combustion. It is only by conceiving of the union, or the synthesis of its parts, that we can understand the properties of water that allow it to extinguish fire (Figure 1: The Vygotskian Metaphor of Water).

Just as one cannot separate water into its distinct parts (H_2O) and still maintain the integrity of water, so, too, one cannot separate the individual from the context and still have a complete understanding of either. The unification of a person within that social, cultural, historical, and political context informs our understanding of this dialectical relationship. We will extend this Vygotskian metaphor of water to our interpretation of pedagogy. In this text pedagogy will not be two separate processes of a teacher, teaching or a learner, learning. Rather, pedagogy, itself a dialectic, is the reciprocal relationship between teaching and learning, creating more than the sum of its parts.

Dialectics

Vygotskian psychology challenges us to see the dialectical union of teaching and learning as they are enacted in human development. In his own work, Vygotsky consistently juxtaposed the work and ideas of others to generate his own views on teaching and learning. "He integrated the ideas of his contemporaries, his collaborators, and his distant teachers as part of his ongoing construction of new ideas" (John-Steiner & Meehan, 2000, p. 38).

Vygotsky saw teaching and learning as braided together in all human development. Therefore, we should study them together as we seek to understand human development through our research and learning. As Moll (1990) reveals, Vygotsky "insisted on the dialectical study of what we could call whole activities…psychological activity in all its complexity, not in isolation" (p. 6). In our study of pedagogical practice, we must look holistically at teaching and learning, learning and developing, and at individuals within their sociocultural, historical, political context. Vygotsky related development of individuals as integrally tied to development of the collective in which they learn and play (Souza Lima,

WATER
Study of the whole:
H_2O extinguishes fire.

Study of the parts:
H - burns
O - sustains fire

- Vygotsky

FIGURE 1   The Vygotskian Metaphor of Water.

1995). In other words, we must look at *mind in society*, in the spirit of Vygotsky's 1978 book of the same name.

In keeping with this Vygotskian practice of making our work dialectical, in *A Vision of Vygotsky* we will examine what we have learned from him as we compare and contrast his ideas with those of others. We recognize that our philosophical perspectives can both support and constrain our thinking process because not any one perspective or theory alone can totally express our experience. Just as Vygotsky compared theorists, we will demonstrate how a Vygotskian perspective can be complementary to and enhanced by a Freirian perspective of critical pedagogy. We will continue to juggle and juxtapose thoughts and theories, all the while maintaining our focus on the centrality of language as our salient theme.

The Overriding Theme

The overriding theme of this book will be language. When we speak of language, we refer in the broadest sense to semiotic mediation within the limitless boundaries of culture, history, and sociocultural context. We see language as a holistic reflection of experiential and cognitive knowledge grounded in sociocultural, historical, and political context. Many different perspectives have been represented in the work of Neo-Vygotskian scholars, which will be further examined throughout the chapters. Although these scholars share a common frame based on Vygotsky's work, they have interpreted his work through their unique lenses, adding a complexity to his original work because of their distinct perspectives.

For our purposes, we will use the words *social cultural* and *sociocultural* interchangeably, and, in so doing, we assume that the historical and political influences are a part of any context. Our intent remains constant: We are referring to the complex relationship of teaching, learning, and human development. In addition, we will use the terms *interactionist* and *constructivism* interchangeably. In the glossary, we will explain how construc*tiv*ism and construc*tion*ism have different meanings in the literature.

Visually Vygotsky: A Road Map for Readers

Throughout this book, a road map will connect the various parts to the whole as we theorize Vygotsky's constructs of teaching and learning within human development. Each chapter will open with a quotation from Vygotsky, which will serve to introduce the readers to the conceptual development to follow.

In working with teachers, we often use visuals to explain the complex ideas and relationships inherent in Vygotsky's work. When we feel we don't have the time to share the visuals, and have them strewn about among our teaching materials, students invariably start to rummage though them, talk about them, and then begin to scribble their own graphic representations of Vygotskian thought.

As one teacher so clearly said to us recently, "Why didn't you just show us these? Now, I get it!"

Given the powerful responses we have had to the visuals, both with students in our classes and with participants in conference presentations, we will share "Visually Vygotsky" with you as part of the path winding throughout the book. While we recognize that a one-dimensional representation is rarely adequate to fully encapsulate the meaning of abstract concepts, the visuals are still useful to generate ideas with others. It is often the very notion that the visuals do not totally capture the essence of the ideas that leads to more discussion, more ways of representing, more ways of understanding the complexity of our own thinking, speaking, knowing, and learning.

What Is New about Vygotsky?

The fact that educators continue to reapply his work in their everyday lives in different ways is what is so enduring and endearing about the man and his vision. Our purpose, however, is to expand the answers to this question by using Vygotsky's own words as he studied psychology to make sense of pedagogy. By doing this, we hope to continue in a Vygotskian holistic spirit and unify the dialectical worlds of teacher education and educational psychology.

INTRODUCTION

Even though so many years have passed, Vygotsky's thoughts, ideas, and works not only belong to history, but they still interest people. In one of his articles, A. Leontiev wrote of Vygotsky as a man decades ahead of his time. Probably that is why that he is for us not a historic figure but a living contemporary (Vygodskaya, 1995, p. 116).

This quote from Vygotsky's daughter, Gita, expresses eloquently our own thoughts about her father, Lev S. Vygotsky. We are almost as fascinated by the history of his life as we are entranced by his theories of learning and development. We never tire of finding more information about him, his work, his relations with his family, students, and colleagues. The more we learn about Vygotsky on a personal level, the more we understand his work. From our readings, we recognize that this was a man who very much lived his theories, and who strived to understand his world in order to make the world a better place for others.

Remembering My Father, by Gita L. Vygodskaya

In recent years, Vygotsky's work and information about his life has become more readily available. Shortly after his death (1934), his writings were banned and his name was removed from scientific journals by the Stalinist regime. Fortunately for us, Vygotsky's family kept his numerous manuscripts safe. After her mother's death, Gita became responsible for the documents, and in 1956 she began efforts to have them translated and published. Gita, herself a psychologist, has recently published a biography of her father, as well as various articles in Russian scientific journals. It is through her devotion to her father that the legacy of Vygotsky continues to grow and evolve.

In her reflections about her father, Gita noted that her memories of Vygotsky are dear to her and have been embellished by the recollections of other family members as well as his students and colleagues. Among those who eagerly shared memories of Vygotsky with her were Alexander R. Luria (a world-renowned neuropsychologist and colleague of Vygotsky), as well as A. V. Zaporozhetch (a prominent Russian psychologist, specialist in early childhood), and N. G. Morozova (an expert on special education and psychopathology). Through Gita's own studies and work with these prominent scholars, she learned about their teacher, her father, and their years of working together. Gita (Vygodskaya, 1995) recounted that the former students and colleagues who shared their memories with her always did so with passion and admiration.

In Gita's recollections of her father, she states that he rarely gave his opinions to his children because he preferred for them to work things out on their own. When they asked questions, rather than give a complete answer he would draw them into discussions that resulted in a commonly agreed-on answer or decision.

Vygotsky's way of viewing schooling can be seen in a reflection that Gita described as a difficult but important lesson for her as a child. She had returned from school after taking a particularly difficult test to find her father at home. Proud of the fact that she had done well on the test, Gita told her father that another child sitting next to her had not done as well on her test. Vygotsky looked very disappointed and told her that she should not be proud of her efforts to conceal information from her peer. He offered her a way to make amends:

> As always in these situations he offered me a solution: he did not want me to feel like once I did something wrong I was now incapable of doing good. He suggested to me that I go and ask my classmate about what she didn't understand, and try to patiently explain it to her, and if I couldn't do it so she would understand perfectly, then he would be glad to help me. "But here is the most important thing", he added, "you must do all this so your friend be sure you really want to help her, and really mean her well, and so it would not be unpleasant for her to accept your help". More than 60 years have passed since this incident and I still remember all of his words and try to follow them as best I can in life (Vygodskaya, 1995, p. 115).

Remembering Our Friend, by His Colleagues

Colleagues of Vygotsky have written their remembrances of him as well. While he worked with colleagues to formulate his cultural–historical theory by providing clinics in which they studied the actions of children, he would also hold lectures on his analysis of the clinical studies. Vygotsky's work was captivating to his audience as "scientific and practical workers, teacher and students from all over Moscow flocked to his demonstrations and analyses of child behaviour at clinics and lectures" (Yaroshevsky, 1989, p. 25). Not only did they fill the lecture halls, but those who could not find room inside the hall would often listen from outside the open windows. One of Vygotsky's colleagues, A. Luria (1979, p. 52), described these lectures as "great occasions" in which Vygotsky would talk from three to five hours at a time, lecturing without notes.

A key point that Luria stressed in his recollections was Vygotsky's insistence that their research should never be limited to laboratory work and divorced from the real world. In his work with handicapped children, Vygotsky "rejected simple quantitative descriptions of such children in terms of unidimensional psychological traits reflected in test scores. Instead, he relied on qualitative descriptions of the special organization of their behavior" (Luria, 1979, p. 53).

Luria also wrote that it was not an exaggeration to call Vygotsky a genius. After five decades in the scientific world, Luria noted that he "never again met a person who even approached his clearness of mind, his ability to lay bare the essential structure of complex problems, his breadth of knowledge in many fields, and his ability to foresee the future development of science" (Luria, 1979, p. 38).

Vygotsky worked tirelessly to bring together theoretical research on learning and development with educational practice as he considered scientific research itself a special form of practical activity (Yaroshevsky, 1989). As Zebroski stated: "Vygotsky was simultaneously immersed in the practical concerns of the clinician, the teacher, and the teacher educator. His 'laboratory' was spread across the Soviet Union in the hospitals, public schools, and universities of a society in transition" (Zebroski, 1994, p. 154).

In terms of how he worked with children at the clinic, one of Vygotsky's students, Lev Zankov, recalled that those who observed were amazed at how Vygotsky conversed with the children while examining them. Through his questioning of the children, Vygotsky established trust with them because he "always talked with them as though they were equals, always paid attention to their answers. In turn, the children opened up to him in a way they never did with other examiners" (Vygodskaya, 1995, pp. 112–113).

Vygotsky has been hailed by Michael Yaroshevsky, a prominent historian of psychology in Russia and a scholar of Vygotsky's legacy, as an intellectual giant because of his participation in building a new culture through his theoretical research. Vygotsky produced an incredible amount of work in his short life. His daughter relates (Vygodskaya, 1995) that "Lev Vygotsky worked feverishly and left behind a great deal: just think of how he must have worked to create, lived only 37 years, 270 pieces of scientific work!" (p. 113). The fact that he worked so hard in spite of the toll that tuberculosis incessantly took on his health continues to inspires us today.

Vygotsky and His Times

The work that Lev Vygotsky began decades ago in post-revolutionary Russia is still relevant and informative today. At least three reasons exist for the popularity of Vygotsky's work among intellectual circles: (1) his emphasis on the active contribution of humans to the development of their own consciousness; (2) the importance of social interaction in development; (3) the notion of the mediational role of language in the communicative process. (Emihovich & Souza Lima, 1995). Throughout the coming chapters we will be addressing these constructs that were central to Vygotsky's work.

Historical Beginnings: A Brief Look at the Background of Vygotsky

Who was this Russian psychologist who continues to influence us decades after his death? Who is this educator from the past who tugs us into the future? The story of his life is a source of inspiration for educators. Looking at the historical context of his life helps us to understand why his work emphasizes the fundamental importance of context and culture on language and learning. His life provides a vivid picture of how one can be highly productive under the most difficult personal and societal conditions.

During his short life in pre- and post-revolutionary Russia, Vygotsky generated enthusiasm and excitement in his continuing search for deeper understanding of the processes of learning and development. From his own experiences in learning to his early career as a teacher and teacher educator, Vygotsky's work touched and changed lives in his own sociocultural context as it does in ours today. His daughter, Gita, notes that those who learned from and with Vygotsky, years after his death still considered the thirty-seven-year-old researcher to be their teacher.

From his passion for learning during his short, difficult life, we learn and re-learn valuable lessons. We discover and rediscover our own courage in the midst of challenging educational influences and societal changes. When we are discouraged with the social, cultural, or political context of our lives, we draw strength from his personal and professional life. In this chapter we will take you through a brief history of Vygotsky's life that includes parts that were most compelling to us as we searched through the sources available (Blanck, 1990; Vygotsky, 1986; Yaroshevsky, 1989).

Vygotsky was born in 1896 in the town of Orsha, in Belorussia in northern Russia, to a middle-class Jewish family. Within the first year of his life, his family moved to Gomel where his father was a banking executive and his mother was a licensed teacher. During these pre-revolutionary years in Russia, Jewish families suffered from outside discrimination. In spite of this repressive environment, his parents surrounded their eight children with books, ideas, and conversation that would influence his work in psychology and pedagogy later in life. Learning, teaching, and collaboratively sharing were central to his sociocultural context at home. His family talked and listened to each other, creating an environment of sharing and collaboration. As the topics of conversations deepened, the language and the ideas of Vygotsky evolved.

Vygotsky's education also was enhanced by his own private tutor, who dialogued with him by implementing the Socratic method of question and answer. His genius surfaced early in his life when he attended private preparatory school after completing the primary level with independent study. Even at this stage, he was interested in a wide range of academic pursuits. During these early secondary school years, his intellect was obvious to the professors who surrounded him. He excelled in math and in classical studies, but was keenly attracted to literature, theater, and poetry. In addition, he was fluent in many languages and was an avid speed-reader. Luria described the books that Vygotsky read as *not exactly adventure novels* (Blanck, 1990, p. 33).

As we reflect on the teenage years of his life, we marvel at the complexity of his ways of knowing and his "otherness." Discrimination was a part of his life as a Jewish teenager. With the support of his family, he had the courage to follow his interest in learning as much as he could. His depth and breadth of knowledge at this point in his life were astounding, yet, according to his schoolmates (Vygodskaya, 1995), Vygotsky was not impressed with his knowledge and never acted superior. He willingly offered what he knew as assistance to others as a youngster and all his life. We imagine that Vygotsky must have believed, "What good is knowledge if you don't share it with others?" An interesting reflection might be, "What would happen to this caliber of student in public schools today?" Would this type of intellectual ability be recognized and validated? Once again, we find that Vygotsky's life speaks directly to us as educators in present-day society. Knowing about his life causes us to reflect on our own educational process.

When Vygotsky first prepared to enter the university, a quota system kept Jewish student enrollment to only 3 percent. This tiny percentage of students needed to have the best scores on tests, which would not have been a problem in his case. However, in attempting to hold down the level of intelligence represented by the Jewish community, government officials changed to a lottery system of admittance just as he was ready to enroll. On hearing this news, Lev was completely discouraged and was convinced that he would never get into a university. In an attempt to offer encouragement, his friend made a bet with Lev to try for the lottery anyway. When he was accepted, he gave his friend a book of poetry with the note: *To Senya, in memory of a lost bet* (Blanck, 1990, p. 34).

In college, Vygotsky wanted to follow his interest in the humanities. However, this area of study would lead to the field of teaching, which was denied to him because of his religion at that time. Instead, Vygotsky entered college as a medical student, but, later, decided to drop medical school in favor of law school. In order to satisfy his avid interest in the humanities, he enrolled in another university at the same time. We often think of the challenges that certainly must have faced Vygotsky as he simultaneously attended two universities. He studied philosophy and psychology while also focusing on literary criticism. Those who read Vygotsky's publications in the field of literary criticism say that it was among his best work, although it has since been lost.

In 1917, Vygotsky graduated from both universities. It is significant to remember the social context of his time: the Russian Revolution of 1917, which caused daily hardship for him, his family, and the Jewish community. His graduation and that revolution are forever joined in our minds. His entire world was undergoing fundamental massive societal changes, just as ours is as we begin the twenty-first century. Vygotsky returned home to Gomel where his family suffered greatly from illness and his town was still occupied by German forces. Both his mother and youngest brother were suffering from tuberculosis, and Vygotsky cared for both of them.

In 1919, with Russian rule finally reinstated, the law now allowed him to become a teacher. He immediately began to teach literature, aesthetics, philosophy, and Russian language in a newly opened vocational school, along with psychology and logic in a local teachers college (Vygodskaya, 1995). At this time, Vygotsky began to suffer from the tuberculosis that would take his life prematurely. During post-revolutionary Russia, there was a tremendous amount of famine, hunger, lack of heat, and terrible suffering, and Vygotsky's family was not immune to the suffering. However, this revolutionary time also produced great intellectual growth and development. Reflection on this time in history and Vygotsky's accomplishments always gives us hope. Each of us has times when our world and our educational space may not be exactly as we would wish. However, we can see how truly great ideas emerged from the people in Russia in spite of their tremendous suffering.

Although his tuberculosis continued to take its toll on his health, Vygotsky was highly productive in research and theory building. He was actively involved with a wide circle of scholars, and his ideas grew from their shared dialogues. His background as a literary critic served him in his work as a teacher of literature and history of the arts. He also organized lectures and literary discussions with the local townspeople, and participated in a publishing company with one of his cousins and a friend. Although the publishing company went out of business for lack of paper, Lev Vygotsky continued his varied activities and became "the central figure in Gomel's cultural life" (Yaroshevsky, 1989, p. 58).

Along with these activities, he continued his study and involvement with psychology, and began a search for a new psychology in order to understand the role of consciousness in child development. Because of his concern and interest in teaching and learning, he organized a special psychological laboratory in the teacher training school in which he was lecturing.

Lev Vygotsky married Rosa Noevna Smekhova in 1924. They had two daughters; Gita the eldest became an educational psychologist, while Asya was a specialist in biophysics. It is said that Rosa kept her spirits up during Vygotsky's illness, and she worked long days taking care of handicapped children after his death in 1934. Rosa died in 1979, and Asya died in 1985. Gita is now retired, living in Moscow, and continues to publish works about her father.

Shortly after his marriage to Rosa, Vygotsky became even more dedicated to developing a new psychology. He was invited to give a speech at a major scientific conference in Leningrad (then Petrograd) in 1924. It is often noted that Vygotsky began his work in psychology at this time, when he first attracted the attention of Alexander Luria (and many others) with his presentations. Later to become an associate of Vygotsky, Luria advised the Director of the Institute of Psychology to bring Vygotsky on board at the Institute in Moscow. However, to label this as the beginning of his work could be misleading, for as Yaroshevsky (1989) pointedly noted, Vygotsky would not have been able to attract such attention from noted scientists

> if he had not focused, during his years of teaching in Gomel, on the needs and tendencies of development of psychological thought under the new historical conditions.... What was conceived and matured in Gomel, saw light, developed and transformed, in Moscow (pp. 94–95).

After his appointment with the Institute of Psychology in 1924, Vygotsky devoted his life to the pursuit of a new psychology, aimed toward the development of consciousness, which was in direct opposition to the behaviorist tradition espoused by his contemporary, Pavlov, that was prevalent at that time. As part of his work in this area, Vygotsky (1997) wrote an educational psychology text for teachers from lectures he delivered as part of his educational psychology course (first published in 1926 in Russian). According to V. V. Davydov (1997), this text-book signaled a significant shift in Vygotsky's creative life. It was after this work was completed that he undertook major experiments in psychology with his colleagues, work that would contradict the concepts that were basic components of many psychology schools, including the influential U.S. behaviorist schools at that time.

Development of Consciousness: A Search for a New Psychology

One of the major contributions of Vygotsky to psychology was his work on consciousness. Because of his Marxist background, Vygotsky focused on the notion that "concrete historical activity is the generator of consciousness" (Emihovich & Souza Lima, 1995, p. 376) and that humans use tools and sign systems in order to transform themselves and to reshape cultural forms of society. This work on the human consciousness has been considered of major importance to those who recognize Vygotsky's attempts to link the natural and social sciences in his conception of a new psychology in order to overcome the reductionism that had been a frequent part of psychology.

Vygotsky sought to address four major areas of reductionism in psychology: that of reduction to the rational, to the individual, to the internal, and to the innate (del Río & Alvarez, 1995). While the behaviorist movement in psychology had sought to reduce the study of the mind to that which could be objectively measured and, thus, labeled as *rational*, Vygotsky insisted that emotion was a crucial part of understanding consciousness, and he "emphasized the development and cultural construction not only of *meaning*, but of *emotion and directivity*" (p. 386). His answer to the reductionist view of the mind as being of the *individual*, without acceptance of the social origins of the thinking process, was to propose that everything that can be considered individual was primarily social. As noted by Yaroshevsky (1989), "the individual constructs the idea of his own person in the likeness of another individual, receiving his speech reflexes, and thus 'settling' the other in his own organism" (p. 87).

His work also addressed the reductionist notion of *all that is developmental is also internal* with his own construct that learning takes place first on what he called an "interpersonal plane" (Vygotsky, 1978), through interaction with others, then moves to what he called an "intrapersonal plane," as concepts are internalized by the individual. "The transformation of an interpersonal process into an intrapersonal one is the result of a long series of developmental events" (Vygotsky, 1978, p. 57).

The issue of *innatist* reductionism was met with his construct of the "social–cultural–historical construction of higher functions" (del Río & Álvarez, 1995, p. 386). In other words, mental functions are socially, culturally, and historically constructed rather than genetically determined. According to Wertsch

(1991), Vygotsky's *general genetic law of cultural development* claims that an individual's mental functioning derives from participating in social life, and that what occurs in internalization is not a mere copying of socially organized processes, but transformations of processes at an individual level. (Note: the term *genetic* in this case has nothing to do with inheritance or innateness, rather it refers to *genesis* or origins).

Through his work, Vygotsky was moving away from the established authority in psychology rooted in the work of Pavlov because he felt that none of the existing schools had provided a unified theory of psychology (Vygotsky, 1978). He studied the works of scholars from many backgrounds and traditions in order to understand what he considered to be missing elements from their work. It was in juxtaposing his own work against theirs, and continually refining his studies, that Vygotsky worked to find ways of explaining the processes of learning and development. From his own studies, Vygotsky believed that

> culture, communication, the organism's life, were all integrated into a whole interpreted as a real equivalent of phenomena relegated by empirical subjective psychology to the inner 'space' of the individual's consciousness as a unique property inalienable from it. The category of cultural sign (revealed in the image of a word) and the category of communication, along with the category of action realised along reflex lines (but not identical with it), were laid from the very beginning as the foundation of his psychological system (Yaroshevsky, 1989, p. 94).

Vygotsky sought a psychology that would take into account the role of consciousness in development, while recognizing the cultural, social, and historical basis of psychological functioning. He also recognized language as both a psychological function and a cultural tool with which we can communicate thoughts as well as emotions to ourselves and others, thus allowing for a transformative notion of learning and development to emerge in the field of psychology.

Psychology to Pedagogy

For some, it may come as a surprise that Vygotsky wrote also about pedagogy. As a student of psychology said to us (June 4, 1999):

> Now, I have just visited the ideas of Vygotsky from a different point-of-view, (i.e., as applied to pedagogy). Previously, I had never thought to use his ideas as a building block or as a tool to enhance practices used in the classroom. I feel I am looking down the other end of the tube now.

Although Vygotsky turned to psychology, he still maintained his interest in matters of pedagogy and solving problems in education.

Bruner (1987) stated: "Vygotsky's view of development was also a theory of education" (p. 1). In his view of development and education, Vygotsky placed great importance on the role of language as being shaped by historical forces and as a tool of thought for shaping thought. The notion of shaping is interesting due to the nature of the word *education*. The English word for education has been traced to two different origins: One is the English word *educe*, meaning 'to draw out' or 'extract from' the child what is already there. However, Webster's dictionary (2nd ed.) gives the etymology of education as the Latin verb *educare*, which is derived from a specialized use of Latin *educere*, meaning 'to assist at the birth of a child.' According to Cole (Moll, 1990), the Russian word for education, *obrazovanie*, emphasizes a process of formation provided by external forces. Cole used the example of an ocean participating in the *obrazovanie* of a strip of land. The root of the Russian word is *obraz*, meaning 'image making.' Further, *obuchenie*, translated as 'teaching,' is interchangeable for the activity of the teacher and students. Thus, the Russian words themselves harbor a sense of reciprocity in terms of teaching and learning.

Vygotsky began his work in psychology because of persistent questions he had as a teacher. He was always concerned with the application of theory in practice, and he directed his developmental constructs toward pedagogy and learning. He wondered how it was that we learn and develop, and he wondered why some children seem to develop faster while others seemed to require more assistance. These underlying questions led him to theorize in new and different ways than what had been published by his contemporaries in psychology.

Meeting Our Distant Mentor:
Joan Meets Vygotsky

I first met Vygotsky in South Dakota when I was in an undergraduate English class in 1965. I particularly remember the context in which I first heard the name, Vygotsky. The highly regarded professor who introduced us to him had white hair and a gentle nature. I remember that in this professor's classes we learned a lot; it never seemed like work, and most of it has stayed with me through the years.

Le and I are often asked: What does a Vygotskian class look like? An example would be this class: The professor never spoke *at* us; he always spoke *with* us. He encouraged us to actively explore our thoughts and our language. As we talked and listened in his class, we didn't realize that we were using words to socially construct our own thinking. We were encouraged to learn from opposites.

Through this collaboration, which focused on dialectical inquiry, we stretched and grew in unexpected ways. Complex meanings for words increased, and thoughts deepened. I vividly recall we were active participants in our own learning, and we cognitively moved to a higher level as we talked with our friends and the professor. We didn't talk about dialectical thinking; we lived it. He didn't teach us about Vygotsky; we experienced Vygotsky.

Second, I met Vygotsky in 1983 at the University of Arizona at a time when the social and cultural context of my life had changed. I was teaching junior high students and going to graduate school. During this revisit with Vygotsky, I was much more aware of theory informing my practice, and my practice informing theory. It was often a toss-up as to whether my students or my professors were teaching me more. The cognitive connections between the university classes and the junior high classes seemed to flow in both directions.

In the rural school district where I was teaching, Spanish was the primary language of my students; they spoke English as a second language. Spanish was the dominant language in their homes, and the students' thoughts were embedded in their primary language. It was clear to me that the students had the thought (in Spanish), but often they did not have the language (in English) to demonstrate their knowledge. This continually put them at a disadvantage when English was the language of the classroom in which they competed with English-only students.

Gradually, we learned together the primacy of thought. Once we had a grounded understanding of the idea, we could develop many words (in English and/or Spanish) around a thought. Connections would begin to grow between the language and the thought, but never in a one-to-one or linear relationship. Often, unexpected meanings would emerge; new linkages would develop. Multiple and unforeseen paths emerged in the process of connecting thought and language.

Above all, the students and I discovered that what really mattered was having the thought. Sometimes we discussed ideas in English, and sometimes in Spanish. The words seemed to stretch the thoughts, and the thinking motivated us all to learn more words. When the thoughts erupted in the use of language, we moved to the next level of cognition. As I reflect on this time, it is ironic that I was studying about Vygotsky in a graduate class, but the junior high students and I were experiencing a Vygotskian class.

Third, I met Vygotsky at Texas A&M in 1990. By this time, I had a fairly good understanding about the importance and interrelationship of thought and language, of dialectical thinking, of the importance of the social and cultural context on teaching and learning. I was firmly grounded in the changes, the process, the development, the richness, and the spontaneity of thought and language. In fact, I was attracted to the search for meaning, which develops from thought and language. Cognitively, I had reached a higher level as my thoughts and language had grown and deepened from the context of my own lived experiences. The professors in my graduate classes and the students in secondary classes had successfully pulled and tugged me to my next higher developmental level.

I was standing in the library stacks, browsing through the Vygotsky section. It was like visiting with an old friend, and I sat down on the floor between the stacks to enjoy his books. As I was paging through *Thought and Language,* I came to Vygotsky's explanation of the Venn diagram (Figure 2). "Schematically, we may imagine thought and speech as two intersecting circles. In their overlapping parts, thought and speech coincide to produce what is call verbal thought" (Vygotsky, 1986, p. 88). I had never been very comfortable with this graphic because, for me, it failed to capture the complex interrelationship between thought and language. I got up from the floor and walked to a large empty library table and started to draw.

I hurriedly drew the picture in (Figure 3) on my yellow legal paper. The purpose of the moving line, which links speech and thought, is to demonstrate the rec-

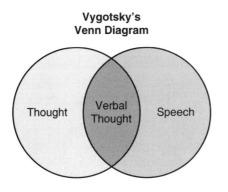

Vygotsky's Venn Diagram

Thought   Verbal Thought   Speech

FIGURE 2   Venn Diagram.

iprocity of the relationship. For example, the language of my students is the moving line that links their language with their newly emerging thoughts. As the students write and talk in their own language, they internalize the ideas. The process is multidimensional, boundless, and dynamic. Language informs thought, and thoughts come to life in language. Meaning springs from the union of verbal thought.

I wanted to capture the Vygotskian concept that all thought and all language have separate roots, but that they grow together and change each other in a multitude of unforeseen ways in a never-ending process (Figure 4). In classrooms, as students talk and write, the pedagogy shifts from teacher-directed to student-centered. As this pedagogy demonstrates, student-generated ideas have the potential to build on each other and to develop even more thoughts and more language. The relationship between thought and language moves in any direction and touches all as it develops. Words expand as thinking deepens.

A few months after I drew this graphic, I suddenly needed it in a moment of academic frustration. I was struggling with the concept of critical pedagogy, and it would be safe to say that my thoughts on this subject were tiny. The language of critical pedagogy eluded me. As I attempted to make meaning of this new concept, the language would slip and slide away from me. I read book after book and was always left with more questions. Finally, in complete frustration, I came to the realization that I would have to find meaning for myself based on my own

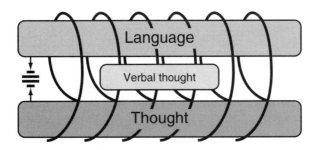

Language

Verbal thought

Thought

FIGURE 3   Language and Thought.

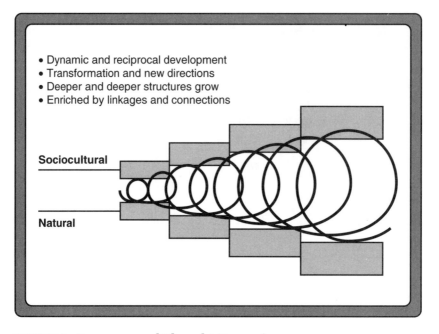

FIGURE 4 **Language and Thought Dynamic.**

lived experiences. I needed my own cognitive coat hooks on which to hang these new thoughts and words. My internal dialogue went something like this:

> "What do I know?" I asked myself. "Well, I know a little about language. Okay, that is a good starting point. Now, what language person, in particular, might be helpful? Oh, yes, my old friend, Vygotsky," I answered myself.

So, I sat down one weekend with my worn and tattered *Thought and Language* (1962), and I started to read and reread. Vygotsky taught me again that if I had one word and only a fragile, fleeting thought, I could begin to generate meaning between the two. The words would multiply, and the thoughts would grow. The dynamic relationship between the two would continue to create new and more complex meanings. This is exactly what I did in the early stages of my study of critical pedagogy. In this case, we could say that language was a tool to help me understand. However, it did not feel like I was using a tool; rather, it felt like a process that enabled me to think more deeply and critically.

The ideas of Vygotsky empowered my learning of the thought and language of critical pedagogy. As I learned each new word and/or thought, new linkages grew with my prior knowledge and existing experiential base. I always knew that by using the language of critical pedagogy, my thoughts would deepen to new understandings. The most important lesson I learned was that I had the ability to create new knowledge by using what Vygotsky had taught me about the relationship between thought and language. By metacognitively using my knowledge, I created new knowledge that was meaningful and purposeful at that time (Wink, 1997).

Meeting Our Distant Mentor:
Le Meets Vygotsky

I first met Vygotsky in the midst of a career move back to my educational roots after thirteen years in the business world. In 1990, I joined the academic world again as graduate student, intent on completing a secondary credential and a master's in multilingual education. My earlier experience of teaching high school students in a Spanish language classroom was a distant memory as I negotiated the courses I would have to take to resume this career.

One of the first courses I enrolled in was designed to inform us about various models of teaching. I remember that first day of class, thinking, "I must have learned this in my first go around at teaching back in the seventies. I have to think back on my own experience as a teacher and as a student to help me make sense of the text we are going to have to read for this course." Then the news came from the professor that we were required to be teaching in a classroom so that we could put into practice what we were learning. How was I going to accomplish that? The next day I was at a local high school, asking if they needed a substitute teacher for their Spanish classes. Indeed, they needed a substitute. In fact, they needed a long-term substitute for two classes, and that suited my needs perfectly. We signed the contract, and I had no idea how much I would learn from that experience!

I was slated to teach two classes: second-period class had twenty-two students, top in the class and eager to learn; third-period class had thirty-nine students; twelve of those students were bilingual, but needed help with their Spanish reading and writing skills. The second-period class was so similar to the classes I had taught before, that I thought it would be a breeze. Nothing in my past experience had prepared me for the third-period class. They were a rowdy group, well known in the school for their ability to run off substitute teachers. I quickly learned that I was number ten in only the fourth week of school. I wrote in my self-reflection journal after my first week:

> (Sept. 17, 1990) They are bored…these kids have had no consistent teacher for four weeks, and they figured I was just another sub. Day two was better and each successive day I could see improvement in their attitude, but the one class is still a major challenge for me because I have to come up with extra materials for them.

I did not know what I was going to do with the students in the third-period class. I knew that I had to tailor the teaching to the students, but my classes prior to this had been similar enough in composition that only minor adjustments had to be made. With this third-period class, I had to throw away the pattern and start over to construct an experience that would benefit their learning and my teaching.

As my graduate course continued through the semester, we studied other models of teaching: information processing, cooperative learning, role playing, mastery learning, and direct instruction. As graduate students preparing to be teachers, we studied numerous ways to assign points for good behavior, ways to increase executive control and learning aptitude. We learned how to determine learning styles so that we would address all the modalities of learning. We learned how to award points for group work and points for individual learning.

In the classes where I was substitute teaching, I tried all of these teaching strategies. I discovered that some things worked, once. As soon as the students caught on to my fancy methods, they would up the behavioral ante, and I would have to comply by doing something even more entertaining the next time to keep them engaged. I found that there was power in giving points for behavior, but the power soon paled for me because the students were more interested in earning points than in learning what I had to offer. Something had to change, and change it did, when I met Lev Vygotsky.

The change came with a class assignment in the methods course I was taking. The professor told us we had to select one of the models we had studied, work with that model extensively as a project, and report on it at the end of the course. The most popular models were quickly snapped up by those savvier than I was about these methods. When the selections were made, peer tutoring and reciprocal teaching were remaining as options, and my name was still not assigned. The professor asked if I would do both of these together. "Sure, why not?" I replied. I figured I had as good a chance with those unfamiliar terms as with any of the others.

Off to the library I went to research those unfamiliar terms: *peer tutoring* and *reciprocal teaching.* I was going to be using them in my substitute-teaching classes so I had to find out how to do so. I found three articles in our library to guide me, and I read them over and over to understand what I had to do. As I studied Palincsar and Brown's (1986) work, I realized that what they were proposing was similar to what I had done in my prior teaching: making predictions about the text by using their prior knowledge, generating questions about the text, summarizing, and then clarifying what had been learned. The teacher was a facilitator, guiding the practice while students were sharing responsibilities of learning with each other.

As I sat in the library musing on these articles, the germ of an idea began to form:

> "Ok, I used to teach Spanish years ago, but not under these circumstances. Let's see what I can use from my experience, combined with what I am learning now," I reflected to myself.
>
> "I know that the bilingual students have expertise in oral language that they could share, but they need to improve their writing skills. The

English-only students need to talk and learn the vocabulary, and I always used dialogues in class so they could practice. Why not have the bilingual students write texts for us to use in class? They can become peer tutors, and if I explicitly model the techniques of reciprocal teaching, they can use the same techniques to teach their texts to the rest of the class. Then the English-only students can construct dialogues from the texts, practice them and get feedback from their peer tutors on their progress," I reasoned.

For the first time since I had taken this job, I was getting excited about teaching and learning with these students. It occurred to me that this "difficult" class was going to teach me far more than the calmer, easygoing second-period class. So off I went, to implement this form of teaching and learning. The project soon became successful as we worked through the initial implementation issues. The bilingual students improved their writing skills, became the local experts in their native language, and honed their tutoring skills with the English-only students in the classroom. The English-only students began to respect the expertise of their bilingual peers as they read the texts and constructed dialogues together. These particular strategies were working with these students. That much I knew. It was in the next class in my master's program that I found out why.

The next class I took was with a newly hired professor at the same university. During that first class, as Joan taught about assessment of second language students, I quickly realized that I had entered a realm of education with a vocabulary unto itself. Questions began to form as I struggled with all new words and ideas, feeling much like a second-language student myself.

From the very start of this class, we were always talking and sharing so that we could, in Joan's words, make meaning for ourselves. We soon found that whenever we verbalized our thoughts about our readings, it was all we could do to stop talking and bring our attention back to the front of the room. Joan never talked at us, but continually asked questions and posed problems. Just when we thought we had answers, she would ask more questions to generate discussion. Through this discussion, I began to make sense of what I had experienced the prior semester.

Vygotsky came to life as Joan shared his concepts about thought and language. Finally, I had encountered a theory that unlocked for me what I had intuitively felt about teaching and learning, but did not yet have the words to articulate. I knew that the learning theories encountered in my education years earlier did not jibe with my own convictions. Working with the bilingual and English-only students the semester before had taught me that what worked with one group of students was not necessarily going to be effective with another group. Now, I knew why. I was realizing then that in his search for a new psychology, Vygotsky showed that learning is both individual and social and, at the same time, natural and cultural. Our lived experience surrounds and touches each of us in different ways, and, as such, influences our learning.

In portraying the importance of social context on language, Joan told us about Vygotsky's idea of the zone of proximal development. This meant that if students could talk and problem-solve with others, who had more experience or knowledge in specific areas, they would be able to reach greater levels of cognition. In our work together in Joan's class, we lived these concepts while we internalized theory that informed our practice. What Joan had learned from her studies was being played out in this classroom each time we met. We realized the value of verbalizing our thoughts, recognizing that we came from differing perspectives because of our lived experiences. Every idea had merit, questions were more important than answers, and the process was more important than the product. We were experiencing transformative education, and most of us were working harder and enjoying it more than ever before in our educational lives.

When asked how I first learned about Vygotsky, I credited Joan with introducing me to his work, and sharing with me a way to theoretically verbalize my practice. Through our sharing over the years and after reading many other's interpretations of Vygotsky's work, it dawned on me one day that Joan was not the one who introduced me to Lev Vygotsky. I actually encountered his ideas for the first time the semester before I met Joan, in my experience with "models of teaching" class. I had been assigned a semester project by an expert in behaviorism, the one model of teaching that actually fit with my theoretical perspective of teaching. In that serendipitous semester, I encountered the "how" of teaching and learning, and, in the next serendipitous semester, I discovered the "why." I am able now to put words to my experience. I still marvel at the convergence of events in that year that have instigated a synergy that continues even to this day.[1]

Conclusion

As you can see from the heartfelt words of Vygotsky's own daughter, and through our own narratives about meeting Vygotsky, his work transforms lives and practice. The purpose of this introduction was to acquaint you with this genius from our past. In keeping with a Vygotskian tradition, we acknowledge that the historical past informs our future. Realizing the historical context of Vygotsky's life helps us make sense of his world, and also reminds us that the past has a way of coming back to teach us if we will listen. In our current educational world, we are reliving a portion of Vygotsky's past with our return to high-stakes testing, deprofessionalizing, and demoralizing of teachers. As Maxine Greene stated on a literacy listserv (Feb. 10, 2000):

> I wonder about the body politic of a system that continues to ignore its children, its teachers, its people. I wonder about good people gone bad, and I wonder as I work for the change, how and what each one of us is willing to pay so that we will not continue to feel so bad for each other. Out of something bad comes something good, so tells us the good book, but then, how long will we continue to justify the futility of ego, and the lack of meaning invested in testing without teaching, of training without understanding, and of prescribing solutions without seeing the root causes and the stages of humanity.

The remainder of this work is devoted to demonstrating how Vygotsky's theories can be carried into classroom practice. We will carve out a path of principles, most dominant in Vygotsky's work, that are the most relevant for students.

ENDNOTE

1. These two stories of how Joan and Le first became acquainted with the works of Vygotsky are adapted from an earlier version, which was originally published in: J. Wink, L. Putney, & I. Bravo-Lawrence. Introduction: La voz de Vygotsky. *CABE Newsletter, 17,* 10–11, 13–14. In addition, the figures in this chapter were adapted from J. Wink. (1997). *Critical Pedagogy: Notes from the Real World.* New York: Addison Wesley Longman, and J. Wink, L. Putney, & I. Bravo-Lawrence. Introduction: La voz de Vygotsky. *CABE Newsletter, 17,* (1994, September/October) 10–11, 13–14.

PART ONE

Why Vygotsky?

Deliberate avoidance of philosophy is itself a philosophy.
(Vygotsky, 1986, p. 41)

There is only one chapter in Part 1. Its purpose is to provide a historical road map of the multiple perspectives that affect teaching and learning in schools. We will chronicle the changes in educational theory since the time in which Vygotsky was working, thinking, and challenging others to think in new ways. This chapter serves as the foundation for the remainder of the book.

Why Do We Do What We Do?

We will describe the evolution of pedagogical and psychological thought of the past century for two reasons. First, we provide this historical background so that readers understand the context in which Vygotsky's ideas developed. As with all evolving ideas, it often happens that contradictory elements exist alongside each other. Our second purpose in beginning with a description of the development of educational thought is to lead readers to focus on one question: Why do we do what we do?

History is helpful in finding answers to this question. The early roots of education shed light on our thinking today. For the most part, beginning in the late 1800s and continuing through all of the 1900s, educational philosophy in the United States resulted in two significant movements, Progressivism and Scientific Management. The leading proponents of each movement, Dewey for the first and Thorndike and Skinner for the second had very differing viewpoints on educational psychology and pedagogy.

In the following, we will examine how different theories of teaching and learning in the United States grew out of these roots. In addition, we will show how a broader range of educational thought developed from these two sources. Specifically, our goal is to establish Vygotskian educational psychology as a link between the early ideas of Progressivism and the Transformative education of today.

Each of us in education is influenced by the thinking that has preceded us. Each of us has periodically done something in a classroom because that is the way it was done to us. Just as Vygotsky laid out a continuum of theories in order to think about new thoughts, we do the same so that readers will reflect on whether their own ideas are a good fit with the students of today, the schools of today, and the society of today.

As we reflect on the history of how multiple ideas affect pedagogy and educational psychology today, we will include a variety of perspectives, while leading readers to reflect on their unique way of seeing the world. At times, we will refer to the historical ideas as theories, philosophies, perspectives, viewpoints, schools of thought, and thought communities (Fleck, 1979), a group of thinkers with mutual interests, jointly constructing knowledge.

Thought at the Turn of the Century: 1900

At the turn of the last century, two contradictory and simultaneous ideas were competing for their place in schools: Scientific Management and Progressivism. At times, it seems that oppositional thoughts are unique to educators of today. However, we come from a long historical tradition of competing ideas striving to turn theory into practice in schools. "[N]ovelty emerges only with difficulty, manifested by resistance, against a background provided by expectation" (Kuhn, 1970, p. 64). Let us say clearly at the outset: Vygotsky gives us a high degree of expectation.

First, Progressivism, led by Dewey, was a school of thought that focused on a child-centered and experiential approach to teaching and learning. This perspective emphasized discovery and a dialectical approach to constructing knowledge. If we think about the way classrooms are organized and managed, we can think in terms of the classroom and what is actually happening there. In a progressive classroom, the desks and chairs would be movable, students might be working in groups on processes of inquiry, the teacher and materials would be resources for learning, and the entire sociocultural context would respond to the needs of the students. In this metaphor, the classroom is a learning place, not a workplace (Marshall, 1988; Marshall, 1992a).

Second, Scientific Management was a contrasting perspective. Those who approached schools with a management-centric approach reasoned that, if the industrial revolution of the late 1800s in the United States demonstrated efficiency in the workplace, then certainly it would improve the efficiency of transmitting information to students in schools. Today, a century later, this way of thinking is often thought of as the traditional perspective because it has had such a profound effect on schools in the last one hundred years (Oakes, 1999).

In contrast to the perception of the classroom as a learning place, the Scientific Management school of thought saw the classroom as a workplace.

> [I]f we put before the mind's eye the ordinary classroom, with its rows of ugly desks placed in geometrical order, crowded together so that there shall be as little moving room as possible, desks almost all of the same size, with just enough space to hold books, pencils, and paper, and add a table, some chairs, the bare walls, and possibly a few pictures, we can reconstruct the only educational activity that can possibly go on in such a place. It is all made "for listening"—because simply studying lessons out of a book is only another kind of listening; it marks the dependency of one mind upon another (Dewey, 1991, pp. 31–32).

This brings to mind the old joke about a potential epitaph for Dewey's gravestone: "Here Lies the Man Who Convinced Americans to Unbolt School Desks from the Floor" (c.f. Newman, 1998).

In classrooms that have their historical roots in the Scientific Management philosophy, the students are *listening* because the classroom is set up for industrial efficiency. The underlying assumption is that listening is the major thoroughfare of learning. While this description fits many classrooms in today's schools, the description was first published in Dewey's *The School and Society* in 1900. Graduate students in our classes have asked us repeatedly: Why has so little changed in the past one hundred years? Why is the metaphor of classroom-as-workplace still so prevalent in our schools? We will explore potential answers in the following section.

Thought at the Turn of the Century: 2000

The Scientific Management approach to society and schools heavily influenced another school of thought, often referred to as behaviorism. The historical roots of the management approach eventually took on other names in schools: behaviorism, positivism, traditional, and back-to-basics.

Today the efficiency movement is no longer grounded in a factory model; rather, it has been appropriated by and infused with a CEO mentality prevalent in the workplace outside of schools. This school of thought now advocates for standards, high-stakes assessment, and extrinsic motivation. This perspective influences and places high value on quantitative measurement, parts-to-whole learning, and outcome-based pedagogy. In our writing, we will show the relationship of this movement to what Smith (1998) has referred to as the Official Theory of Learning.

The opposing idea, Progressivism, has also influenced society and schools throughout the last one hundred years. Its legacy is seen in holistic/dialectical learning, reflective assessment, and intrinsic motivation. This approach eventually resulted in other perspectives known as cognitivism, social cognitivism, interactionism, generativism, constructivism, social constructionism, sociohistorical, cognitive developmental, and transformative education. These are terms that we will examine in later chapters.

Evolution of Thought: 1900 to 2000

Certainly, educational philosophies have more influences than Scientific Management and Progressivism. However, it is also clear that these two perspectives have fundamentally affected all who have an interest in schools today. The legacy of each remains strong. The proponents of each are committed. The divisions are deep. As readers reflect on the past one hundred years, it is clear that these two contradictory ideas have each played a fundamental role in educational philosophy and practice in the United States.

As we reflect on the various ideas of history and the ideas of today, we again ask that readers reflect on: Why do we do what we do? In many cases, we are thinking the thoughts of one hundred years ago and doing the same as we did one hundred years ago. However, from a Vygotskian perspective, we note that the entire sociocultural, historical perspective has changed drastically. In addition, the political context of today is vastly different from then. As the world has changed, our questions and answers need to reflect the monumental changes in society. In looking at school renewal, what kind of renewal do we want? Do we want renewal that reflects lifelong learning practices, or do we want renewal that results in short-term learning as seen in quantifiable test scores? Effectiveness or efficiency? Intrinsic or extrinsic? Classic learning or official learning? We invite educators to find their own answers based in the sociocultural context of our shared history and implicated future.

Maxine Greene eloquently summed up the issues for us in an electronic dialogue:

> Teachers who are consciously and reflectively choosing themselves as participants in school renewal are being challenged to clarify their beliefs and (more and more often) to defend their practices. If the discourse they are developing can be infused with the kinds of metaphors that reorient ordinary common-sense thinking, if they can break through more often what John Dewey called 'the crust of conventionalized and routine consciousness' (1954, p. 183) when attention is turned to the school, neighborhood or district, then discussions may be moved beyond the customary and the self-regarding. If the fears and suffering of local people, some of them feeling themselves to be ignorant and powerless, can be taken into account, what Paulo Freire called a 'pedagogy of hope' might even take form, and dialogue of a different sort might take the place of the language of prescription or complaint or demand. (Greene, M., 1997, p. 2)

Conclusion

Smith (1998) compares the two previous schools of thought by linking Progressivism to the long tradition of what he refers to as the Classic Theory of Learning and connecting Scientific Management and Behaviorism with the Official Theory of Learning. In Chapter 1, we will provide an overview of the development of educational psychology in its historical context. We have chosen to incorporate various theories into three large, ever-changing schools of thought: transmission models, generative models, and transformative models. While we recognize that these three perspectives are not all-inclusive, we present them as perspectives familiar to many educators. However, we are attracted to the thinking of Nieto (1996), who reminds us always to keep the number seventeen in mind, as it so well reflects multiple perspectives on complex realities. The past century was indeed a complex reality for the evolution of Vygotsky's legacy. The complexity of the past century has been visually represented by Chris, a graduate student (Figure 5).

ENDNOTE

1. The authors wish to thank Chris for her artwork on this time line.

Official Theory of Learning
(Smith, 1998)

Scientific Management	Behaviorism	Back to Basics Standards
Taylor	Black box theory	Controlled Language
Memorization	Stimulus–response	
	Quantify–measure	

| 1900 | WWI | WWII | 1950 | 1980 | 1990 | 2000 |

Progressivism   Frankfurt School   Cognitivism
of Critical Theory
Dewey   Interactionist
Experiential   *Piaget*   Constructivism
                                   Constructionism
                                           Social Cultural Learning
        Sociocultural Learning   Critical Pedagogy
                                           Democratic Pedagogy

Vygotsky
Dialectical Learning

Reciprocal action between thought and language

Classic Theory of Learning
(Smith, 1998)

FIGURE 5 **Official versus Classic Theories of Learning.**

1 Theorizing Theories and Thinking Thoughts

[H]e who considers facts, inevitably considers them in light of one theory or another (Vygotsky, 1987, p. 55).

Years ago Vygotsky laid out the various theories of educational and psychological thought; he was theorizing about theories. He was critically reflecting on the various theories available, because he believed that synthesis was central to the creation of novel ideas. He continually juxtaposed his reasoning against opposing viewpoints to lead him to a new integration of ideas. In his collaboration with his colleagues, he established what John-Steiner (1996) refers to as a "thought community," a group of scholars jointly creating a body of knowledge.

In this chapter, we will use Vygotsky's psychological and pedagogical concepts as the unifying paradigm for many otherwise divergent theories of learning and development. Our goal in examining educational theory is similar to Vygotsky's. We invite the reader to think about thought, to theorize theories, to ponder pedagogy. We do this in the spirit of Vygotsky, who was once a teacher who researched learning and development to inform pedagogy.

> [I]n education it is far more important to teach the child how to think than to communicate various bits of knowledge to him.... Thinking, you see, denotes nothing less than the participation of all of our previous experience in the resolution of a current problem, and the distinctive feature of this form of behavior is simply that it introduces a creative element into our behavior through the construction of every possible connection between elements in a preliminary experience, which is what thinking is essentially. By this very fact, it multiplies the limitless possibilities of all those connections that may be produced out of human reactions, and makes a man's behavior inexhaustibly multifaceted and exceptionally complicated (Vygotsky, 1997, p. 175).

Vygotsky continued in this line of reasoning by writing that thinking is difficult; it is through learning made difficult that learning takes place, i.e., when teachers present problems to be solved as opposed to information to be memorized. Vygotsky also noted how complex we are because of how we use our experience to help us create knowledge. This complexity leads us to Vygotsky's work to help us make sense of an increasingly complex educational space that cannot be reduced to simplistic bits of knowledge.

Central to this chapter will be the evolution of ideas, theories, philosophies, and thought communities that affected, not only the thinking of Vygotsky's time, but also the ideas that undergird pedagogy in the schools of today and tomorrow. Together we will examine how these philosophies of yesterday still affect us today in our everyday lives. This chapter serves as the foundation for further development of the Vygotskian thought examined throughout this book.

We begin this chapter with a historical journey through a jungle of educational paradigms, questioning why we think the way we do about issues in education. Often we have found, when working with educators, that the mystery of the various "isms, ologies, and ists" is so profound that some will discredit them as too esoteric to be meaningful, falling back on what is perceived and a more pragmatic approach, "just tell me how to do it." However, in the long run, *methods* will not sustain teaching in the always-changing social cultural context. However, *theory* will provide a discourse to understand, articulate, and adapt practice to meet the needs of students, even as the world changes.

We continue the chapter with a look at how Vygotsky studied the work of others to make sense of his own thinking. To help us understand the major concepts that we will work with in later chapters, we will provide a glimpse into the similarities and differences between Vygotsky's work and that of one of his most influential contemporaries, Piaget.

Why We Juxtapose Theories and Theorists

Vygotsky believed that to understand any concept it is vital to trace the concept to its origin, if at all possible. In studying the historical background, we can make sense of what we are studying, and we bring perspective to what we are learning. We can reflect on what we are doing in classes. Eventually, we can ask ourselves: Why? Multiple ways of talking about educational theory are available for our reflection. What are the various perspectives? What question does each answer for me? What questions are left unanswered?

Finding Answers in a Historical Journey

We invite readers to take a historical journey through the various educational ideas of the last century. We encourage each reader to see how multiple perspectives have influenced schools and thinking. We will look at these ideas and ask ourselves: What questions will that school of thought answer for me? What questions will that school of thought not answer for me? Then we will move on to another theoretical perspective, and see if that might answer our questions. As we do this, we will continually be relating the historical grounding and theoretical perspectives to our actions. Perhaps, one of these perspectives will cause you to do something as a teacher or as a learner in a certain way. Our question is: If you could develop a broader perspective on the possibilities and uncover the assumptions underlying your current understandings, might you have more options for your own teaching and learning?

Multiple Perspectives to Multiple Learners

We will push you to think about how the thought communities of educational history affect you, the curriculum you use, the methods you use, the community of learners you create with the students in your own classrooms, and the effect of all of this on diverse learners. Just as we ask you to expand your thinking about the multiple perspectives available to each of us, we also ask that you reflect on the broad diversity of students filling schools today. Students of many cultures, languages, and ethnicities are the norm for many schools. Not only has the world changed; the students have changed, and our philosophical questions and answers must reflect these changes.

We will think about our thoughts; we will ponder our pedagogy; we will theorize our theory. And, in so doing, we will learn about other theories that will broaden our perspectives and open the door to greater possibilities. "We challenge schools and communities to look at education in a whole new light. Our goal is to nurture innovative—even radical—new approaches, not reward entrenched conventional wisdom" (Sarason, 1990, p. 176).

Transmission Lens: Behaviorism/Positivism

The transmission lens, more than any other, has profoundly affected why we do what we do in schools. The ideas of behaviorism, a direct descendent of Scientific Management, provide the bulk of school experience for many in the United States. Often referred to as positivism, it is the status quo; it is the way we have always done things. It is the rationale for the underlying assumptions behind the oft-heard comment: "Well, when I was in school...." Behaviorism accounts for the many myths that drive educational policy.

Behaviorist theory posits that learning consists of patterns, memorization, and imitation. This type of learning can be seen as a response to an outside stimulus, and is reinforced by extrinsic reward. Thus, motivation for learning is in response to a desire for reward. The teacher, being trained in scientific method, monitors events, transmits information, and presumes to objectively assess learning outcomes. Teachers ground their lessons in behavioral objectives and instruction is programmed.

Those mostly commonly associated with the early school of behaviorist thought in the United States are Taylor, Thorndike, Watson, Skinner, and Pavlov. Their work flourished during the early twentieth century. During this same time in Russia, Pavlov was conducting experiments in classical conditioning that greatly influenced behaviorism. In the 1930s to 1950s the behaviorists in the United States (Guthrie, Hall, and Skinner) continued to study learning as behavioral change. Remarkably, a world away, Vygotsky was formulating his theories in the 1920s and 1930s and coming to completely different conclusions about educational theory. When Vygotsky examined the behaviorists' ideas to see which questions they answered and which they did not answer, he recognized a limitation.

For Vygotsky, learning is more than just passively receiving information and responding to it; learning includes the ideas generated in the process of dialectical discovery. In addition, from a Vygotskian perspective, learning and development are inherently tied to the sociocultural context. In contrast, the behavioral theorists posit that learning is how a student responds to an outside stimulus. However, their lens does not include what people construct in their minds, which is influenced by their lived experiences. Focusing only on a stimulus/response model does not allow the lived social, cultural, historical, and political context of our lives and those of our students to show through.

To increase our understanding of each of these perspectives, we find it useful to apply the theories in an educational setting. For each of the perspectives presented we offer the following activity, followed by the responses actually given by a group of inservice and preservice teachers in a graduate learning theories course.

Through a transmission lens, knowledge is _____ .

The learner's role is _____ .

The teacher's role is _____ .

The learning process consists of _____ .

The learning environment looks like _____ .

The responses from the learning theories class were as follows: In the behaviorist realm, knowledge is transmitted. The learner's role is as a sponge to soak up the information or as a responder to the teacher, whose role is giver of information. Learning, then, is memorizing facts and applying them in different situations. Classrooms are arranged with individual seats in rows separate from others because interaction is not desired as it slows down the rate of giving and receiving information.

Using the extreme of the behaviorist position, learning is defined as acquiring facts, skills, and concepts, often through drill and guided practice with discrete elements. In addition, teaching is assumed to cause learning in rather passive students (Marshall, 1992c). To summarize the behaviorist perspective: Outside stimulus is the primary agent responsible for learning (Gredler, 1997). Its motto could be:

It's the outside stimulus!

Generative Lens: Cognitive to Interactionist to Constructivist

Continuing with the juxtaposition of ideas, just as Vygotsky did, we move from the transmission lens to the generative lens. The behaviorist perspective eventually began to evolve into an approach, initially referred to as cognitivism or social cognitivism, that eventually developed into cognitive psychology, a prominent perspective today. The historical roots of constructionism can be traced back to cognitivism, which flourished in the 1930s. Gestalt theorists believe that people organize information into patterns and relationships so that they perceive meaningful wholes rather than just unrelated bits of information. As with all evolution-of-thought communities, the ideas take shape, define themselves, and redefine themselves. The varying theoretical constructs often affect pedagogy and psychology concurrently.

On the continuum of pedagogy, the cognitive perspective moved beyond the stimulus–response model and made it possible to focus on the actions of individuals in their environment. "Cognitive learning theorists focus on the human mind's active attempts to make sense of the world" (Woolfolk, 1998, p. 282). From this perspective, teachers attempt to engage students in active learning. The roles of attention, retention of information, and schema learning, connecting new knowledge with old knowledge were all associated with various cognitivists.

Through the shift from behaviorism to cognitivism, one notable difference is that students are asked to engage more cognitively with their learning. Extrinsic rewards began to shift toward intrinsic motivation. The cognitive approaches are called by various names: social cognitivism, Gestalt learning, and information processing. Some of the early people associated with this school of thought are: Gagne, Piaget, and Bandura. "In summarizing the cognitivist perspective: the learners' mental processes are the major factors in learning" (Gredler, 1997, p. 13). Their motto could be:

It's mental processing!

Eventually, cognitivism began shifting to a much more interactive process that led to the constructivist or interactionist approach, which assumed the interrelatedness of behavioral and mental process with the environment. In the late 1980s, educators began to place even more emphasis on the active construction of knowledge within the classroom. "Older cognitive views emphasized the *acquisition* of knowledge, but new approaches stressed its construction" (Woolfolk, 1998, p. 247).

In the Vygotskian tradition, we continue with the inquiry: What questions does this perspective answer, and what questions does it not answer? In the cognitivist viewpoint, the environment is backgrounded and not an integral part of what is being learned. One difference from behaviorism and cognitivism, which emerged with the interactivist or constructivist lens, was that it assumed that the individual was doing the constructing within the mind, perhaps in relationship with others, but not necessarily so. Also, the cognitivist perspective does not in-clude a theory of culture, and so it assumes individual differences to be capability differences.

After studying cognitive theory, which eventually developed into interac-tionism and/or constructivism, the learning theories class used the same prompts to apply their knowledge of the generative lens. If knowledge is individually con-structed, then the role of learner is as an experimenter, a researcher, constructing and testing hypotheses. The role of the teacher is the "guide on the side" to help each individual come to her own conclusions about the experiment. Learning then, is hands-on experimenting, applying what you know to what is being con-structed. Classrooms will be set up so that students can move to stations or learn-ing centers to work on experiments, but not necessarily with each other.

In summary, the constructivists believed in the interrelatedness of behavior, mental processes, and the environment (Gredler, 1997). Their motto could be:

It's constructive!

Transformative Lens: Social Constructionist

As we move into the transformative section of our pedagogical continuum, we see that, from a Vygotskian perspective, the social constructionist lens enables us to see the cultural component of language use in relationship to thought, and the individual in relationship to others. This relationship is not only social and cul-tural, but also historical, because we use the cultural tools of communicative signs and symbols handed down to us to construct our learning. This focus makes it possible for us to see the context as an integral part of our learning. We build col-lective knowledge together; then, as individuals, we use whatever part of that collective knowledge that is meaningful in our own lives. This lens also shows us learning through problem-solving situations, but not necessarily in problem-posing situations.

What did the learning theories class have to say about the social construc-tionist portion of the transformative lens? As they reflected on their own learning about social constructionism, they again answered the previous prompts to dem-onstrate their knowledge. Through the social constructionist transformative lens, knowledge is collectively constructed by individuals whose purpose is to share their expertise in order to construct and negotiate meaning. The learner role, then, is to bring what you already know into relationship with new information through interaction with others in the classroom. A learner is an apprentice, as well as researcher and experimenter, and an inquirer, an interviewer, and an in-vestigative reporter.

The teacher's role is similar in some respects to that of the cognitive con-structivist teacher, although as a more experienced leader, researcher, inquirer, interviewer, and investigative reporter. The purpose is different because the re-sponsibility of the teacher is to facilitate the students' learning process and to co-ordinate the learning with others around a particular content.

In summary, the social constructionists believed that "the signs and symbols developed by a particular culture and the child's interaction in learning these symbols are essential in developing…higher mental functions" (Gredler, 1997, p. 13). Their motto could be:

It's sociocultural!

Transforming Transformative: Critical Pedagogy

At the far end of the continuum is the critical lens that will continue to expand on the various principles and practices that affect educational thought and action. As in the Vygotskian perspective, teachers are learners, and learners are teachers. However, not only do we reflect on our practice, we also act on our reflections. In so doing, we move beyond merely understanding the words we read. We also understand the influences and the power structure of the world.

This critical lens, combined with the developmental and educational theory of the sociocultural, gives us our current best shot at taking our educational practice out of the one hundred-year abyss and moving it toward a Freirian vision of the pedagogy of hope.

The irony is that what is perceived as new and radical—critical pedagogy—has its roots in the progressive ideas of one hundred years ago. Dewey's Progressivism was fertile ground for the seed of critical theory that flourished in Europe and Latin America throughout the middle of the past century. Not only did Dewey's idea connect tightly with critical theory, but also with democracy. Dewey saw the connections between democracy and pedagogy. Democracy was not a subject to be studied, but rather a value to be lived. Dewey believed that the theory and practice of democracy should be nourished by the power of pedagogy.

The irony continues. Vygotsky, although he died at the beginning of the twentieth century, very much fits into the model of critical, transformative thought communities. At first glance it seems contradictory that anyone who lived so long ago would have ideas that are at the forefront of education today. However, recalling Smith's (1998) categories of educational theory, we see that the Classical Theory of Learning includes not only the critical thought of the antiquities, but also the critical thought of today and tomorrow. To finish our continuum we encouraged this group of educators to move another step beyond the social constructionist perspective. We asked them to repeat this process from a critical pedagogy approach.

As they discussed the transformative lenses, the students in the learning theories class noticed that looking concurrently through a social constructionist and a critical lens was like having two eye contacts, one for reading and one for distance. In this case, one eye contact is for critical close work and the other creates a sharp, distant vision. Together they give a critical and focused look at complex realities.

After the discussion, here are the answers the students generated: From a critical perspective, knowledge is power. The teacher and learners seek to use this power for self- and social transformation. The generated pedagogical knowledge is grounded in social justice. The philosophy that supports transformative teaching and learning is founded on the principle that theory and practice are joined to form praxis. Not only must democracy be taught, it must be lived within the classroom, the school, and the community. Lesson designs that spring from this philosophical basis seek to break down the harmful forces of marginalization. This model of lesson design seeks to assure all learners of equity and access to both the academic resources and power structures of society.

In summary, the social constructionists believed in the social, cultural, historical context as the determinant in development and learning. The critical pedagogues assumed all of this and included the political context. Their motto could be:

It's political!

Theory Is Practice: Example Lessons

Given the theory we outlined above, what would classroom practice look like if it reflected the three models previously presented? In a transmission model of education, the teacher is standing in front of the classroom, and the students are at their seats, which are in rows. They listen to what she says and write it down in their notebooks.

> A carrot is a root. We eat many roots. It is orange, and it is good for you. Other roots we eat are onions, beets, jicama, and potatoes. Class, are you writing down everything that I tell you? Today I will classify plants as those you can eat and those you can't. Make two columns on your paper and be sure to get every word I say for your homework. You will have a test on these exact words tomorrow. Who can name some other roots that we eat?

Now, imagine a generative classroom with small groups of students clustered around various learning centers. At each center, students are exploring the properties of edible roots.

> One group is cutting a potato, a carrot, and an onion and dropping iodine on the pieces to see if they contain starch. Another group is sorting through an array of vegetables to determine which are edible roots. At still a third center, a group is setting up jars to sprout potatoes. The teacher moves around the room, quietly observes, and periodically interacts with various groups. She moves to the group that has jars for sprouting potatoes. "I see your group has used different amounts of water in your jars. Can you predict which potato will sprout first? Why?"

Now, let's visit another classroom that is also studying carrots, onions, and roots. The educational model that is being used in the following classroom is historically rooted in the transmission and generative models. However, this model reflects, not only the changing world, but also our more complex understandings of meaningful teaching and learning. This transformative model reflects today and prepares for tomorrow. Imagine a classroom in which small groups of students are outside working in their garden, which they planted several months ago.

> The students are digging the potatoes, carrots, and onions and weighing them. Based on their production costs, the students will determine their price per pound later in math class. The group has decided in their class meeting that they will sell a portion of the roots in order to earn money for the scholarships for a field trip. The remainder of the garden vegetables will be donated to the local food kitchen (Wink & Swanson, 1993, cited in Wink, 2000, p. 17).

In a second example of a transformative classroom, a student explained how his fifth-grade classroom community is different from the classes he has had in his prior experience.

> Our Tower Community is very unique and different from most other classes. This is why…The teacher of the Tower is usually Ms. Yeager, but everyone gets to play different roles, like teaching. Lots of times we have to work in groups and we have different roles in that, too…When you're in the Tower you have to look at different points of view…Most of all, in our community you need to know respect for everyone and everything and be responsible for what you do.

In the opening lines of this essay describing his classroom community, Chris described four ways in which this classroom community differed from others: (1) They work in groups in which students take up various roles such as facilitator to help them function as a community; (2) they are able to understand and express their particular points of view; (3) they treat each other with respect; (4) they take responsibility for what they do in their day-to-day work together (Putney & Floriani, 1999, p. 17).

In other words, Chris's teacher used an approach to teaching in which she created opportunities for learning (Tuyay, Jennings, & Dixon, 1995) so that she and the students together engaged in constructing knowledge rather than simply transferring knowledge. She engaged students in constructing a community each year that afforded them opportunities for transforming knowledge of their civic roles and relationships—the norms and expectations that define community membership—and their knowledge of inquiry processes necessary for academic work in their classroom.

A transformative approach such as that used in Chris's classroom encourages teachers and students to be lifelong learners. As Freire (1998) argued, teaching from a transformative approach means that the teacher is acquiring new knowledge while engaging students in a "continuous transformation through which they become authentic subjects of the construction and reconstruction of what is being taught, side by side with the teacher... (p. 33). A transformative approach, then, is one in which teaching and learning are in a dynamic and reciprocal relationship, and one in which learning and development are essential to both teacher and students (Lankshear & McLaren, 1993; Putney & Floriani, 1999; Shor, 1999).

In contrasting these differing perspectives, we turn to a view on rethinking teaching and learning, in which Marshall (1992b & c) argued the need to reconceptualize learning as a process that occurs as learners interact with others and materials over time. She further maintained that research on learning needs to move beyond investigating isolated teacher behaviors or clusters of teacher and student practices toward a more holistic and dynamic examination of the learning process as it occurs in the times and spaces of classroom life.

Journals: Reflections on Theory to Practice

We initially said that one of our purposes in looking at evolving educational perspectives was to lead readers to ask: Why do we do what we do? We conclude this section of Chapter 1 with comments from the journals of teacher/graduate students who were coming to grips with the reality of putting theory into practice in their own ways.

In the first example, Ksenija realized what happens when an educator does *not* link theory with practice. While theories are often contradictory, sometimes theories exist simultaneously within the same classroom. Such is the case for Ksenija, who reflected in her journal on her philosophy class (July 7, 2000):

> I vividly recall a previous Philosophy class where we were taught the Classical Theory of Learning. The irony is that the professor used behaviorist methods to teach it. There were 35 students arranged in 3 straight rows, and we had to stay in the same seat throughout the semester. He never walked among the rows of students; he never crossed the invisible line which separated us. He walked in and began pouring knowledge into our heads: Kant, Hegel, Erasmus. We were expected to write every single word because we had to repeat it back to him on the tests. The students who could write faster were rewarded with better grades. The class was agony. I felt like a plant with no sun. There were no discussions; questions were banned. We had thoughts and were not allowed to express them.
>
>   For him, memorizing was learning. For us, it was a simple drill. Our only goal was to get a good grade. I don't remember much of what he taught; I do remember how he taught.

For Ksenija, the philosophy professor, who had claimed to be a progressive and critical teacher, demonstrated no connection between his espoused theory and his real practice. In the second journal selection, Tammy, a teacher, learned to articulate her own theory and practice better only after she learned of the major ideas that continue to influence schools. Tammy wrote (March 20, 2000):

The first year of teaching, I was simply there to get the job done, but the behaviorism and progressivism came clashing head-to-head at my school. In college I had learned that beginning readers needed access to books, lots of literature, and a print-rich environment. At my school, I was mandated to teach only phonics and phonemes in a systematic and explicit manner. At first I was happy to read the script and teach what and how they told me. I was a puppet, transmitting knowledge to my students, most of whom did not understand English: implicitly or explicitly. My first year of teaching was the ultimate example of Scientific Management. I was forced to live the Official Theory of Learning (Smith, 1998).

However, I am in constant conflict because I believe that the students in my classes will learn better about language and ideas if their experiences in class are meaningful, collaborative, nonthreatening, and interesting. My mandated curriculum is none of these. I see the needs of the students and want to adapt. I need to use manipulatives, vibrant picture books, literature, hands-on experiments to teach language, math, and science. My students need to experience it and talk about it before they can read and write about it; they are only in kindergarten.

Now, that I have learned about the big ideas of the past century, I am seeing my classroom with new eyes. Today, I still recognize my "gut instinct," but I also know the historical roots of the ideas in my school. My goal will always be transformational, although I am now in a context of forced transmission. For me, simply good teaching comes from Dewey, Vygotsky, and the Classical Theory of Learning.

The conflict for Tammy was that she was not allowed to turn her own theory into practice because of the mandated curriculum in her school. Her theory and the school's practice are in conflict, which leaves her in conflict as a teacher. We can only imagine what this might do to the students.

In some of our examples, we are aware that our classroom observations demonstrate the extreme of a particular theory. While we know that this extreme is not true for all teachers in all schools, we use it to make the point that not all strategies are appropriate at all times, and that philosophically and theoretically grounded teachers will be able to make the choice of what is pedagogically sound for their students. However, we do know of teachers for whom the extreme of being told what to teach and how to teach it is daily reality. These teachers have been forced to conduct their classrooms through a transmission lens that does not fit their pedagogical perspective. We feel the need to demonstrate their reality to make visible the drastic differences in philosophical, ideological, and theoretical positions that structure schools, classrooms, and curriculum.

Classroom Application of Learning Theories

For his time, many probably would have said that Vygotsky had some extreme ideas. Some might even say that today. He was not a traditional educational psychologist and educational philosopher. His unconventional way of studying, comparing, and contrasting the works of others opened up avenues of thought that led him to a new psychology, to develop his own unique pedagogy. However, before sharing his new psychology, we want to explore further the more traditional approaches to philosophical ideas, leading up to more transformative systems. In what follows we consider how these various approaches might appear when incorporated within a classroom.[1]

The following questions are typical of those teachers ask when they are teaching during the day and taking graduate classes at night, a context with which we are very familiar. These questions often arise when teachers reflect on their own beliefs and behaviors. As students and teachers grapple with others' educational thinking, they are often encouraged to evaluate their past and current principles and practices. This critical reflection can open the door to a better understanding of the teaching and learning process. We hope that readers of this text will enter into inquiry with us and ask: Why do I do what I do in the classroom? What are my beliefs about the theory and practice of quality education in my own context? How can I change, improve, and adapt my methods?

To this end, we offer the following list of typical questions teachers might ask. A graduate student, Chris, proposed hypothetical answers from her study of several well-known theorists. Her answers typify their respective philosophical beliefs, which are based on their own research (Gredler, 1997).

1. How can I promote reading for pleasure in the classroom?

From a *behaviorist perspective,* John Watson (1913) might suggest that teachers associate pleasure reading with an atmosphere that elicits positive emotional conditioned responses. This can be done by setting up a special reading corner in the classroom with comfortable chairs, beanbags, or pillows.

B. F. Skinner (1969), with his ideas of *operant conditioning,* might add that students who read on their own during class should be rewarded. They can be given the opportunity to choose something they enjoy reading and then read to younger students in other classrooms.

As we approach a more *interactionist perspective,* Robert Gagne (1985) could draw from his *learning conditions* and say that the goal is to impress a love of reading on the minds of students. This could be accomplished by reading enjoyable books to students. So that students are properly motivated, the teacher needs to set the stage by creating a positive outlook on reading. Teachers can create opportunities for students to choose their own reading. The teachers could make the library central to all learning. Teachers could be encouraged to share books from their own personal collection.

Albert Bandura (1977), representing what many refer to as *social–cognitive theory,* would suggest that the teacher first be a good role model. Teachers need to sit down and read during Sustained Silent Reading (SSR) time. Teachers are encouraged to reinforce appropriate reading behavior with positive comments to students about their reading.

Lev Vygotsky (1986), representing the school of thought often known as the *developmental–interactionist approach* or *sociohistorical theory* would suggest that children learn to read as they experience reading in meaningful contexts. Teachers need to give students opportunities to use reading in social situations. For example, students can read with partners or in small groups; they can read with older or younger students; students need opportunities to talk to each other about books they have read. It is through this social interaction that students use speech as a tool for thinking. Discourse in the classroom is an important aspect of reading comprehension. As students interact with each other, they build vocabulary, establish a foundation for written text, and eventually link spoken language to what they read.

Teachers can: (1) give students opportunities to write about things that are meaningful to them; (2) encourage them to share what they have written with others; (3) provide opportunities for students to ask purposeful questions about what they read and write; (4) model the questioning process. Become a participant in class discussions. As students experience this process with each other, they will learn to ask questions of themselves about what they are reading and writing.

2. How can I encourage students to exercise appropriate school and classroom behavior?

B. F. Skinner, representing *operant conditioning* of the *behaviorist perspective,* might suggest that teachers need to create positive classroom environments that encourage acceptable behavior. Teachers can focus attention on what students are doing right, rather than on what they are doing wrong. Appropriate behavior needs to be reinforced. List positive reinforcers that can be used to reward appropriate behavior. One way to do this is to observe students in order to understand what they like to do. For example, if extra computer time is valued by students, teachers can create opportunities to provide more time on the computers as a reward for good classroom behavior.

Edward Thorndike (1905), also representing *behaviorism,* might add to this by asking teachers to articulate appropriate classroom behaviors. For example, if students are to enter the classroom in an orderly manner, take out a book, and read for fifteen minutes, the teacher might note the students who are successfully carrying out those three behaviors and comments positively. The goal is to clarify a connection between appropriate behavior and a positive word. Consistency on the part of the teacher should eventually eliminate many inappropriate behaviors.

Albert Bandura, speaking on behalf of the *interactionist perspectives* and/or *social–cognitive theories* would suggest that teachers need to take care of behavior problems immediately and be consistent in carrying out discipline procedures because students will be influenced by the behavior they observe. If a student breaks a rule and the consequences are fair and consistent, the other students will be discouraged from breaking the same or other classroom rules. Conversely, if a few students misbehave and nothing is done, the other students will soon follow their example because they see that there are no consequences for their actions.

Teachers need to model expected behavior. For example, if students are to talk quietly in the classroom, the teacher must do so as well.

Lev Vygotsky, often labeled in survey textbooks as the voice of *developmental, interactionist, sociohistorical,* or *sociocultural theory,* would advise that students be responsible for and have control over their own behavior. Appropriate conduct should be the result of their ability to regulate themselves. Students need to know the rules and be a part of creating and implementing them. Students need to understand that there are logical purposes for rules. They need limits, but should see that limits are set for their own good and for the good of others, not so that teachers can assert their power and control over them. Students may need more guidance at first, but will eventually learn to take responsibility for their actions and regulate their own behavior.

3. What can teachers do to make lessons interesting and meaningful for students?

Robert Gagne (1985), using his ideas about *learning conditions,* often considered to represent the *cognitive* and *interactionist perspectives,* would suggest that teachers need to do things that help students focus their attention on the lesson or activity. For example, he would encourage the use of visual aids such as real objects or pictures. He would recommend demonstrations that help illustrate important concepts. It is important to ask questions that require students to use their imagination. Teachers need to provide experiences that allow students to use their five senses. New ideas and instructions need to be written on the board.

Jean Piaget (1971) representing the *interactionist, developmental,* and *cognitive perspectives,* would say that students need to have an active part in their learning, and they need to interact with each other and with the environment. For instance, the best way to teach students about animals is to take them to the zoo. Teachers could arrange follow-up activities for this experience with meaningful classroom activities that connect what they have observed to specific curricular areas. Students could draw or write about animals; compare and contrast animals; or make a class graph of favorite animals. Applying one concept in a variety of ways helps reinforce the concept and, thus, increase learning.

Classroom materials and situations should be organized with specific objectives in mind. Free exploration in the beginning is fine, but students need guidance in what they are doing if overall goals are to be met. This can be done by asking thought-provoking questions that help students construct new knowledge from what they already know. This requires careful planning on the teacher's part. Teachers need to decide ahead of time what students are to learn and devise questions that will elicit thinking. For example, if students know that lions have fur, ask what other animals have fur. It is important to use examples that are concrete, familiar, and meaningful.

Be aware that students' errors are important steps in their overall understanding. In other words, they can learn from their mistakes. It is good for students to struggle a little—that is how they learn.

From a *sociohistorical perspective*, Lev Vygotsky would say that the acquisition of new concepts is most meaningful to students when they are given an opportunity to construct their own knowledge and to discover things for themselves. This is done as they interact with each other and participate in activities that are of interest to them.

Teachers will need to develop the habit of observing students as they involve themselves in various classroom activities throughout the day. By critically observing, teachers will come to understand and be able to articulate when an activity is a bit too easy or too difficult. If teachers know what students are capable of doing on their own, then they can take students to a new, more difficult level, with some assistance. For example, if students can easily create an AB pattern, they can learn to make an AAB pattern. At first, some may need help, but they will eventually be able to carry out this task on their own. Likewise, if students can independently write two related sentences, they can learn to write three.

The responses to common questions teachers ask are varied. As has been shown, no one theory answers all questions, and the theories are not exclusive of each other. Teachers need to be flexible, knowledgeable, and critical in applying theory to practice. One theory can be utilized in certain situations and another may work best in other contexts. Knowledge of the various theories of learning is essential to understanding that more than one can be put to use in the classroom.

Searching for a New Psychology

In the introduction, we highlighted some of the cultural aspects of Vygotsky's life. These early ways of being had profound effects on Vygotsky's work as a teacher, philosopher, and psychologist. Vygotsky turned to psychology so that he could combine scientific knowledge of the discipline with his own common-sense knowledge, intuition, and inspiration from his experience as a teacher. So convinced was he that theory and practice are interrelated, he declared that the motto of this new psychology would be "practice and philosophy" (Yaroshevsky, 1989, p. 15).

As we discussed earlier, Vygotsky began his work in psychology because of persistent questions he had as a teacher. He wondered how it was that we learn and develop, and he wondered how best to teach all children, including those who were in need of more assistance to solve problems. During Vygotsky's time, the citizens were reconstructing and renewing their society. It was during this post-revolutionary period that Vygotsky began his quest for a new psychology that would move away from the established authority in psychology. He reasoned that none of the existing schools had provided a theory of psychology that brought together a unified notion of how we learn and develop (Vygotsky, 1978).

Throughout the time that Vygotsky was theorizing about learning and development, he was constantly questioning. He not only questioned himself, but he questioned what others were studying. He studied the works of scholars from many backgrounds and traditions (e.g., Freud, Koffka, Lewin, Pavlov, Piaget, Stern, Thorndike, etc.), in order to understand what he considered to be missing elements from their work.

Vygotsky was influenced by the work of Hegel. This influence was evident in the way that Vygotsky thought in dialectics. He often looked at what seemed to be divergent ideas, and then questioned why they were divergent, and what could be learned from juxtaposing one idea against the other. It was not a matter of reducing the world into one or another way of thinking and believing. Rather, juxtaposing his own work against that of other scholars helped Vygotsky to continually refine his studies. This is how Vygotsky worked to find ways of explaining the processes of *learning* and *development.*

Vygotsky sought a psychology that would take into account the role of consciousness in development, while recognizing the cultural, social, and historical basis of psychological functioning. He also theorized language as both a psychological function and a cultural tool through which we can communicate thoughts as well as emotions. This new psychology encouraged a transformative notion of learning and development.

In his search for a new psychology, Vygotsky continued to look at the theories of psychologists of his time and studied their work as he developed his own concepts. He categorized their works into major positions on the theory of child development reflected in the works of Piaget, Thorndike, and the Gestalt school (Vygotsky, 1978). In what follows we will explain what Vygotsky actually wrote, and we will interpret his words with our illustrations.

The first theory is a perspective on learning and development proposed by Piaget as interpreted by Vygotsky. We have read his interpretations and have illustrated his thinking (Figure 1.1).

As the visual illustrates, development and learning are separate systems in which cognition influences language development as a natural part of the maturation process. Learning then involves the mastery of skills attained in that particular level of development.

According to Vygotsky (1978, 1986), viewing development and learning from this angle suggests that the educator teach to the lowest ability in the child. Another way to express this is that education aims at mental functions or intellectual operations that have already matured in the child. Thus, Piaget's theory indicated that development or maturation is viewed as a precondition of learning but is

PIAGET

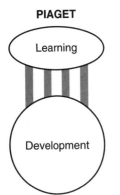

FIGURE 1.1 Piaget's Theory.

never the result of it. To summarize this position: Learning forms a superstructure over development, leaving the latter essentially unaltered (Vygotsky, 1978, p. 80). Piaget proposed that a level of cognitive development must be reached before learning could take place.

Vygotsky focused on not only the actual level, but also on a potential level. In addition, Vygotsky espoused that learning leads development.

> For Vygotsky, learning first, and then development.
>
> For Piaget, development first, and then learning..

The second position, taken by Thorndike, interpreted by Vygotsky (Vygotsky, 1978), showed development as being reflexive; learning was a natural reaction that followed development. In Figure 1.2, the circles of learning and development are identical figures that coincide. This is the essence of Thorndike's theoretical position, based on the concept of reflex, which posits that learning and development occur simultaneously.

The third theory represents the work of the Gestalt School. Vygotsky interpreted the Gestalt theory as viewing learning and development as a complex relationship of two different processes, rather than a process of acquiring habits and skills (Figure 1.3). In the Gestalt view, maturation makes possible the process of learning. In turn, learning pushes development forward. While the two processes were now considered to be interactive, development was still considered to be the more important, primary process.

While Vygotsky studied all three of these theories advanced by his contemporaries, he extended their work in order to make meaning for himself, based on his experience. Vygotsky brought to the theories his focus on historically shaped and culturally transmitted psychology. Figure 1.4 illustrates Vygotsky's theory of learning and development as a reciprocal process. His view included the concept of children as active participants in the developmental process in which language has a direct affect on cognition. Learning and development are interrelated processes, which begin from the first day of a child's life. Vygotsky (1978, 1986) argued that, while learning systems may be similar among children at certain

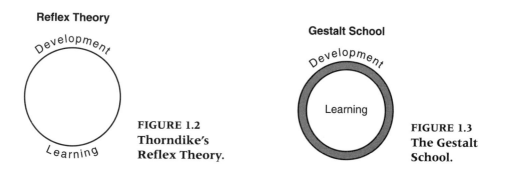

Reflex Theory

Development

Learning

**FIGURE 1.2
Thorndike's
Reflex Theory.**

Gestalt School

Development

Learning

**FIGURE 1.3
The Gestalt
School.**

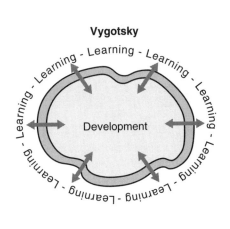

FIGURE 1.4   Vygotsky's Theory.

phases of their developmental process, these systems cannot be identical for all children because of their differing social experiences. He further maintained that learning leads development, a departure not only from Piaget, but also from all the theorists he had studied.

Psychology to Pedagogy

At the beginning of this chapter, we used a quote from Vygotsky to emphasize the relationship of theory and practice. Zebroski (1994) interpreted it further: "Theory is not the opposite of practice; theory is not even a supplement to practice. Theory is practice, a practice of a particular kind, and practice is always theoretical.... Vygotsky believed that theory was inevitable and important" (pp. 15–16).

As early as 1962, Bruner called Vygotsky's conception of development a theory of education. As we have discovered in reading his text on educational psychology, Vygotsky (1997) not only was developing a new psychology, but, in directing his work to teacher educators, he also was reconceptualizing pedagogy.

A Vygotskian Perspective on the Work of Piaget

Modern educators often compare the works of Vygotsky with his most famous contemporary, Jean Piaget. They were born in the same year, but they lived in different cultures, under very different circumstances. As Jerome Bruner noted in his keynote speech to the Second Congress of Sociocultural Research, celebrating the centennial of their birth, educators everywhere are indebted to the legacies of these two theoretical giants who studied the complexities of the human mind. As Bruner (1996) noted:

> Piaget and Vygotsky dedicated their lives to the study of how human beings grow to construct and exchange theories about the world and about each other. Each proposed an epistemology that recognized the essentially developmental nature of such theory building. Both were as full of awe at the cognitive constructions of the growing child as they were at the insights of a Pythagorus, a Pascal, a Tolstoy.

Their respect for the growing mind changed the study of human development, indeed the intellectual climate of our times (p. 2).

For all of their similarities, there were also profound differences. For example, both theorists concentrated on intellectual development. However, they each pursued this interest with differing questions and problems, and from very different sociocultural paths. Wadsworth (1996) noted: "Piaget was primarily interested in how knowledge is formed or constructed. His theory is a theory of invention or construction, which occurs inside the mind of the individual" (p. 10). Vygotsky, however, was interested in the cultural and social influences on learning and development as well as how individual children actively internalize what they learn from others. Bruner (1996, p. 2) described the differences in their outlooks as their particular genius:

Piaget: to recognize the fundamental role of logic-like operations in human mental activity.

Vygotsky: to recognize that individual human intellectual power depended upon our capacity to appropriate human culture and history as tools of mind.

Vygotsky: Learning First, Then Development

How did Piaget and Vygotsky come to view learning and development? How did their views differ? Why does it matter to us?

One of the significant differences in theory between Piaget and Vygotsky is that: Piaget believed that development preceded learning, whereas Vygotsky believed that learning precedes development. For Piaget, a student could not learn something until she was developmentally ready. However, Vygotsky believed that learning pulled development to higher levels. This difference has the potential for profound impact on teaching and learning today. We offer the following vignette to demonstrate how this theoretical difference might look in classrooms.

Theory Is Practice: An Elementary Classroom.   Jean and Pia are student teachers in first-grade classrooms. Dr. V is their university supervisor. Dr. V was once a first-grade teacher, and her teaching is grounded in Vygotsky's sociohistorical theory. Dr. V arranged for both student teachers to meet together throughout the semester with her so that they could learn from discussing their experiences with different mentor teachers and in different classrooms. Dr. V knew that both student teachers came from a Piagetian background and had not yet had the opportunity to study Vygotsky. Therefore, her goal was to share a Vygotskian perspective on learning and development with them. Dr. V hoped that their learning would enhance their own development.

DR. V: Jean and Pia, you've both had one week of student teaching. How is it going so far?

PIA: I'm trying to discover where my students are developmentally and then go from there. They need experiences with the real world and using things they are familiar with to demonstrate the concepts of addition and subtraction.

DR. V: It also helps to talk through what you are doing. The students will use the language they hear from you to internalize the concepts. In other words, it will get them thinking. Try some predictions and problem solving.

JEAN: I thought that requiring first graders to think about two things at once is beyond their ability. They're not yet at the stage where they can do it. It's just going to take them more time.

DR. V: Talk with the students about what you as a group are doing. Ask questions along the way. Have the students do an activity in pairs so they can talk with each other.

JEAN: I'm doing some graphing activities, and I started with real objects.

DR. V: This is good, you are both thinking about what you can do to make your lessons meaningful. Don't forget that speaking and thinking go together, and if you get the kids talking about what they are doing, they'll take it in and understand it better. How is reading going?

PIA: I can't seem to get the low readers interested in reading. During silent reading time I have to force them to read. Most of them sit and stare at their books or just talk to each other.

JEAN: Silent reading doesn't work too well with first graders; developmentally, are they ready for it?

DR. V: What would happen if you encouraged the students to read aloud so they can hear what they are reading, and try partner reading?

PIA: Make sure the books they have to read are on their level.

JEAN: Yes, but I found some children's magazines about animals that they like to talk about. I know these magazines are too difficult for them to read so I wasn't going to use them for reading class. But Kwan keeps going to those magazines. Yesterday he sat next to Beto, and they both looked at those magazines together. They kept whispering about those animals, and I was wondering if I should send them to the time-out center.

DR. V: What happened when they whispered about the animals? Talking helps them reflect on what they know and helps them think about things in new ways. Did they learn from each other through this informal conversation?

Much later in the semester, Dr. V met with Jean and Pia in order to assess their student teaching. First, she needed to listen to them.

DR. V: How is it going with your student teaching?

PIA: I'm beginning to see the importance of observing my students. I learn a lot by watching them. I try to ask myself questions: What can they do on their own? What can they do with a little help?

JEAN: I've also seen how important it is for students to learn by doing. It was hard at first, because I felt like I didn't have control over anything. Eventually, I saw that if I structured classroom materials and situations so that they are in line with my objectives, learning took place and I was able to guide students in the right direction.

PIA: I also found it helpful to ask questions. This encouraged my students to grow in their learning and develop new ideas. Of course, it helped to have them interact with each other. Many students are very creative, and I sometimes find myself learning from them.

DR. V: Pia, how is the silent reading going?

PIA: It's going really well, but it's no longer silent. The students seem to enjoy reading more when they are reading aloud and reading to each other.

JEAN: Remember Kwan and Beto? I didn't think they could read those harder magazines, but in science the other day, they were both going on and on about how a baby kangaroo incubates in the mama's pouch for weeks. Did they learn by talking about those pictures?

DR. V: Could be that more was going on there than met the eye. Ok, and the math lessons?

JEAN: I'm seeing how important it is to use concrete examples—especially when I'm introducing something new. It really helps them understand. Oh, and after explaining something, I have a few students demonstrate to the whole class.

DR. V: Modeling is always important. Having some students model for the others helps them feel that they are an important part of the group.

PIA: I have a few students who always seem to get things right away. I've grouped them with the students who need a little more help. They enjoy being the 'teachers.' Makes me wonder if the students sometimes learn more from each other than from me.

JEAN: And it takes a lot of time and planning to figure out how to connect concrete experiences to symbolic thinking. Children think differently from adults. What makes perfect sense to me might be totally foreign to my students.

PIA: I'm amazed at what they learn from each other. Learning really is a social experience and I think using language in this way expands their thinking.

DR. V: Hmm, seems like learning leads development. Do you see any connection between your students learning from each other and the meetings we've had together?

JEAN: Well, I hadn't thought of it before now, but I guess we have been learning from each other.

PIA: We've taken ideas from these discussions and used them in our own classrooms.

DR. V: If you think about it, you have been learning in several ways. You have applied what you learned in your courses, and you observed your mentor teachers and conferenced with them about your lessons. Then you talked with me and with each other here in our debriefing sessions. Throughout your student teaching, I have been giving specific directions so you could scaffold your learning. Soon you will be able to teach without my help.

PIA: Having people to talk with has been helpful.

DR. V: Learning for teachers never ends. I agree that talking with others enhances our learning. Our meetings have encouraged me to try new things in my graduate classes. I'll bet you didn't know that I was incorporating some of your ideas into my Classroom Assessment course for teachers, did you?

JEAN: You mean that you learned from us?

DR. V: Of course! We all learned from each other through our collaboration around real-life problems you were having in the classroom. Remember, novices contribute to mentors in their own ways. Good job, both of you![2]

The above conversation illustrates the difference in the starting points of these two theorists. Both Jean and Pia began their student teaching from a Piagetian perspective. They originally understood development from the point of view of preparation for learning. As they interacted with each other and their supervisor, they came to recognize how learning leads development in a Vygotskian sense. Their supervisor asked questions, responded to their reflections from the starting point of learning leading development, and helped them connect their classroom experiences to learning theory through their discussions. "Thus, for Vygotsky, learning is the driving force of intellectual development, whereas for Piaget, development is the driving force" (Wadsworth, 1996, p. 10).

Vygotsky: Active Use of Language

Another major difference between Piaget and Vygotsky was their thinking about how we use language. Vygotsky's social/cultural/historical perspective was evident in his conviction that all learning was first accomplished through the language that flows between individuals. Language and action, for Vygotsky, were tools of mediation for learning. Speaking reorganizes our thinking, and our language comes to us as a cultural heritage through our interactions with others. Because we actively use language, it changes our thinking, and our thinking and actions change language. This belief is the cornerstone of the difference Vygotsky made in conceptualizing how we think, learn, and develop. Keep this important idea in mind as we make some comparisons between theories.

Theory Is Practice: A University Classroom. What does a Vygotskian class look like? We have seen the following example in which language was the tool of mediation for students making meaning from their experience. Wells (2000, pp. 60–61) enumerates several characteristics of such a classroom:

- constructing a collaborative community
- engaging in purposeful activities involving whole persons actively forming identity
- incorporating activities that are situated and unique
- using curriculum as a means for learning, not just an end result
- producing outcomes that are both aimed for and emergent
- constructing activities that must allow diversity and originality

From a Vygotskian perspective, the classroom would have teachers and students learning together through exploration and collaboration in an inquiry-based curriculum.

The following describes a conversation in a postsecondary class that had experienced a Vygotskian pedagogy, but did not see it nor recognize it until they articulated it.

"What does a Vygotskian class look like?" the graduate students asked after they had studied Vygotsky.

"Well, what have we been doing since day one in this course?" the professor replied.

"We keep an issues log each night as we read our assignments," the first student replied.

"Then, when we get to class, we sit in small groups and discuss the issues each of us has highlighted," replied the second student.

"Next, our whole class discussion is determined by our logs, not by the text and not by you because we are asking significant questions about our own understanding," the third graduate student said to the professor.

"Then would you say that our discussions of your issues from the logs were important for you to make sense of what we are studying?" asked the professor.

"Well, I know that I understood the issues much better in class than I did when I wrote them in the logs by myself," answered a student.

"Ok, and how did we create the midterm project?" the professor asked the class.

"Oh, yeah," the first student replied, "I remember that we created six different possibilities for a midterm, and each student could choose. Some of us renegotiated our choices a couple of times."

"How did we decide to grade the various projects?" the faculty member queried.

"We created a rubric together one night in class," a student answered.

"I remember that some of us read the same difficult journal article and then got together and talked about it and then presented it for our colleagues in class," another student observed.

"I knew, when I assigned those readings, that, on an individual basis, they might be a bit beyond you because you would be grappling with new academic thought and language. But, I remember that each group had a dynamite demonstration of the materials so that your colleagues could do their own sense-making of those same articles. Together, it seems that you, collectively, have generated meaning of some very heavy readings that you all complained about from the first day," the professor said. The students smiled knowingly.

"But look at how much we learned," the professor concluded. "And, now my question to you is: What will you do with the new knowledge that you have generated?" (adapted from Wink, 2000, pp. 100–101).

In other words, language was how they mediated their understanding.

Major Points of Child Development: Vygotsky/Piaget

In the next section we briefly diverge from the major perspectives we have addressed thus far in order to analyze the similarities and differences between the two foremost developmental theorists we have studied, Piaget and Vygotsky.

While both of these theorists looked at children's interaction with their environment, Piaget based this interaction on the maturation of the individual's inherited genetic program. For Piaget, intelligence matured in an observable pattern, allowing the child to adapt to changes in the environment (Phillips, 1975). He believed that understanding occurs through development of the cognitive structures of the individual. In addition, interaction with physical objects, with the environment, and with others is key to developing knowledge, and this cognitive development influences language use and thinking.

Vygotsky (1986), on the other hand, believed that the child's reasoning was socially constructed through interaction with adults and peers. The development of higher cognitive functions was a mediated activity, which occurred first during social interaction. Understanding occurs through our historical, social, and cultural relations with others. Our language is more than a symbolic system through which we make meaning. Language also carries with it the meanings and intentionality of those who came before us, and who now use that same tool to make meaning with us.

In light of both views of cognitive development that we have discussed, Piaget is noted as seeing children advance in development, not necessarily through the use of language, but through action with physical objects in their surroundings (Wadsworth, 1996). Vygotsky, on the other hand, theorized that our learning leads our development through the use of language as a cultural tool. What we need to understand in this case is that Vygotsky did not separate language from action, but saw them in a reciprocal relationship. The Russian word that Vygotsky used for language is more correctly translated in English as "speech act"; the notion of action is implied in the Russian word for language (Bruner, 1987).

At the educational level, Piaget's view of cognitive development as a necessity before language can be acquired tends to make classroom instruction dependent on the child's natural level of cognitive development. In contrast, Vygotsky believed that instruction leads and supports development through the interaction of two kinds of concepts: scientific, or schooled concepts, and spontaneous or everyday concepts (Kozulin, 1990). The everyday concepts were those that emerged from the child's own observations and experiences. These generalizations about everyday events were necessary, but not sufficient, for children to begin acquiring scientific concepts. The two types of concepts then work in harmony with each other; the spontaneous concepts creating an experiential path for the development of the scientific, which would offer organization to the child's thinking.

In Vygotsky's view, relying on the spontaneous concepts alone to gauge the child's progress lead to the faulty view of development leading instruction. Vygotsky theorized that assessment should focus on what the child is able to do with the assistance of an adult when the spontaneous concepts come into contact with the scientific concepts introduced in education. The difference between what a child can do with assistance and what she or he can later do alone is a measure of the developing psychological functions. This was known as his zone of proximal development, which we will discuss in depth in Chapter 4. This notion takes into account individual differences, and focuses on the communicative nature of learning in which the participants come to an understanding of the operations they are performing. He also charged educators to anticipate and teach to the proximal level, to that which children are beginning to understand, so that education "emerged as activator of development" (Yaroshevsky, 1989, p. 278).

The value of Vygotsky's work in relation to epistemological forms of pedagogy stems from the very way in which he viewed learning and development as dynamic processes—social, cultural, and historical by nature—and in dialectic relationship with each other. He acknowledged learners as interactive agents in communicative, socially situated relationships. This was a move away from a view of the learner in terms of what can be measured objectively, as a lone individual, genetically predisposed to develop and act on the environment. Rather, Vygotsky's view of the individual was in terms of the emotional combined with the rational, as social and cultural beings who learn through interaction with others as they socially construct meanings through the use of the mediational tool of language.

To further differentiate the perspectives we have represented in this chapter, we offer a contrastive chart to illustrate the differences in the potential positions one could adopt through these perspectives. Think of the three categories presented as different lenses one could wear to view teaching and learning from the different perspectives.

Durán and Syzmanski (1995) differentiate the terms *social* or *cognitive constructivism* and *social constructionism* as founded on two distinct perspectives: social constructivism is derived from Piaget's developmental theory while social constructionism is linked with Vygotskian theory. The social constructionist theory places emphasis on learning as a process that includes "appropriation of cultural beliefs about the world and how to function competently in activity settings that constitute the 'lived experiences' of particular communities of practice" (p. 150).

Another way to think of the difference between them has been described by Hruby (2001, personal conversation with J. Green) as a difference in how knowledge is perceived and constructed. "That is to say, while constructivism deals with knowledge formation in the head, constructionism deals with knowledge formation outside the head between participants in social relationships" (p. 51).

We demonstrate how these perspectives differ across various elements of classroom actions in Table 1.1. This chart is meant to be a tool to compare and contrast the views, and is not exhaustive of all the points that could be compared. We invite the reader to add more to the chart as you learn more through your studies about educational perspectives.

In Table 1.1 we depict three of the perspectives for comparison to illustrate some of the differences in the ways these perspectives are played out in the educational setting. We have labeled the perspectives as *behaviorist-derived, cognitive constructivist* (based on Piaget's work), and *social constructionist* (based on Vygotsky's work). We have seen Piaget and Vygotsky differentiated by the terms *constructivist* and *social constructivist,* but we are using the term *social constructionist* for Vygotsky's work, as suggested earlier by Durán and Syzmanski (1995), to more easily differentiate these perspectives.

In this summary chart, we highlight how the lens you choose to view teaching and learning will change what you practice in the classroom. For example, knowledge itself is either a fixed body of knowledge to acquire, or it is mutable and constructed by individuals in a social world. From a social constructionist perspective, the difference is that the expectation for construction of knowledge is in collaboration with others.

In terms of teaching, the behaviorist-derived viewpoint tends to position the teacher as the adult in authority, presenting the information for students to memorize. The teacher becomes the *Sage on the Stage,* encouraging students to stay on task, and correcting wrong responses from students in a recitation style. The teacher in the cognitive constructivist arena becomes the *Guide on the Side,* challenging students to individually construct knowledge in a hands-on environment. The teacher creates opportunities for meaningful interaction with ideas, materials, and other students. From the social constructionist perspective, the teacher becomes a mediator, an *Actuator of Learning.* That is, the role of the teacher is to construct *with* students opportunities for interacting with meaningful ideas, materials, and collaboration with others.

From a behaviorist-derived standpoint, students act as receptors of information, working to actively listen, follow directions from the teacher, and complete

TABLE 1.1 Comparison Chart of Perspectives

Construct	Behaviorist-derived	Cognitive constructivist Piaget	Social constructionist Vygotsky
Knowledge	Fixed body of knowledge to acquire	Changing body of knowledge, individually constructed in social world	Changing body of knowledge, mutually constructed with others
Learning What	Acquisition of facts, skills, concepts	Active construction, restructuring prior knowledge	Collaborative construction of socially/culturally defined knowledge and values
How	Through drill and guided practice	Through multiple opportunities and diverse processes to connect to what is already know	Through socially and culturally constructed opportunities, tying to students' experience
Where	Within individual's head	In interaction with others and environment	In collaboration with others through the social/cultural setting
Teaching	Transmission, presentation, telling (sage on the stage)	Challenge thinking toward more complete understanding (guide on the side)	Coconstruct knowledge with students by sharing expertise and understanding (actuator of learning)
Motivation	Rewards, grades, jobs	Self-development, competence	Collective and individual development through collaboration
Role of Teacher	Manager, supervisor	Facilitator, guide	Mediator, mentor, actuator
Actions	Encourage on-time task completion, correct wrong answers	Create opportunities for interacting with meaningful ideas, materials, others	Construct with students opportunities for interacting with meaningful ideas, materials, others
Role of Peers	Not usually considered or rigidly structured	Not necessarily encouraged, but can stimulate thinking, raise questions	Assume part of knowledge construction, contribute to definition of knowledge, help define opportunities for learning
Role of Student	Passive receptor of information	Active construction within mind	Active coconstruction with others and self-negotiating meaning
	Worker	Generator, constructor	Cogenerator, coconstructor, reformulator
	Active listener, direction follower	Active thinker, explainer, interpreter, questioner	Active thinker, explainer, interpreter, inquirer, active social participator

(continued)

TABLE 1.1   Continued

Construct	Behaviorist-derived	Cognitive constructivist Piaget	Social constructionist Vygotsky
Student View of Self	Remember/forgetter, algorithm follower, worker	Sense-maker, problem solver	Sense-maker, problem solver, socially appropriate member of collective
Evidence of Learning	Products	Process of inquiry	Process of inquiry, socially competent participation in collective
	Performance: answers on worksheets, standardized tests	Performance: explanation of reasoning	Performance: explanation of reasoning, social performance over multiple sites
	Assessed in single setting at one or periodic points	Ongoing assessment	Ongoing assessment over multiple sites
Purpose of School	Transmit, reproduce a common body of knowledge	Create new knowledge, learn strategies to continue learning	Create new knowledge, learn strategies to continue learning
			Prepare individuals as social members with expanding repertoires of appropriate ways of interacting

Adapted from Marshall (1992b) and Woolfolk (1998).

the tasks that are assigned by the teacher. The student view of self is as a worker, completing tasks assigned and remembering what was discussed in class. As constructivists, students act more as generators of information, actively constructing within their mind the knowledge that comes from actively working on projects, both individually and with others. Their view of self is as a problem solver and sense-maker. In the social constructionist outlook, students are actively negotiating meaning and coconstructing knowledge with others. They are reformulating ideas as they individually internalize what they have learned in collaboration with others. Their view of self, while similar to the constructivist view of sense-maker and problem solver, is also as a socially competent participant in the classroom collective.

The evidence of learning changes between perspectives. For example, through the behaviorist-derived lens, products of student work demonstrate learning: answers on standardized tests, completed worksheets, and reports. These products are assessed either in a single setting or at periodic points throughout the school year. From a cognitive constructivist lens, the evidence of learning appears more as performances to demonstrate evidence of reasoning on the part of the student. Assessment here is ongoing throughout the year. In the social constructionist view, evidence of learning is also performance-based, but it also includes appropriate performances as collaborative projects with others. Ongoing assessment occurs throughout the year, in multiple situations, both as individuals and as collaborative efforts with others.

Finally, the purpose of schooling is also different in these contrastive positions. In the behaviorist school, the purpose is to transmit a body of knowledge to students so they can reproduce that knowledge to demonstrate their readiness to move forward through school, and eventually to graduation and beyond. The cognitive constructivist outlook on schooling is to provide opportunities for students to create new knowledge and to learn strategies so that they can continue learning after their time in school. While similar to this outlook, the position of the social constructionist school is that, beyond creating new knowledge and becoming lifelong learners, students are prepared to be social members. They are continually expanding their repertoires of appropriate ways of interacting with others in constructing knowledge.

Thus, the perspectives presented in Table 1.1 offer a contrastive view of what teaching, studenting, and schooling look like, depending on how one views the roles and purposes of teachers, students, and schools themselves. We invite readers to add to the chart as they study and reflect on their own schooling experiences.

Multiple Perspective for Multiple Realities

The purpose of this chapter has been to illustrate the multiple perspectives that affect teaching and learning in schools. By looking at the various theories, we hope that readers will understand how existing theories affect their own classroom practice. In our experience of working with teachers, we see that teachers are developing a discourse that allows them to articulate not only others' theory but also their own. However, many teachers that we know, who can articulate masterfully the relationship between theory and practice, still are unable to make effective change in their educational space because of a sociocultural context that is tenaciously holding on to unexamined assumptions and past educational practices. In far too many cases, local teachers are controlled by mandated policymakers who not only reside in far-away communities, but who are removed from the sociocultural context of classrooms of today.

What this exemplifies is a paradigm struggle of multiple perspectives. The teachers are living a local reality of teaching the children in their district while the policymakers are looking to the past for a vision of a single *ideal* reality that they once knew. Vygotsky understood well that we cannot make the schooling experience into a "one size fits all" garment for students. In his book on educational psychology for teachers he stated:

> The goal of the school is not at all a matter of reducing everyone to the same level, on the contrary, one of the goals of the social environment that is created in the school is to achieve as complex, as diversified, and as flexible an organization of the various elements in this environment as possible. It is only necessary that these elements not be in any way irreconcilable, and that they be linked up together into a single system (Vygotsky, 1997, p. 79).

Thus, we have to realize that the local reality of teaching and learning in classrooms is a complex process that cannot be reduced to a single curricular program that attempts to place every student in the same place at the same time. Rather, we have to understand the multiple realities that exist for classroom participants and try to prepare all students for the realities that they will encounter beyond the schoolyard.

Understanding the notion of multiple realities may be, for some, a difficult procedure. For example, as Frank (1999) related:

> I have lived in the United States for my entire life, and I had a difficult time with the idea that there is no one right reality.... I had trouble thinking that there might be a different reality than the one I saw and created every day of my life.... Wasn't something either true or not true, factual or not factual? For me to understand multiple perspectives took help from a good friend who was able to talk to me about my reservations. It was not a quick process and took time. I had to be wrenched away from my mainstream way of looking and my 'one-way-only' of understanding the world. It was difficult to see life from a different viewpoint. The world was always OK for me without having to know from a different perspective. What I did not see was that the world was not OK for some others (p. 4).

What Frank came to recognize through her work with classroom teachers and preservice teachers was the importance of viewing situations from multiple perspectives to more fully understand what is happening in a classroom.

In the ethnographic glimpse that follows, we expand on the notion of multiple perspectives beyond the educational context to demonstrate how pervasive ethnocentricism can be. In trying to make sense of the notion of multiple realities, one graduate student told us that she and her husband were discussing multiple realities, coincidentally, in the grocery store. She related her experience to her graduate student classmates:

> Last week in the grocery store I was sharing with my husband our classroom discussion about the concept of multiple realities. "I was excited and told my husband all about it in the cereal aisle," she related. "He so did *not* understand that his reality, being the 'correct one,' was *not* the same as my reality in that moment," she told them as she continued, "Here is how the exchange went between us."
>
> "But dear," I said to my husband, "our experiences, our culture, our thinking, our speech have an effect on our way of thinking about the world."
>
> "No, can't be. There is just one reality, one truth to be found," he retorted. "You have to adjust your thinking to understand my way of seeing it," he continued with a wry smile.
>
> "See, we are experiencing it right now. Your reality and my reality are totally different because you cannot and will not even conceive of what my reality could be," she sighed.
>
> She and her fellow students laughed together about not only the multiple realities of their classroom but also the multiple realities of their lives. They were amazed at how learning in schools suddenly can emerge at unexpected times in unexpected places.

As the graduate student related her experience, the others began to understand that to take up a different method, a different paradigm, one has to accept the notion of multiple realities. Just as the husband in the grocery store could not comprehend another possible reality we realized that for some, tenaciously clinging to assumptions—particularly when they are initially challenged—is what keeps us from learning and developing. The Vygotskian perspective has challenged us in the past to juxtapose different ways of knowing to construct new ways of understanding.

Conclusion

This chapter serves as the foundation for the remainder of the book. We chronicled changes in educational theory since the time in which Vygotsky was working, thinking, and challenging others to think in new ways.

In taking up a Vygotskian perspective, we realize that the entire sociocultural, historical perspective has changed drastically. In addition, the political context of today is vastly different from the past. We have expanded on the different perspectives that have contributed to our understanding of the relationship between learning and development. Having examined various perspectives in a historical look at education, we now turn to specific principles of the Vygotskian legacy.

E N D N O T E S

1. The authors wish to thank Carrie for her design of the different learning perspectives as Vygotsky described them in *Mind in Society.* She originally drew them to lead to her own understanding, and, in sharing them with us, she has increased our understanding.

2. The authors wish to thank Chris Kerfoot, who created not only the three questions and answers that primary teachers often ask about philosophy and practice, but also the Vygotskian/Piagetian student teacher vignette as part of two longer research assignments she conducted for a graduate class. We also wish to thank Dr. Granger Dinwiddie, the professor for one of her classes, who provided the freedom of opportunity for Chris to write what she needed to write.

PART TWO

Three Principal Principles

Thus is the educational process an active one on three levels: the student is active, the teacher is active, and the environment created between them is an active one (Vygotsky, 1997, p. 54).

In Part 2, we explore three principles of Vygotsky's work that are most salient for learning and development. These chapters are meant to be progressive; i.e., each builds on the previous one. We begin with the dynamic and reciprocal relationship between thought and language. From there, we move to the complex implications of the sociocultural context that embodies, not only our thought and language, but also the sum of our experiences. The first two principles culminate in the third, the zone of proximal development.

We will focus in Chapter 2 on the Vygotskian notion that language and thought are central to learning; they are woven together—a fabric of experience and culture; they are joined to make sense of our past, present, and future. As Karen, a teacher, said, "Half of thought and language is something that goes on inside a person and is not visible or measurable while it is happening." She continued, "You see the results of what happens in the brain through speaking and writing." We think she is partially right. Thought and language is more than simply what happens in the brain; it also takes place in a person's heart and a person's soul. Bialystok and Hakuta (1994) write that learning takes place in language, the brain, the mind, the self, and culture. This chapter will promote ways of guaranteeing language and learning for all students.

If language is denied, thought is denied; culture is diminished; identity is endangered. Bilingual and hearing-impaired students are two examples of those who are sometimes denied access to language, thought, culture, and identity. As Sonia, a beginning bilingual teacher said to us, "I know many of my peers, who in an effort to become 'Americanized,' have lost their language, heritage, and cultural roots. As they were denied their language, they were denied a part of themselves."

Priscilla, mother of Martín, a profoundly hearing-impaired child, has shared with us many examples of ways in which Martín cannot access (oral) language to enhance his thinking. It is only through signing, his language, that he can enhance his thinking. She often watches him sign to himself when he is involved in a problem-solving activity. Martín is using his language of signing to help organize his thoughts so that he can solve problems.

Sonia and Priscilla have helped us value the immense contributions of thought and language to learning and developing. As will be seen in Chapter 3, the sociocultural context for thought and language is another way in which educators can make a difference everyday for the students in their own classes. Chapter 4, the zone of proximal development, will demonstrate how all of the three principal principles are related. However, we begin with Kelly, a teacher in Germany, who said it as well as it can be said.

> "The Vygotskian perspective opened a door in my mind," Kelly told her graduate classmates. "For me, the three concepts are so intertwined, that I can only discuss them as a whole. I tried to understand one at a time, and just when I thought I had it, and the dust was just beginning to settle, a door would open beyond. I felt like Alice in Wonderland as I made my first journey though Vygotsky's house."

With these words, we invite readers to open the door to their minds and beyond.

2 Thought and Language

Thought is not merely expressed in words; it comes into existence through them. Every thought tends to connect something with something else, to establish a relation between things. Every thought moves, grows and develops, fulfills a function, solves a problem (Vygotsky, 1986, p. 218).

In this chapter, we explore the centrality of thought and language in all development. Vygotsky theorized the relationship between cognitive development and language, and he considered external dialogue to be both a psychological tool as well as a psychological function. Initially, we will inquire visually into the connections between thought and language with a series of graphics, beginning with Vygotsky's own portrayal and expanding to other illustrations of the reciprocity between thought and language. Unique Vygotskian language is further explained in Chapter 6, which also serves as a glossary.

Near the end of this chapter, we examine thought and language by looking in classrooms. Our goal is to integrate this reciprocal relationship in actual classroom social practices that we have experienced with teachers and students who daily face the daunting challenge of turning the principles to practices.

Thinking about Words

The use of the English word *language* can be problematic when discussing Vygotsky's work. According to Rieber and Carton (1987), the use of the English translated title, *Thought and Language,* does not capture the essence of the meaning that Vygotsky intended. The Russian title, *Myschlenie i Rech',* is more correctly translated as *Thinking and Speech.* The difference here is the notion of language as a semantic and grammatical system, and speech as the action of utilizing the language.

Minick (1987) further distinguishes between Vygotsky's work and that of his linguistic contemporaries: Vygotsky studied the *relationship* between thinking and speech, rather than viewing them as distinct functions. We call this to the reader's attention because it is this notion of teachers and students interactively shaping their worlds, and each other's worlds, through their active speech that will come into focus as we explore more of the concepts that inform this book. Therefore we use speech and language interchangeably, but recognizing that our intention is to convey the *active* and *interactive* nature of communicating.

> **Language is the skin of thought.**
>
> Oliver Wendell Holmes

The Vygotskian Venn Diagram

Early in his work, Vygotsky was interested in the relationship of thinking and speaking. As Luria (Vygotsky, 1987) explained, Vygotsky was trying to investigate the study of thinking by first locating the component that should be studied that contained all the elements of thinking and speaking in the child's activity. To do so he began with a proposition that was opposite to the ideas suggested by his contemporaries. While Piaget viewed children's verbal development as egocentric, directed toward the self and not to others, Vygotsky began with an opposite thesis. He argued that children are social beings from the beginning, and that their egocentric speech is an attempt to verbally figure out an answer to a problem. These early studies are what led Vygotsky to study the relationship of thinking and speech.

In *Thought and Language,* (1962) Vygotsky represented schematically the relationship of thought and speech with two intersecting circles in which "the overlapping parts, thought and speech coincide to produce verbal thought" (Vygotsky, 1986, p. 88). The Vygotskian notion of verbal thought is made visible with this Venn diagram: one circle represents thought; the second represents language; and, where the two overlap, verbal thought occurs. Verbal thought is central to understanding the connections between thought and language, just as it is central in the Venn diagram.

To study the concept of verbal thought, the interconnectedness of thinking and speaking, Vygotsky (1986) searched for a unit of analysis that would contain the properties of verbal thought as a whole, much like the metaphor of water that we discussed in our introduction. That most elementary form of the unity of thought and speech is word meaning. When reciprocity between thought and language is achieved, when the two circles are joined, when things make sense, thought and language have come together to create verbal thought, or word meaning. It is the point at which words begin to work. This is the notion Vygotsky realized; that language was both a tool and a psychological function. Constructing language is a cognitive function for communicating our thoughts to others and, at the same time, language is a tool for constructing more thoughts. In Vygotsky's (1986) words, "thought undergoes many changes as it turns into speech. It does not merely find expression in speech; it finds its reality and form" (p. 219).

Those who know the legacy of Vygotsky also realize that the Venn diagram illustrates the union of thought and language, but not the dynamic process that he envisioned and referred to in his writings. For Vygotsky, language informed thought, and thought came to life through language. Both thought and language were influenced by our sociocultural experience. The entire process was active and situated in the interactions and human connections of the sociocultural context.

For this reason we wish to go beyond Vygotsky's graphic with what we perceive to be more interpretive visual representations that emphasize the dynamic and interactive relationship between thought and language. Every thought is altered as it moves into the realm of language. The opposite is also true. Language is changed as it moves into thought. The relationship between thought and language is reciprocal, dynamic, and constantly changing. As students learn and use new language, the process impacts their thinking, and vice versa. It is through the fusion of thinking, speaking, and our experience that we construct our knowledge.

Expanding the Venn Diagram

Another illustration of the reciprocal development of thought and language is included to demonstrate how one graphic can serve as a springboard to another. Vygotsky's original Venn diagram encouraged Joan to continue graphically in order to grasp the dynamic relationship of thought and language (see Figures 2, 3, and 4 of the Introduction). So, too, did others continue to expand on their own understands with further drawings. While the concept illustrated in Figure 3 shows the reciprocal nature of the relationship of thought and language, it also includes the product of the process, word meaning.

The process of thinking and speaking and, thereby, generating word meaning is also depicted in Figure 4, with the addition of the sociocultural environment that also affects what we think and come to know. In addition, this graphic demonstrates the expanding nature of our learning. As we think and discuss through our experiences with others, our learning expands and deepens our knowing and our development.

These graphics have expanded students' understanding, also. We have used them in various settings, which has generated other ways of thinking about the concepts. For example, after seeing the four graphics, an international teacher in a graduate course immediately drew a whirlwind on her paper (Figure 2.1).

When she showed it to her colleagues in class, at first they did not understand her ideas. She began by explaining to them.

> Well, you know how new thoughts and, perhaps, vocabulary, come to us. Oftentimes these ideas are a challenge to our long-held assumptions. It is contrary to all our beliefs to that point. It is like we had an idea, and all of a sudden someone tells us an anti-idea. The anti-idea churns; it tries to germinate; sometimes it explodes. We struggle and grapple with it. It triggers anger, defensiveness, and resistance.

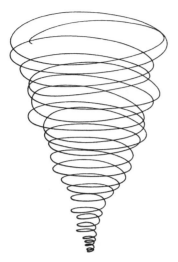

FIGURE 2.1   Closed Whirlwind.

The other international educators in the graduate class nodded their heads in agreement. They understood the struggle with new ideas and vocabulary, with new thought and language. The woman who drew the graphic continued.

> When this happens to me, I discuss the idea with someone. I usually choose a peer, another teacher, who also clings to some of my myths. Thus, my peer validates my instincts to reject the idea. Thus, after much agony, I often retain my previous thoughts and belief system.

"No, I'm not like that," another teacher announced to the class. She left her desk and walked to the chalkboard where she hurriedly drew the graphic in Figure 2.2.

> For me a new challenging thought comes in like a whirlwind when there is an opening—when I am receptive. Usually, I learn a new idea as someone is sharing a personal experience with me. I usually come to awareness as I visit with someone—or, through a dialogue. For me a new thought emerges as a new perspective is shaped.

In Harriet's version of the open whirlwind, a new idea can open our minds to a different perspective if we are receptive to it. This new idea first expands our thinking, and then narrows as we begin to make sense of it. The idea expands again when we share what we have learned with others.

After first sharing her conceptualization of thinking, Harriet, an ESL teacher who grew up in the United States and has lived the last twenty years in the Czech Republic, then shared her ideas on how *knowing about* is different from *experiencing*. Her colleagues asked her for some examples.

FIGURE 2.2   Open Whirlwind.

"Swimming, cancer, and reproduction," she replied. "There is a big difference in knowing about those three things than *experiencing* them. Another example was Helen Keller. To know about 'water,' she needed a knowledgeable teacher who gave her, not only the experience, but also the language.

Harriet continued by sharing the story of a young immigrant student in her class who had had horrific experiences with family in their war-torn homeland. The young student had experienced fear, pain, and hate. However, she needed the language to express her past life in order to grow into her new one. Harriet shared how the girl's thoughts about fear and safety were much deeper and truer than her classmates' due to her own personal experiences with war. Harriet's knowledge of the Vygotskian concepts of thought and language enabled her to support the young victim as she healed from her past and acquired language to express her experiences.

At this point, the class, filled with teachers from all over the world, began to share their personal experiences with *their knowing about* and their *experiencing*. They agreed that it helped them grow cognitively when they could talk with a friend or colleague. They agreed that they all needed time to cogitate for any new idea to be internalized, interpreted, and accepted. In their experiences, an idea can take a long time. It is as if an idea needs to lie around and rest before being born; learning and developing take time. They agreed they needed a language to articulate a thought or an experience. As they carried on this discussion, Harriet suddenly realized: "The problem with the graphics thus far is that they don't visually portray the primacy of experience. There is a big difference between knowing about something and experiencing it."

As she talked, she walked to the whiteboard and quickly sketched a braid with strands of three different colors. Harriet used red for thought, green for experience, and blue for language (Figure 2.3).

FIGURE 2.3   The Braid.

Harriet continued:

> "We must acknowledge the primacy of experience in thought and language. However, even if you have had the experience, you have to have the language to express it. That is what we're trying to do in this class—learn new thoughts and language to express our experiences, past and present."

Through her talk and her illustrations, Harriet showed that she had internalized Vygotsky's conceptualization of the relationship of thought and speech, and how it is grounded in the totality of experience, the sociocultural context.

Cognitive Development and Language

A particular language was used by Vygotsky as he thought about thought and language, as he theorized the relationship between cognitive development and language. This language continues to be used by later Vygotskian scholars and will be explained in Chapter 6.

During the process of development, children become active participants in their learning through the use of language and interactions with others. Rather than viewing language as merely a semiotic function of cognition, Vygotsky viewed the use of signs and symbols as mediators of human cognition. In other words, we use language, in our action of speaking, as a tool for developing thought, and, at the same time, we develop language through thought. This reciprocal relationship allows us to realize that the social action of using language could lead cognitive development. Interaction of thinking and speech results in experience for the learner, and Vygotsky viewed this experience as a key factor in further impacting the relationship of thinking and speech. In the classroom, as well as in interaction with others away from the classroom, learners use language to communicate thoughts, and, through the social act of verbalizing those thoughts, combine their experiences with those of others, a continual, lifelong learning process.

The use of language as a mediational tool was central to Vygotsky's cultural–historical perspective. Vygotsky (1978) noted that using language actively represented two distinct manifestations of the social realm. First of all, psychological tools (e.g., language, algebraic symbol systems, counting systems, etc.) are social in the sense that they are products of the social/historical/cultural system. Individuals have access to these products through their participation in the cultural practices in which the tools are culturally transmitted (John-Steiner, Panofsky, & Smith, 1994). At the same time, the tools are social in the sense that they are utilized in the process of social interaction. Learning and development, then, are thoroughly situated in culture, and development of the individual is "a process in which children grow into the intellectual life of those around them" (Vygotsky, 1978, p. 88).

According to John-Steiner and colleagues (1994), a mediational tool (e.g., language, signs, practices) is one that "contributes to qualitative changes in development" (p. 139). Vygotsky viewed mental functions—reasoning, attention, memory, and so on—as activities of consciousness, which are originally social and are mediated by cultural tools, mainly language, thus becoming intrapsychological. In other words, the use of language, in interaction with ourselves, with texts, and with others, actually transforms mental functioning.

This notion of language as a mediational tool was a revolutionary concept in itself. Prior to his work, the major theorists shared a common philosophy of individualism, lacking any focus on the communication between people mediated by language (Yaroshevsky, 1989). Vygotsky, on the other hand, brought into focus the nature of our being as cultural, social, and historical, with an emphasis on the communicative practices of the individual as part of a collective. As cited by Shepel (1995), Vygotsky named this system of relationships of the individual with peers and adults as the *social situation of development*. This social situation of development "defines totally those forms and the means by which the child gains new characteristics of personality, derived from the social reality, as the main source of development, as the way for the social to become the individual" (p. 431). This notion of activity as first collective, then internalized by the individual, became an integral part of another Vygotskian construct, the zone of proximal development.

Autumn Leaves

An analogy will illustrate how semiotic tools mediate language acquisition; specifically, we are speaking of how one acquires an additional language. If you are relatively new to understanding how one acquires another language, this analogy is for you. If you already have mediated your own knowledge of language acquisition, we hearken back to our more capable peer, Harriet, who taught us that knowing about was far different from experiencing. Finally, if you know about language acquisition and have experienced the process of acquiring another language or two, we hope this analogy will simply be another tool for you (Wertsch, 1991).

Watching a child acquire a first language resembles the study of a natural phenomenon, such as leaves falling from branches on an autumn day. If one were to watch a leaf as it fell on a still autumn morning, the movement of the leaf would be smooth, seamless, and even soothing. However, when one acquires an additional language, the process could be compared to watching leaves fall on a rainy, windy, chilly autumn afternoon. In this case, the leaves are tossed wildly by the wind and rain. The elements are so unpredictable and intense we often have no way of knowing how or where the leaves will land.

First-language acquisition for most is like breathing. It is an unconscious, natural process of interacting with others to communicate. Other language acquisition is often a turbulent process as we consciously attempt to generate new thoughts with a language we do not yet understand. The legacy of Vygotsky is clear: Language and thought are interactive, dynamic, and bound together.

Additional language acquisition is facilitated and enhanced by first-language learning. The greater the depth of first language competence, the faster the acquisition of all others proceeds. As Vygotsky noted, "success in learning a foreign (*sic*) language is contingent on a certain degree of maturity in the native language" (Vygotsky, 1986, p. 195). Vygotsky continues by saying that children can transfer to other languages the system of meanings they already possess in their native language. He demonstrates that the reverse is also true: a new language facilitates mastering the higher forms of the native language, expanding the mental abilities in both languages.

The secret of acquiring an additional language is meaning. That's it. The new language has to become meaningful. Fortunately, there are multiple ways of making meaning; there is no one perfect way that works for everyone. However, using the language we know best certainly is one that works well. For example, we will assume that most readers of this book know English well. If this book were written in Punjabi, or Cambodian, or Spanish, would you find any meaning in it? However, that is exactly what happens every day in many schools to many students. If they do not make meaning in the time allowed, they do not learn; they may fail; their culture may be blamed; they may even be blamed for being poorly motivated. Krashen (1996) has pointed out that, when we give children quality education in their primary language, we give two crucial variables for academic success: knowledge and literacy, both of which transfer across languages.

Cummins (1999) expands on this when he posits that we come from a tradition of bilingual education research that places value on a limited approach to research and then assumes that policy-relevant conclusions will be forthcoming. He refers to this approach as the Research Policy Paradigm, which looks only at methodologically acceptable studies. Studies of this type, while a good approach to inquiry, have limits in providing answers for policymakers. The problem with this narrow approach is that, even though the studies may be methodologically acceptable to many, it is simply impossible to apply rigorous controls to the multiple human, administrative, and political variables that affect a student acquiring an additional language. Or, from a Vygotskian perspective, we would say that the sociocultural context is central, and often overlooked, in the process of thought and language acquisition. An alternative paradigm is what Cummins calls the Research Theory Policy Paradigm in which *theory* mediates research so that it is applicable for policymakers. Cummins argues for research grounded in theory, and not in isolation.

Several classroom examples illustrate how learners approach language acquisition. We have chosen these authentic learning experiences for two reasons: First, they demonstrate the primacy of language informing thought, and thought informing language, i.e., when learners do not understand the language, they do not have access to the thought. Second, they demonstrate the fundamental importance of context in language and learning.

> The relation of word to thought, and the creation of new concepts is a complex, delicate, and enigmatic process unfolding in our soul (Tolstoy, 1903, p. 143).

Unless It's Just a Language Thing

We will share two seemingly isolated experiences that capture for us the complex ways in which language has primacy in our learning. The two following experiences initially may appear to be unrelated, however. We will then show how they each are tied together in a Vygotskian framework, demonstrating the dynamic and reciprocal relationship between thought and language.

A national radio station invited a group of educators, policy leaders, and journalists to discuss the education of minority and majority students in public schools. We welcomed the discussion and listened with rapt attention, not only to hear what answers might be shared, but also to discover who they referred to when they said *minority* and when they said *majority*. Only the night before one of us had read of a school with 82 percent "minority" students, so obviously the semantic grounding is other than numerical.

However, the participants of the radio discussion were not focusing on the semantics of *minority* or *majority;* rather, they had one central question: Do "minority" students receive the same education as "majority" students? During the broadcast, they phoned several states and interviewed various school personnel who felt that schools were quite enlightened about the subtle (and not so subtle) ways that "minority" kids do not receive the same education.

Basically, those interviewed and those on the panel discussion were building consensus on the fact that the *same* curriculum given to students with vastly different experiences did not result in equity of access for all. The participants were discussing their belief that the curriculum seemed to work for those for whom it was developed. If the curriculum had been normed for "majority" students, it seemed to be fairly effective with them. However, the "minority" students had such diverse experiences (cultures, languages, thoughts) that "sameness" did not include their ways of knowing.

> It is a wise man who said that there is no greater inequality than the equal treatment of unequals.
>
> Justice Felix Frankfurter

At this point, the host announced invited phone calls from the listening audience.

"Of course, *those kids* get the same education—unless it *is just a language thing,"* glibly asserted the caller from a high socioeconomic suburb north of New York City to the assembled radio panel and national listening audience. Suddenly, the *other* entered the discussion. With this one flippant comment, he had trivialized and reduced not only language, but also many learners' experiences to irrelevancy.

As we listened, we knew that, one day, in the context of the classes we teach, we would find a time and place to revisit the assumptions of that radio caller. Weeks later, Andrea, a graduate student who teaches high school art classes provided that opportunity for us in a graduate course.

Andrea and Art: More than Just a Language Thing

Andrea had recently moved to California, an area in which schools often are filled with students who represent many languages and cultures. Often these same classrooms have teachers with limited experiences with languages and cultures. Because of this, various classes are available for the teachers to broaden their understandings of the world of learners who come from highly diverse ethnic, cultural, and linguistic experiences. Andrea had just moved from a state that still has a very Eurocentric tradition and seeks to maintain it. However, now she finds herself in a new context that challenges some of her previously unchallenged assumptions. Specifically, she is struggling to understand why she needs to take some of *these classes* that are designed to prepare credentialed teachers with a knowledge of language acquisition.

"Why do we need to study this?" Andrea asked her professor on the first night of class. Her question seemed more laden with her own past assumptions than it was filled with honest inquiry. Sometimes, students ask questions to send a message, rather than to find an answer. The professor, who had heard this question several times before in her career, could not help but smile at the irony of the required text sitting on the Andrea's desk: *I Won't Learn This from You* (1994) by Herbert Kohl. Thus began the semester.

Throughout nine weeks of the semester, the professor tried in multiple ways to open the door for Andrea to internalize and integrate the ideas of the class. Andrea clung to her assumptions: I am an art teacher and learning about language diversity does not relate to me. The professor tried to demonstrate that language was central for all teachers and learners. The professor tried to show that a good art class is also a good language class. The professor painstakingly explained why and how any art class is a natural place for those who are acquiring English as an additional language. The professor explained how art was expression, just as language is. Nothing. Andrea believed her world did not include a need for understanding this new knowledge. Finally, in the seventh week of the semester, the professor quit worrying about Andrea's resistance and selfishly focused on her own needs. The professor had an editorial deadline looming and desperately needed some drawings to share for possible inclusion in a book.

> "Just draw and sketch for the next three hours of class, Andrea," the professor said as she placed blank sheets of paper, pens, and pencils on her desk as she entered class. "Ignore us. Just draw," the professor firmly reiterated.
>
> "Just draw?" Andrea quizzed the professor.
>
> "Just draw," the professor affirmed, as she experienced twinges of guilt and ambivalence at her own self-centeredness. Secretly, she was worrying about whether it was the right thing to do to ask Andrea to draw during class to meet her own needs.

For the next three hours, Andrea drew as the class continued with its normal pace of questioning, interaction, and reflection. The class ignored Andrea, and she ignored them.

"Andrea, we have a few minutes of class remaining," the professor said to all. "Will you please share with your classmates what you have been doing?" (Figure 2.4).[1]

"Well," Andrea began, "the volcano represents how thought and language join together and erupt into something that Vygotsky called *verbal thought.* This is where real cognition takes place. The ashes spew out of the volcano and work like hot bits of knowledge to push learning and development along its path. It is like what happens when we get into the zone of proximal development and one of us helps the rest of us to understand something that we just couldn't get reading the text alone."

FIGURE 2.4   The Vygotskian Volcano.

The class and the professor sat in stunned silence as Andrea synthesized the learning that had occurred during the past seven weeks of class.

"Now, I finally get it," responded one her classmates. Several other students silently nodded in affirmation.

"Next week, Andrea, would you please draw some of the ideas you have been learning in your other class—the theory class?" the professor asked.

"Okay," Andrea answered, "but, in that class, we are talking about the big ideas that have evolved over the last century and how those ideas have affected schools. I'm not sure that I can draw theory."

However, the next week, Andrea returned to class with a drawing (Figure 2.5).

"This picture of a rainbow represents how the Scientific Management thinkers and the Progressivists were each at opposite ends of thought with their different theories. Get it?" she asked her classmates who sat staring at her.

"Get it?!" one of her classmates blurted out. "I don't get how you *got it.*"

"Well, I finally got to use my own language in this class. It took seven weeks," she said with a wry smile, glancing at the professor. "For me," she told her peers, "art is language all in itself. It is how I think. You think in words; I think in pictures. I'm going to carry this Vygotsky stuff with

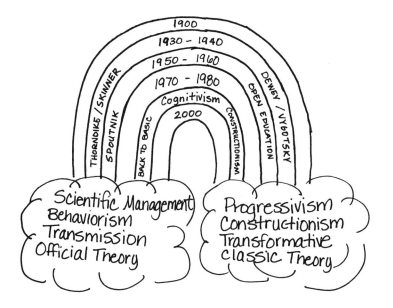

FIGURE 2.5 The Thought Community Rainbow.

me to my high school and create lessons that explode like small pieces of confetti from a firecracker. It will be like watching thoughts gently drift down over the top of the students."

Why was Andrea suddenly able to demonstrate her knowledge when she had appeared so resistant to learning about language acquisition? Suddenly, Andrea was using her own language: art. She was graphically signing the symbols that were meaningful in her language and linking them to the thoughts of her graduate class. In addition, she made her language meaningful for her peers. In this case, she used the symbols of her world of art to mediate her understanding of thought and language.

> At rare intervals, the most significant factors in determining the future occur in infinitesimal quantities on unique occasions (Mumsford, 1956).

Language is how we make sense of the world. It is how words work to let us see, and know, and learn. Language is never "just a language thing." Many of us come from a tradition that encouraged us to believe that language was really less than it is. We may have once believed that language was only neutral, single words we used like handy tools to talk with people. While language is, indeed, a tool for communicating, the past decades have taught us that it is far more. Language is a privilege; language is a right; language is a tool; language is a resource. Language is thought; language is culture; language is identity. Often we only come to realize this when (1) we are in a place where our language does not work so well with others, and/or (2) when someone tries to take our language from us. Denying language is denying access to thought.

> Thought is not merely expressed in words; it comes into existence through them. Every thought tends to connect something with something else, to establish a relationship between things. Every thought moves, grows and develops, fulfills a function, solves a problem (Vygotsky, 1986, p. 218).

The message is clear: Language must be meaningful for thought development.

In our work with Vygotsky, we are continually struck by the complementarity of his work with that of critical theorist Paulo Freire. In the spirit of the Third Sociocultural Conference (July, 2000, Brazil), during which the research presentations focused on the importance of linking the work of these theorists for enriching both sociocultural and critical perspectives, we will provide a framework for reflection on practice as it relates to sociocultural theory. From a Vygotskian perspective, "reflection is a 'becoming space' for the new thinking and imagining. It is a living force of consciousness" (Shepel, 1995, p. 434). By combining the works of Vygotsky and Freire, we promote critical action for solving problems named through reflection. We will first discuss the reflection framework, and then use examples of situations to frame issues through reflective practice and critical inquiry. In the examples we share, we will also model this framework as we reflect on the connections between thought and language as they play out in authentic classroom experiences.

Framework for Critical Praxis

The following process of NoteTaking and NoteMaking has been adapted from Frank (1999), who incorporated it from writing project activities in her own practice for student teachers to use in their observations and reflections about their student-teaching experiences (Dixon & Horn, 1995). Shepel (1995) described teacher education from a Vygotskian perspective as needing to provide the space for teachers to become *teacher–researchers*. Because understanding, in Vygotskian terms, means to change, for teachers to change and develop curriculum, "it is necessary to have the cultural and educational tools to change and develop as a professional" (Shepel, 1995, p. 438). To facilitate this process of change, we have extended Frank's process of reflection for student teachers to include a critical perspective. Adding a NoteRemaking element shows how critical reflection can be turned into action in our own lives. Praxis is the union of reflection and action. Our purpose for including the framework is for our readers to use it in reflecting on the following examples, and to connect these examples to their own experiences. In a Vygotskian sense, this framework becomes a tool for mediation of this text in the context of your teaching and learning.

Critical Praxis Framework

NoteTaking
- Describe
- What?

NoteMaking
- Interpret
- Why?

NoteRemaking
- Transform
- How?

The first step in the process of enacting the critical praxis framework is to describe what is taking place in each of the following examples. The description is based on the perspective of the participants in the situation. You have to look at the situation from the other's perspective; just as Vygotsky juxtaposed theories to learn from the opposite, so, too, here, we are asking that you think about what is happening based on the perspectives of the other. Don't rush to interpret what is happening, don't judge the participants because they present an opposing view. In this first step, just state what is.

The next step is for you to interpret, to question why it happened based on your own lived experiences and the knowledge you have gained. Your interpretations must be based on the evidence you gathered in the first part of this exercise. Again, we are not asking you to judge what is happening, merely to offer potential explanations based on evidence.

The third step is to transform your learning from this experience so that you can improve your own pedagogy and practice. In other words, reflect on what we learned from another's experience, or from reflecting on our own experience, that could result in self- and social transformation in a future situation.

A Papi's Problem Posing

The first example demonstrates how a Latino father posed a problem to school administrators based on the experience of his children in their school. This *Papi* used his own version of our framework to critically reflect on the practices of the school in relation to his family's experience. What follows is a retelling of a real event for us to use to critically reflect and to think about how we would transform our own practice.

NoteTaking: Describe.   This event took place in a Latino barrio school auditorium filled with the local families, the teachers, and the staff from the school. Most of the teachers and staff lived far from the barrio. The educational practices at this school occurred in English only, a language that most of the students did not yet understand.

> **What:** At this school open house, a Latino professor from the local university began by speaking with the group about various ways they might want to improve the curriculum and instruction of their school. Next, the families and school personnel generated future directions of their school; the idea of teaching the children in a language they could understand was not an option available based on a mandate from the district. After the group discussions, the Anglo principal spoke at the group about the various "good" things going on at the school. At the very end of the meeting, just as families were preparing to leave, one of the fathers of the group raised his hand to speak. The principal, who did not speak Spanish, and the father, who did not speak English, looked at each other. Very respectfully and quietly, the father asked the principal, *"¿Por qué enseña a los niños en una lengua que no entienden, y entonces los retienen?" he asked.* (Why do you teach in a language that the children do not understand, and then retain them?) The principal did not have an answer. The open house ended abruptly as the participants silently left the auditorium (Wink, 2000).

NoteMaking: Interpret.   An uncomfortable silence permeated the auditorium as it emptied. No one could articulate an answer to this question. The few in the room who did not speak Spanish could not answer the question. The many in the room who could understand the father's question knew that an answer would not be forthcoming, given the constraints placed on this school by the district.

> **Why:** The children in this particular context were denied language and thought, even though the school was labeled "bilingual." Pedagogically, this school did nothing to lead us to say that it was bilingual. The classes were in English; the teachers predominantly spoke English; the children spoke Spanish.

NoteRemaking: Transform.   As a result of this *Papi's* problem posing, the school transformed itself from an English-centric school to a truly bilingual school through the facilitation of primary language content instruction, while adding English language development for all. Implementation of bilingual instruction also consisted of staff development and parental involvement processes. The few English-dominant children in this school also became a part of the bilingual processes when the community celebrated all children maintaining their first language while adding a second. An ethnocentric practice transformed itself into a pluralistic critical praxis.

> **How:** In our own work we continued to reflect on the question posed by this concerned and quietly articulate father. At first glance, one might have believed that this was a bilingual program, as most of the students spoke Spanish. After putting on our critical lenses, which enable us to see more clearly, we recognized the school was bilingual in name only. In a Vygotskian sense, we had to juxtapose this bilingual program with other bilingual programs in order to see which questions were not answered by this particular program. In what follows, we are again using the critical praxis framework to bring the context into clear view.

Pat's Problem Solving

The socioeconomic, cultural, and geographic context for the next example is vastly different. Whereas the previous school was in an impoverished, Spanish-speaking community of recently arrived immigrants, the next example takes place in an affluent, English-only community of immigrants who arrived several generations ago. The first example is from the East coast; the second from the West coast. In the first example, a father took a risk to problem pose because he saw that the school was not providing what was needed for the cognitive development of his children. In the second example, a teacher took action to problem solve for a student.

NoteTaking: Describe.   Quang came from Vietnam, a literate student ready for fifth grade, who spoke no English. His teacher was English-dominant, and English was the only language used for learning in this classroom. Pat, the teacher, is well versed in how children acquire an additional language and the time necessary to accomplish this. Pat also understood and clearly articulated that she would not be able to assure Quang's continued cognitive development in all the content areas, as she did not speak, nor understand, his language.

> **What:** A Vietnamese-speaking parent volunteer knew Quang's family. She offered to bring a Bible to class, as she knew Quang's family read the Bible. Quang knew the thoughts of the Bible, but did not know the language in English. In addition to reading these stories, Quang also used a computer program, went to an extra teacher, was read to by a parent volunteer, used his English–Vietnamese dictionary, and was given time. Pat arranged for peer tutoring in his native language. He flourished.

NoteMaking: Interpret.   Because of her knowledge of second-language acquisition, Pat knew that Quang's literacy and knowledge would facilitate his understanding and acquisition of English. She found ways to provide content area support in his native language to facilitate his learning of English.

> **Why:** Quang, unlike the children in the previous example, was not denied access to his thought and language development. The teacher's critical reflection on the pedagogy in her school and her own language abilities led her to take action, even though she worried that her community would attack her for using the Bible.

NoteRemaking: Transform.   Quang changed from an isolated child who was unable to access thought and language in the classroom to a child who was able to continue to grow cognitively in content areas, while, at the same time, focusing on English language development.

> **How:** Each situation needs to be problematized and critically analyzed to understand if learners' needs are being met. We must make pedagogically sound decisions for all students. One size does not fit all.

Reflecting on these two seemingly opposite contexts, we see that much can be learned if one reflects critically. In the first case, the school appears to be bilingual, but, in fact, is not. It is only after the problem posing of a concerned parent that the school and community joined together to work toward transforming itself into a bilingual context of primary language support and English language development. In the second case, the school appears to be promote only immersion in English, but, in fact, it was only after the problem solving of a concerned teacher that the student had a de facto (Krashen, 1996) bilingual education program in an English-only context. The teacher transcended the pedagogical confines of her district. In de facto bilingual education the first language is used to make the second language more meaningful. We often hear of cases in which someone "made it" without bilingual education, which happens. However, when all the complicating variables are presented, it is not uncommon to find someone in the background of the student who made the new language comprehensible by the inclusion of knowledge and literacy in the first language. For parents to read in the primary language at home with their children is one of the best ways of supporting their academic achievement in the new language.

Conclusion

In this chapter, we unfolded the complex and dynamic relationships between thought and language. We have used visuals and authentic classroom examples to enhance our understanding of the ways Vygotsky's legacy can become classroom practice. Our use of language determines our learning, and our learning determines our use of language. None of this takes place in a vacuum. From Vygotsky we have learned the importance of the whole when understanding the thinking and speaking that takes place in classrooms.

However, an even more complex whole surrounds the classroom. We began to touch on the surrounding community in the critical praxis examples. We were just beginning to uncover how the greater sociocultural context influences the learning and development of teachers, students, and schools. In the next chapter we will further develop the influences of the social and cultural context.

ENDNOTE

1. The authors wish to thank Andrea for her willingness to help with her artwork even though she had a new baby and out-of-state house guests, and it was two days before Christmas.

3 Sociocultural Teaching and Learning

Instruction, after all, does not begin in school (Vygotsky, 1986, p. 208).

Just as Vygotsky's life was surrounded by many variables that influenced him and his ideas, we also are surrounded by a larger world that touches each of us. We live and work with our own families and those of our students, with our local, state, and national governing bodies, with all the accepted norms, beliefs, and behaviors of society, and with ever-changing demographics. As educators, we feel these influences daily; we act on them; and we are acted on. As each of us experiences life, whether it be the macroworld of society or the microworld of the classroom, we are influenced by and we influence the surrounding environment. We create our own life's path as we live it. No one's path is more valuable than another's, nor is it exactly the same as another.

Vygotsky believed that our life experiences affect and influence our development. Our use of language determines our learning; and our learning determines our use of language. None of this takes place in a vacuum. In this chapter we examine the social and cultural environment of students, teachers, and schools through ethnographic observations that place each of these in the center of a system to illustrate what consequences can result from the interaction of people and their environments.

Two Senses of the Term Social

The notion of *social* is key to the work of Vygotsky, and it takes on different characteristics in a sociocultural perspective. In terms of learning and developing, one sense of *social* incorporates the idea of interpersonal relationships. For example, when we read a good book, the first thing we might do is run and tell a friend about it. We talk about the book with others, and, as we do, we create new knowledge. When we sit in staff development in-services, and the presenter shares a thought or a concept with us, we try to patiently wait until the presenter gives us permission to discuss the idea with our colleagues sitting beside us. When children actively generate knowledge through meaningful classroom discourse and activities, they hurry home to tell their families. They are more excited about what they have done in the classroom when they have been part of the learning process because they own the knowledge, not because a teacher told them so.

Reflecting critically on Vygotsky's perception of the importance of the sociocultural context raises questions about some of our traditional assumptions about schools. Reflecting critically on the sociocultural context also leads us to recognize that we are a part of the world in which we live, what Horton and Freire (1990) referred to as creating our own path as we walk.

Let's go back to a prior example to bring sense of social into focus. We stated earlier that when we read a good book, we want to share what we have read with others. That is one kind of social interaction. However, the notion of genetic development from Vygotsky indicates that being social is also being cultural and historical. As Wertsch (1991) stated, "…even when mental action is carried out by individuals in isolation, it is inherently social in certain respects and it is almost always carried out with the help of tools such as computers, language, or number systems" (p. 15). So, when we read that good book alone in our favorite reading nook, we are not really participating in an individual mental process. We have a cultural artifact in our hands, the book, that employs a cultural tool, language. When we "individually" read the text, we are using our cultural/historical tool of language, which is also a social/cultural/historical artifact. We are, in a sense, interacting with the author and constructing our own version of the text before us as we think about the words and ideas we are reading from our own experiential base.

Our life experiences influence our learning. We talk to each other; we listen to our friends and colleagues, and we develop new thoughts and new ideas. When we don't understand something, we discuss it with a friend and often we discover the answer as we talk. The primacy of being human is how we use language in social context to make meaning. As we talk, we manipulate, not only our language, but also our thoughts, which lead us to higher cognitive processes.

This is often how we think of *social*—what we do with others rather than what we do individually. The view of being social as a secondary process to the individual is so inherent in our Western cultural thinking that we often use the word *social* to distinguish between work carried out by an individual and in direct relations with others. For example, an observer in a classroom might distinguish between "social talk" and "academic talk" to indicate that, when students carry on personal conversations with each other, they are being "social" and when they talk about the learning activity in which they are engaged, they are not being social, but being academic.

However, Vygotsky charged us to think of learning as processes that we carry out first on an *inter*mental plane—in relation and cooperation with others. The individualization of our thinking happens as a result of our intermental processing of information. Learning becomes an *intra*mental processing as we begin to internalize what we have learned through our interactions with others. As Wertsch & Tulviste (1996) state, this view is one in which mind is understood as 'extending beyond skin.' Mind, cognition, memory, and so forth are understood not as attributes or properties of the individual, but as functions that may be carried out intermentally or intramentally (pp. 57–58).

Therefore, in our first look at the word *social* we come to understand that, from a Vygotskian perspective, everything about learning and developing is social. His "general genetic law of cultural development" established that development occurs first between people, then within the individual (Vygotsky, 1981). Individuals then actively transform what they have realized through interactions with others. As Zebroski (1994) noted, "Social relations are always transformed when they are internalized by the individual" (p. 160). We individually decide what is important to understand, and we actively reconstruct for ourselves the information we have taken up from interactions with others.

Vygotsky's premise of cultural development leads us to a second way of looking at the term *social* that often evades our Western thinking. That is to say that not only are we social beings, but at the same time our being social is also cultural and historical through the mediational role of artifacts that we construct. For example, language that we speak, texts that we write, numbers we use to compute all help us learn to use more language, create more texts, and solve more complicated problems. Wells (2000) stated: "Human beings are not limited to their biological inheritance…but are born into an environment that is shaped by the activities of previous generations" (p. 54). The cultural artifacts produced by previous generations bring with them the past, and, through their use, we bring the past into the present (Cole, 1996). Through our interactions with others and with the cultural artifacts produced, we continue to learn and develop, and we construct more cultural artifacts for future generations to use. Vygotsky's conceptualization of mental processing as primarily a social/cultural/historical intermental function that becomes an intramental function as we continue to internalize and reconceptualize what we have learned from others leads us to the purpose of the rest of this chapter.

Through the observed experiences to come, we will take you on a path of social/cultural/historical development. However, you will note an extra pebble added to our construction of the path, a political component that cannot be ignored. In this sense we combine the work of Paulo Freire with that of Vygotsky because the two perspectives inform each other and help us make sense in our reading of our world.

Socioculturally Learning and Developing

The value of Vygotsky's work in relation to pedagogy stems from the very way in which he viewed learning and development as dynamic processes, social, cultural, and historical by nature, and in a dialectical relationship with each other. He acknowledged learners as interactive agents in communicative, socially situated relationships. This was a departure from viewing the learner as a lone individual whose abilities could be measured objectively and who was genetically predisposed to develop and act on the environment. Instead, he viewed teaching as an active process of exploring student activity, while guiding students to levels beyond their current ability to solve problems. Vygotsky did not view students and teachers as separate entities. Instead, he worked to identify "the social environment that linked the two together" (Vygotsky, 1997, p. xxiv).

From a Vygotskian perspective, then, we see that the sociocultural context is very complex. What influences schools and the influence that schools have on the students, teachers, and parents is a complex study. Likewise, what influences classroom outcomes, and the influence those classrooms have on the participants within, is a complex study. Simplistic answers will not suffice for complex questions. As we have indicated before in our work, "for every complex question, there is an answer which is obvious, simple, and wrong." However, what seems to happen in our complex and fast-paced society is a search for quick fixes and fast results. Throughout this chapter, we demonstrate why this approach is not a beneficial one for educational purposes.

A Puzzle of Learning

To begin our journey, we can visualize classrooms as part of a very complex puzzle that is very much like an intricate web of contexts. It is within this puzzle that learning and developing take place. We begin to conceptualize this web, and we will be adapting it as we go, depending on the particular components that are made visible through the athentic classroom moments (Figure 3.1). It is virtually impossible to capture *all* of the pieces of the puzzle that interlock, and that is why we leave the puzzle pieces unbounded: to indicate that there are other interlocking factors that may be unknown to us, or that are not specifically stated.

Throughout this chapter, as we introduce readers to the Vygotskian premise of the sociocultural nature of teaching and learning, we will repeat and adapt Figure 3.1 to demonstrate the complexity of sociocultural teaching and learning. The student, the teacher, and the school will be portrayed in light of the influences of the sociocultural environment. Based on the Vygotskian notion of sociocultural teaching and learning, students, teachers, and families act in dialogue with each other, jointly constructing what counts as knowledge in their life world, what Moll and colleagues (1990) refer to as funds of knowledge.

Throughout their interactions, these participants also bring with them their own experiences, which have combined to bring them to this point in their lives. They have been learning with others and making sense through the language of their social worlds as they are combine these implements of learning, their literate practices, their language, and their ways of being with others in this classroom community. The authors seek to demonstrate the impact of social processes on cognition, and how we influence, and are influenced by, the surrounding environment.

Sociocultural teaching and learning has various names in the literature: socially grounded learning; social–cultural context of learning; social–cultural–political,

FIGURE 3.1   Puzzle of Learning.

historical learning, social constructivist, social constructionist, and sociocognitive. Particularly, the most recent Vygotskian scholars, who are often referred to as Neo-Vygotskians (see Chapter 6), have socially constructed unique understandings of the various terms that are used. However, we will use the various terms referring to social learning interchangeably. For our purposes, the primacy of the social world surrounding us, how it affects us, and how we affect it, is fundamental to understanding Vygotsky's legacy.

Classrooms as Cultures

The classroom is one of the complex pieces of the puzzle of learning; it is part of a much larger world, and it has many worlds within it. From one perspective, the classroom is a very small space situated within a very large and complex world that influences it. From another perspective, the classroom is a very large culture that is filled with multiple relationships and a myriad of complex processes all contributing to learning and developing (Collins & Green, 1992; Santa Barbara Classroom Discourse Group, 1992a).

From a social constructionist point of view, teachers and students together construct the knowledge of the classroom through their interaction, blazing their own educational paths (Wells and Chang-Wells, 1992). In classrooms such as these, teachers are guiding students, rather than transmitting knowledge, and students are actively generating knowledge, rather than passively storing information for possible future use. As noted by Green and Meyer (1991):

> from this perspective, members of a classroom form a social group in which a common culture is constructed. This culture is reflected in the patterned ways members of the social group develop for acting and interacting together, for interpreting what occurs, for evaluating what is appropriate to know and do in the classroom (p. 142).

We also take the position that particular classroom cultures are socially constructed through the interactions of participants. Throughout this chapter, we demonstrate that the participants bring with them their own social and cultural backgrounds, their personal historicity. What we have experienced in the past will influence how we participate in the present. We can unlearn some of those lessons from the past as we will see in the story of Pedro, but those lessons have a strong grip and may take a long time to loosen. In the following look into one classroom, Pedro is featured as one member of the classroom culture. His experiences within that classroom are vastly different from others who are in the same classroom.

The Puzzle of Pedro

In the back of the sixth-grade classroom, Pedro sat alone.[1] His jacket covered his head to shut out the classroom and the world during the first two weeks of class. He did not speak to his new classmates, nor did they speak to him. Any attempt by the teacher to draw him into interaction with others was met with resistance on his part, as well as on the part of the other students. The context of his life had influenced him, and, likewise, he influenced those around him. Much of the world had treated Pedro badly. Because he had been shifted from town to town, he did not want to make ties with anyone for fear that these ties would soon be broken by yet another move to a different school. Instead, he sat at his desk, using his jacket as a shield to isolate him from anyone who dared to get too close.

Pedro is surrounded by many factors that touch his life (Figure 3.2). He is in the middle of a larger sociocultural context. The world has sent him many messages; he has read his world. Some, in education, would blame Pedro for not doing his homework, for not sitting up straight, for not *caring* about learning. However, we cannot view Pedro in isolation; we have to look at all the influences that affect Pedro on a daily basis. This particular student cares a lot; it is just that no one in this school has learned it yet.

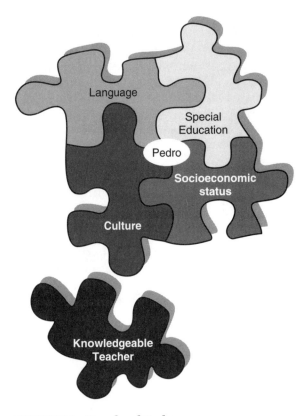

FIGURE 3.2   Puzzle of Pedro.

After many years of being moved from one teacher to another, in and out of resource and special education classes, Pedro found a home in a sixth-grade mainstream classroom. At first he was able to write only two- or three-word sentences when assisted by his teacher, Kathleen. In her classroom, students working collaboratively took on specific roles to complete inquiry-based projects. These roles were frequently changed so that all students could realize equal status and opportunity to lead their groups. Kathleen placed great emphasis on collaborating and valuing whatever abilities each student brought to the group, as well as arriving at consensus for group reports while maintaining individual accountability.

Kathleen was aware that another student in the class, Angela, understood Pedro's language, his culture, and his world. Kathleen placed Pedro in a group of four students: Pedro, Angela, and two of the nicest English-dominant boys in her class. She was hoping that this combination of student resources would be the best possible social situation she could offer this troubled student.

At first, Pedro contributed very little, but taking the coat off his head and joining the group was a victory. Angela offered assistance to him during group activities, and she listened when he spoke. The two other boys in the group were supportive and yet respectful of his space, and somehow understood that Pedro needed time. Soon, the four began to have fun in their group; they were creating their own group dynamic. After several weeks, Pedro started to take responsibility for himself and his group. Angela translated when necessary, but the group was more and more often focused on the problem-solving activities, and they made meaning in their own way.

Pedro finally removed his coat during class. He next volunteered to be the reporter so he could relate the group findings aloud in front of the class. Initially, he reported with some prompting from Angela. Later, he was able to complete an individual report of their project alone, rather than having to ask for Angela's assistance. After his interactive work in the safe environment of his group, Pedro was able to construct his own paragraph of five sentences based on what he had learned during the activity.

Group learning does not always work for all students, but sometimes it can be very helpful, as in this case. Pedro eventually worked at levels others had not thought possible. The sociocultural context of the class had a powerful effect on Pedro and his learning. Not only did Pedro construct his knowledge in this classroom, but also he was able to begin to reconstruct his world.[2]

When we last saw Pedro, he had moved on to seventh grade at the junior high school. We were driving by his school in the afternoon while students were outside waiting for school buses to take them home. There stood Pedro, alone, in the blistering valley heat, with his coat tightly zipped up, as if to close off the world. Once again the sociocultural context of Pedro had placed in him a vulnerable position. He tightly pulled his coat around his shoulders to protect himself from influences of his new educational world. Sadly, we watched Pedro and were reminded that if we are to reach our potential as a society, each Pedro must have an opportunity to realize maximum potential.

The story of Pedro demonstrates that putting together the puzzle of learning and developing for any student is a complex and challenging task. The social cultural context of Pedro's world is very large and very small at the same time: simultaneous and contradictory worlds to mediate. Pedro has read the macroworld, and he is responding in his microworld. He has received messages from his multiple environments, and he is sending messages back to his multiple worlds.

As the participants construct a particular culture through their classroom interactions, they are also bringing into the classroom the influences of their prior and current sociocultural experiences from outside the classroom. The reason Pedro removed his coat in the culture of Kathleen's class was because suddenly he was experiencing a social–cultural context that valued him. He no longer needed to only react against previous and real influences; he was free within *this* community to become a full and contributing participant. However, once he was back in a classroom culture that did *not* value him in the same way, he wrapped the coat, as protection, tightly around himself again.

Teachers often ask: "What can I do?" Pedro and Vygotsky provide part of the answer. The interrelationship of all students and all languages, in a safe and secure environment, is fundamentally important for literacy and cognitive development. It is also important for our future.

Always, our individual and collective journey is surrounded by a larger world that has an effect on each of us. For example, Kathleen, Pedro's teacher, knew that she had to make a new path for *Pedro* in her classroom. She knew that she could not control the context of the macroworld surrounding him, but she could control the microworld of their classroom, which changed the interaction between Pedro and his fellow classmates.

Classroom teachers, as Kathleen demonstrates, have the power to create a supportive sociocultural environment in which students are encouraged to mediate their world. Andrew Heard, as chancellor of Vanderbilt University, was quoted in *Newsweek,* May 25, 1970 as having said, "There is no use trying to make ideas safe for students. You have to make students safe for ideas" (p. 69). Classrooms need to be safe and secure for all voices, even the most wounded among us, such as Pedro. The interrelationship of all students and all languages, in a safe and secure environment, is fundamentally important for literacy and cognitive development. As so clearly stated by Cummins (1999), "Human relations are at the heart of schooling" (p. 1).

As students talk with each other in meaningful, problem-solving contexts, they construct their own cognitive path. Language cannot be viewed in isolation from the sociocultural context of the classroom or the larger world. Vygotsky (1986) stated that higher levels of cognition are both formed by and expressed through language, which is developed in social processes. The very core of Vygotsky's theory was the influence of social processes on higher mental functions and the development of these cognitive capacities, which are social in origin and mediated by changing uses of language (Wertsch, 1985).

In a Vygotskian perspective, Pedro entered Kathleen's class with his learning experiences reflecting his *inter*mental processes of learning. After time in this safe classroom, he shifted his learning to the *intra*mental plane. He internalized the security and the respect of this classroom culture so that he could emerge as the agent of his own social construction of knowledge. Within the culture of this one classroom, Pedro's experiences are unique. The answers for his learning are unique. Teachers and administrators could easily assume that they understand classroom cultures, and yet understand very little about Pedro or his world. The complexity of this web of contexts that makes up the puzzle of Pedro's worlds leads us to understand that one size does not fit all.

High-Stakes Testing

In far too many of our educational contexts, there exists a demand for one-size-fits-all. For example, in numerous school districts across the nation we hear a clamoring for a reading program that forces teachers to adhere to a packaged set of books with an established script. There are "coaches" who observe classroom teachers to ensure that all teachers of the same grade level in the same school are literally on the same page in their teaching of these reading programs.

Interestingly, the students have not been given the script, so it is still their job to try to figure out what the teacher means by the particular vocabulary of these teaching scripts. In one instance, we were told of a first-grade teacher who was admonished by a coach after asking the students to "tell me about what we have just read." The scripting coach told the teacher to tell the students that they were "to sum it up" after reading a passage. A wise but unscripted first grader answered, "But teacher, I didn't know we were doing math now."

Implementing such a canned program would not fit Vygotsky's notion of quality teaching and learning. Vygotsky (1997) suggested that, when teachers are "simply setting forth ready-prepared bits and pieces of knowledge," they have given up being teachers because their role should be that of directing the students in mindful and purposeful activity (p. 339). Furthermore, he stated that good pedagogy results in teachers relating the school and the real world through the subjects that they teach.

Aside from standardized content programs, an even greater threat to individualized learning is the proliferation of standardized testing as a means of judging whether students should advance from one grade to the next. Adhering to one test to decide a student's future basically "ignores the work that shows that individual students do not live large-scale, replicable lives. They live local and situated ones" (Putney, Green, Dixon, & Kelly, 1999, p. 375). Furthermore, large-scale research studies and high-stakes assessments can mask differences that shape student lives.

According to Vygotsky (1997), relying on standardized testing alone to determine children's mental functioning serves to "intellectualize the personality of the child in one-sided fashion, and, therefore, represents it in a false light" (p. 334). The use of standardized testing as the sole determinant of a student's future negates the professional judgment of educators (Kohn, 2000). The use of standardized testing to evaluate teachers and school effectiveness is ill-advised and a practice that should stop (Popham, 1998). As Kohn (2000) states:

> if bonuses for high scores are dangled in front of teachers or schools—or punitive "consequences" are threatened for low scores—the chances are far greater that a meaningful curriculum will be elbowed out to make room for test-oriented instruction (p. 30).

In the following ethnographic moment, we demonstrate what happened when a "testing coach" came into a fifth-grade classroom to prepare the students for taking a standardized test.

Going to the Movies

One of the difficulties students have in taking objective and standardized tests is in determining whether they have substantial information to answer a question. Often in these testing situations, extraneous information is added into the problem, and students must determine exactly what information is useful for providing the correct response. In this fifth-grade classroom, a testing coach was preparing students for an upcoming standardized test. She began with these directions:

"Ok, kids, we are going to ask you to think about the following problem and give us your answer to the question," stated the testing coach. The purpose of this particular example was to help them realize that they did not have enough reliable information to answer the question.

"So, here's the problem: One movie begins at 5:30 P.M., and a second movie begins at 7:30 P.M. Can you attend both movies?" asked the testing coach.

"Heads together and talk about it first," reminded the classroom teacher. The room buzzed with the fifth graders talking about the exercise. Soon each group had an answer for the testing coach. However, they were not necessarily the answers she expected. She assumed that the students would realize that they did not have enough information to answer correctly.

"Well, if the people going to the movies are kids, they probably have to go home after the first one because the second movie will be over past their curfew," stated Jose Ramon at table one.

"What if one movie was on the north side of town, and the other movie you wanted to see was on the south side of town (sixteen miles away)? It might take you too long to drive from one movie theatre to arrive at the other one on time," announced Jeannette at table five.

"But some of our parents work until 8 P.M.," said Rashawnda at table three. She continued solemnly, "They wouldn't be able to take us on time to either of those movies."

"Wait, we know," Maria Elena stated as she stood up to answer at table four. "We could go to the first movie, and if we really wanted to see the second one, we could just leave early enough from the first movie to get to the second one. They always have those other cartoons at the beginning of the movie anyway so we could make it."

The testing coach shook her head and reminded them that they had missed the point of the entire exercise, which was to recognize that the *correct* response was that they didn't have enough information to correctly figure out an answer since they didn't know how long the first movie lasted. We think the testing coach was missing the point that the divergent, creative, and thoughtful answers the students jointly constructed in this situation were far more intellectual than the simplistic and standardized question asked in the first place.

In the next personal experience, the one in the middle of the sociocultural puzzle shifts from a student, Pedro, to the teacher, Sam. As the puzzle pieces change, so, too, does the perspective. In this teacher's world, the puzzle minimally consists of his pedagogy, the curriculum, the students, and the political leanings of his school district, which are about to shift and radically change his world. Through the four-year time line of his teaching experiences, Sam grows professionally as he reflects critically.

Sam: A Teaching Time Line

The university professor had asked the graduate class of experienced teachers to reflect with a Quick Write on their learning during the semester. After about ten minutes the professor noticed that Sam was sitting quietly and was finished; she passed by him, and he whispered to her, "Maybe I'm not doing this right; everyone is still writing." She took his paper and told him to go up to her office and browse through her bookshelf. She looked at his paper and saw a series of faces accompanied by short paragraphs depicting his painful four-year experience as a classroom teacher in Figure 3.3:

1996: First Year of Teaching
I began teaching in Elementary; I was fresh from the University; I came with a generative/constructivist perspective. I was full of fresh, new ideas. I had many second-language learners; half of my curriculum was devoted to teaching language skills.

1997: Second Year of Teaching
Reading Recovery is introduced to my district; test results are low for students in the district. Instruction and testing are standardized. All teachers, myself included, are mandated to use a district-approved method of teaching and material. Bilingual education is being phased out.

1998: Third Year of Teaching
I am sent to a three-day guided reading workshop. I am required to use a highly scripted, heavily formatted method of teaching reading. Bilingual Ed is gone. I still attempt to teach second-language skills, but it is getting harder to fit into limited time periods. The fun in teaching is getting harder to find.

1999: Fourth Year of Teaching
The pressure is on schools/districts. They are being held to strict standards. Whose standards, I wonder? Fun, interactive classroom activities are almost nonexistent. Students' poor behaviors are escalating. My bilingual students are showing little growth in all areas of academics. I find that I have become the teacher in the school that I hated so much when I was a child. I have moved from generative to transmission. What will next year bring?

FIGURE 3.3   Sam: A Teaching Time Line.

What Sam shared with us is not new, but more than ever schools are faced with being held to strict standards with very little recourse if these standards are not met. Who is making the standards? Are they educators in the schools who work with students everyday in their social cultural context? Are they educators in the universities who are teaching and researching? Or, are they policymakers in a distant city with little connection to the classrooms, students, and teachers whose lives are being affected by the policies enacted?

The Sociocultural and Pedagogical Puzzle

As the social cultural context of his world changed, Sam was led to reflect critically on those changes and their effect on him and students in his classroom. The last we knew of Sam, he was discouraged and was seriously considering walking away from the very big puzzle of education.

In what follows, we will meet Fred, who, while reflecting on the esoteric meaning of sociocultural context for a graduate class assignment, suddenly realized that he was living it authentically (Figure 3.4). Fred, like Sam in the previous

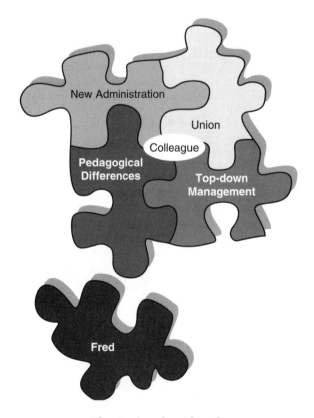

FIGURE 3.4 The Sociocultural and Pedagogical Puzzle.

story, is learning about the complex influences of the macroworld that flow in all directions among all involved; it is a constant process of action–reaction. Sam and Fred, in very different contexts, are each learning that the world is greater than their own classroom. The puzzle has many pieces and is open-ended on all sides. They are coming to understand that these influences are not only social, cultural, and historical, but also political.

As we look in on the teaching world of Fred, we see how he is being called on to defend a coworker whose views do not fit the neat and tidy puzzle that the school district administrators have conjured up for schools. In Fred's case, he is a piece of the puzzle. The following is his story as it was told in his interactive journal for the class assignment.

The Pedagogical and Political Puzzle

I was getting ready to write about the importance of social–cultural context in teaching and learning for a graduate class when a colleague called me and asked me to attend a meeting between her and the assistant superintendent. It suddenly dawned on me that, as I was trying to understand theory, it was turning into practice in my work. My colleague did not know the purpose of the meeting, but she sensed trouble as she had been asked to bring a union representative and a colleague.

We were perplexed, because during her four years in this district she had received great evaluations from various principals at the sites where she worked. She was in charge of a successful academic and girls' sports program. She had been a student in this district who chose to return to her community. She has a credential, a master's degree, and an administrative credential.

When I arrived at the assistant superintendent's office, the superintendent, his secretary, and the union representative were waiting. We could feel the tension. After we sat down, the superintendent handed my colleague a sheet of paper that read *involuntary transfer* to an extended education program.

"Why?" my shocked colleague asked.

"The principal does not believe that you and the district have common goals," the assistant superintendent responded.

Fred later told us that this district had had a long history of collaborative and democratic traditions. Fred and the woman teacher had been hired at a time when the district was open to teacher/student/family empowerment constructs. However, recently a change had taken place. The board of education, the district, and a new administration had adopted a top-down managerial style. Other experienced teachers had recently been moved involuntarily despite the fact that each of them had received very public commendations at a community event the previous year. Fred, like Sam, has only taught for four years, but is rapidly learning the importance and significance of understanding the social–cultural context of learning.

Manuel: To Name, to Reflect Critically, to Act

This scenario played out early in the evolution of La Paloma School District, at the high school level, but it could also take place on a much smaller scale in the classroom. Manuel is a student at the center of a puzzle of politics who demonstrates for us Vygotsky's notion of motivation in relation to language. Vygotsky (1986) stated that, to understand another's speech, it is not enough to understand the words, or even the thoughts; we have to understand the motivation behind the thinking and speech.

Manuel, a ninth grader, was among the students at La Paloma High School who were actively voicing their opinions of the underlying assumptions of school personnel regarding Mexican American students. Even though the population of the town and La Paloma School District was largely Mexican American, the teachers, administrators, and support staff were mostly Anglo-American. The lack of role models, lack of understanding of the Mexican American experience, and especially the high school's disciplinary procedures, were perceived as discriminatory toward the Mexican American population. The student/parent protests led to a three-day boycott of the school involving over one hundred students. For a dozen or more of the students, the protest carried on for months while they were home-schooled.

The people involved in this turmoil were each viewing it from their own experiences and perspectives. However, the lives of the teachers and administrators were as different from the students and parents as was their culture and heritage language. The administrators presented a scenario of discipline and a successful school in which *some* of the students moved on to higher education. The students and parents talked of teachers and counselors who told them that they were not in need of a higher education because they would never leave the orchards, fields, and packinghouses of their local agricultural community.

In the midst of their activism, we were invited to interview Manuel, who saw himself as a revolutionary, attempting to make changes in his school. We asked Manuel why the students felt more successful in their home-schooled environment.

"Our home classes are better than the school because we now have a teacher who will answer our questions." He continued, "Teachers need to respect students in order for students to respect teachers." When we asked Manuel what he thought of people saying that he would turn next to gang involvement, he smiled a knowing smile as he noted, "We have knowledge, with knowledge we have power, with power we don't need to belong to a gang."

The administrators at La Paloma High School viewed fourteen-year-old Manuel as a troublemaker, and they labeled him as a gang member; we viewed him as a teacher. This young man was teaching us what his life was about and what his motivation was so that we could understand his actions and words. Through our interaction with Manuel, we came to internalize Vygotsky's (1986) concept of how language reflects reality and consciousness. "If perceptive consciousness and intellectual consciousness reflect reality differently, then we have two different forms of consciousness. Thought and speech turn out to be the key to the nature of human consciousness" (p. 256). To understand completely a person's words, we must come to recognize the motivation behind the words.

In the previous chapter, we shared a process, the Critical Praxis Framework, in which critical reflection leads to action for self- and social transformation. In this scenario, Manuel was living this framework. In a Freirian sense, Manuel was problem posing: to name, to reflect critically, to act.

Students live their lives in the social context of a much larger world. A multitude of people, ideas, assumptions, and events influence our students, and, the students, their larger world. The ebb and flow of influences from the outside world to the culture of the classroom never ceases; the forces of the environment move in complex, and often unseen, patterns. The influences from the macro- to the microcultures constantly move; schools are acted on, and schools react. Those in education receive messages from the social–cultural context, and they send back other messages (Figure 3.5).

As portrayed with the arrows in Figure 3.5, the influences of the social–cultural context move in all directions. Often, the person in the center is perceived to be the culprit, for example, Fred's teacher friend. A simplistic view would blame her inquiry-based, critical approach to teaching and learning, while ignoring the entire change in philosophy and practice consuming the school. The same is true in the case of Manuel. It is easy to imagine that the dominant group, in this case Anglo-American administrators and teachers, might blame him for his defiant behavior, while at the same time ignoring the influences to which he is reacting. These two examples, familiar to many who know schools well, are only too real for Fred and for Manuel. Just as Vygotsky developed his cognition and his perspective from his social context, so do we all. Until Manuel and his family and *compañeros* took a stand to tell the story from their perspective, not much was going to change at La Paloma High School.

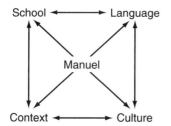

FIGURE 3.5 **Student in the Center.**

> Power concedes nothing without demand. It never did. It never will.
>
> Frederick Douglass

Life would have continued in much the same way as before. However, none of the teachers, counselors, or administrators will look at their school in quite the same way now. How much they will change will depend on how many more Manuels speak up and attempt to show their point of view. We personally hope that many more do so, and soon. While school did not immediately change for Manuel,[3] a change was occurring for his cousin, Oscar, who was a second grader in an elementary school in La Paloma School District. The following is his story.

What Oscar Taught Retta

Retta was a first-year teacher in a bilingual elementary school in a barrio that was part of La Paloma School District. She was hired for this bilingual job, somewhat to everyone's surprise. She had her ESL certificate, but was not bilingual. In spite of the availability of two native-speaking Spanish bilingual candidates, the district was "unable" to find a bilingual applicant.

On the first day of school, her new colleagues, in attempting to prepare her, were sharing their opinions of the students she had not yet met. The socially constructed portrait of one of her students, Oscar, made her physically grimace every time his name was mentioned. The negative comments about Oscar's terrible behavior quickly established her initial relationship with him. At this early point in her professional development, Retta never stopped to reflect on how the picture she brought with her to the classroom would affect her relationship with the students. Her preconceived notions came into the culture of the classroom with Retta and had the potential of altering the human connections with students, and particularly with Oscar. Schools in La Paloma School District are complex enough, without having as an added burden the challenge presented to Oscar: all those in authority were against him without ever having met him.

This was how Oscar's year began in second grade. Fortunately for him, he had a teacher who, although she carried some stereotypical and historical assumptions with her, was also open to rethinking and relearning. Simultaneously, Retta's own learning and developing continued in the culture of the classroom of her graduate work. There, she was challenged and quick to relate the theory of her graduate coursework to the reality of life for Oscar.

Blame the Victim

The social process of schooling often leads educators to look only at the child-in-the-middle and forget about the greater social context, just as Retta's cohorts in the teacher's lounge were doing when they were coloring her perspective with their stories of Oscar. Looking only at students rather than acknowledging the effects of the social context in which they live and interact daily is called blaming the victim (Ryan, 1976). The Blame-the-Victim literature, which has continued to grow, blames the student (or her family or culture), instead of critically looking at the sociocultural context and the pedagogy. In this case, bilingualism was the scapegoat used to rationalize the poor school performance of Oscar.

As we have shown throughout this chapter, the learning and development of students should be understood as a product of the interaction of many factors: the student's language and cultural background, the educational setting, and the wider sociocultural influences. We argue that schools need to embrace an inclusive pedagogy that not only benefits everyone, but acknowledges the role that each of us plays in the entire educational process. This is what Retta came to realize in an activity that was part of a teacher in-service she attended early in the school year.

Structure for Success

In the teacher in-service, the purpose of the activity was to demonstrate the importance of the influence of the social context on students. To do so, participants attempted to build a structure in a hands-on activity, representing the need for a strong support system for our schools. The five participants, including Retta, were asked to choose one of five cards containing a category title and an explanation of the societal function of the persons or group of people represented by the category.

Their objective was to form a star structure as shown in Figure 3.6. The five people were spaced apart so as to form a widely spread circle as follows: beginning with the person holding the *community card,* the *educator* stood to the right of *community.* To the right of the educator was the person representing *culture and language,* and to the right of that person was the *administrator.* The person representing *parents* stood between the *administrator* and *community.* After forming a broad circle, they were given instructions to form the star structure, maintaining a hole in the center of the star with a diameter about twelve inches.

FIGURE 3.6   Structure for Success Star.

The facilitator instructed the participants to listen for the name of their category and, when their category was called, catch the ball of rope, then read what was printed on their card. After reading, they were to hold tightly to one end of the rope, then toss the ball of rope to the next person called by the facilitator. The next person would likewise catch the ball, read the card, and prepare to hold the line with one hand while tossing to the next name called until all the cards had been read and the star was formed.

They began the activity with the person who had the card titled "Community." She deftly caught the ball and read:

Community
Community members establish the philosophy of the school district by mandating to the district school board policies and procedures under which the schools will operate. Community members who rethink traditional values and update attitudes to include and value multicultural populations will encourage a school district to be responsive to the needs of all the students in their diverse schools.

The community representative held her end of the rope and tossed the ball to the person representing administrators. That person caught the ball of rope and read:

Administrators
Administrators carry out the will of the community by enforcing policies established by the school board. Clear philosophical guidelines constructed throughout the district make visible the academic expectations. Administrators who keep in touch with the reality of today's classroom and who support current research and development will also be active in supporting the learner.

The administrator held one end of the rope and tossed the ball to Retta, who was representing educators. Retta caught the ball and read her card:

Educators
Educators research and implement theories and models, which support academic growth and development. Teachers who are confident of their professional knowledge about student welfare with regard to academic and social success will be better prepared to meet the individualized needs of their students.

Retta then tossed to the individual representing parents, who caught the ball and read:

Parents

Parents, as first teachers, realize the important role they play in the educational future of their children. When working with parents we should consider how we invite them to participate in the education of their children. If we emphasize the importance of their teaching, and encourage them to provide input into the academic success of their children, then they will have the opportunity to participate more fully as partners in the educational system.

The parent tossed the ball to the person representing language and culture who then read:

Language and Culture

Language and Culture are an important focus in the development of positive psychosocial values and academic growth. When heritage culture is valued for both parent and child, then language and culture will become more than isolated celebrations within the school environment. All who are aware of the importance of primary language and academic success will understand that, whenever possible, students must be engaged in building on previously acquired knowledge through their primary language in order to continue to improve in their newly acquired language.

The language and culture person made the final toss back to the community representative who held the two ends of the rope together. The formation seen before the group was a large star, representing the structure upholding children in the schools. The participants were instructed to hold tight to their ropes and to keep the line taunt unless instructed to let it go. They positioned themselves so that the hole in the center had a diameter the size no larger than eight inches. Then the facilitator brought out a giant beach ball and placed it in the center of the structure. Retta could see they had a structure that represented a well-balanced, nurturing environment in which the student could mature and thrive, with all the groups cooperating and working together for the benefit of that student.

However, the facilitator suggested that this student might not be thriving in their system, but falling behind academically. Rather than immediately blaming the victim, the facilitator suggested they look closer at their structure to find a cause of academic slippage. She began with the example of a student whose culture and language were not valued in the community. If the student is met with disdain for his or her identity, then he or she would have a weakness developing in their structure. (She instructed Community to allow the rope to go slack.)

The facilitator then suggested that, if the administrators held a philosophical stance that did not value the student's language, then chances are that the educational system would lack development of the student's primary language. At this point, they discovered another weakness in the administrator side and the language and culture side. As these participants slackened their ropes, the beach ball tee-tered precariously.

The facilitator asked them to tighten their ropes again so they could suppose that both the community and the administrators were strong, but that the teach-ers and parents believed that their students must be mainstreamed as quickly as possible in order to learn English. As they allowed the rope to go slack, the partic-ipants could visibly see the weak points in the structure on the Educators, Par-ents, and Language sides. She told them that moving students away from their heritage language into English as quickly as possible may appear to be logical to those who are not aware of language acquisition principles. However, the non-English-dominant students who were conversant in English on the playground were struggling with academic literacy in English. As she explained this point, the beach ball fell to the floor, with an audible gasp from the participants.

As they quickly realized, it is easy to *drop the ball* if these five groups do not work together to support students in our educational system. What is needed is to move from an educational perspective that is detrimental to one that is beneficial as illustrated in the following table.

Beneficial	Or	Detrimental
Cultural Validation	Or	Cultural Assimilation
Transformative Class	Or	Passive Class
Teacher/Learner	Or	Teacher/Transmitter
Questioning	Or	Memorizing
Parents/Participants	Or	Parents/Spectators

In their discussion following the activity, the participants realized that to Structure for Success, the following components would need to be in place: collab-orative classrooms, interdependence among students, valuation of primary language and culture, community participation, parental involvement, and educators and administrators committed to serving all students in the best possible manner (Wink, 1997).

Retta and Success

Retta was moved by her participation in the Structure for Success activity. As she and her colleagues "dropped the ball," she suddenly pictured Oscar as the child in the center, represented by that beach ball. The person chosen to represent the par-ents in the activity was Margarita (Manuel's mother from La Paloma High School), a first-grade teacher at Retta's school. As they interacted after the activity, Retta began to describe Oscar to Margarita, and to make the connections with the ideas she had learned about blaming the victim. Margarita asked Retta if she would like to meet Oscar's parents at the parent meeting coming up. Retta agreed to meet Marga-rita in her room before the meeting, and together they would meet Oscar's parents.

Margarita was one of the initiators of the parent meetings. They had started slowly at first, but by this time the parent group was strong, and Margarita had stepped into the role of advisor. Retta met Oscar's parents, yet, at first, she kept a great distance between herself and the parents. During the September meeting, she maintained three rows of auditorium seats between herself and the families. In the October parent advisory meeting, there was only one row of seats between them. In November, Retta actually sat by the families and a friend translated for her. By the December meeting, she was freely roaming and visiting with the families with the aid of her limited Spanish and her "new attitude" (Krashen, 1990). The parent meetings were helping Retta and the families to develop mutual respect and understanding. These meetings triggered the interaction that triggered the transformation in Retta. This transformation enabled Retta to arrange for a visit to Oscar's home to visit with his mom about his behavior.

Retta told us about the home visit. She was astounded to discover that he had a good home environment, with a loving and supportive family; his brothers and sisters were successful in school. She was relieved to learn that Oscar's mom shared her concern for Oscar. The mother could not understand why Oscar was not learning at the same pace as his brothers and sisters did. However, Oscar's mom was too uncomfortable and alienated to come to the school and discuss her concerns. Retta told us that, before the visit, she assumed that Oscar's behavior was a result of his home.

Now, Oscar is a different person when he is with Retta. Whereas she used to be outraged by his bad behavior, she now understands why he behaves that way and tries to develop strategies that serve his needs better. Retta has moved from blaming-the-victim to critically examining the educational system. She is attempting to transform the system so that Oscar can learn more effectively. Retta and Oscar together are mediating their environment. Oscar is moving through the zone of proximal development (Vygotsky, 1962, 1978, 1986) by the interaction with adult guidance. Because of the implementation of a parent advisory committee, Oscar is changing from disabled to empowered (Cummins, 1989). We watched Retta and Oscar talk quietly and stare out of the window, and remembered how she used to talk about him; now, she visits with him. Retta thinks that Oscar has changed. We think that Retta has changed.

However, Retta still has a critical step to take. She still thinks that Oscar has changed. She needs to critically examine herself and recognize that she is a part of the process of transformation. In Oscar's search for knowledge and literacy, she is a significant variable in the process.

Library Mapping

In the previous examples, we have used students and teachers as symbolic centers of their sociocultural context. We have chosen to do this in order to share the hidden (and, not so hidden) influences that affect, and are affected, by all of us.

For our final example in this chapter, we purposely move to a sociocultural context that is more grounded: libraries.

Le taught a summer course for preservice teachers in Foundations of Bilingual Education, which focused heavily on the social, cultural, historical, and political contexts of language acquisition in the United States. One specific assignment for the future teachers was designed to lead the students into the community—not necessarily "their" community—but the community of the students who were in the process of acquiring English as another language. Le started concretely with maps, representing various neighborhoods. On the maps, the library or libraries were highlighted. Slowly the students began to realize that the "neighborhood map" was that of the schools in which they were being placed for student teaching.

The maps were clearly marked with the bus routes, the homes of the students, and the locality of the libraries. The first thing that the preservice teachers noticed when looking at the maps was the proximity to the school and library for many of the students.

Le's assignment for the future teachers was deceptively simple: They were to visit the library and map where the bilingual books were located. If the students wanted to simply read a book in a language that they could understand, where were those books located? She told the preservice students to ask for help from the librarians for bilingual books and then to map the area made available for families to sit and read.

The range of findings by these preservice teachers is worth noting. Of the eighteen in that university cohort of learners, two came back with glowing reports of how esthetically pleasing and inviting the reading areas were. The bilingual books were easy to find; the librarians wonderfully helpful; the library even had outreach programs in place that invited the parents to come in and read with their children. Not surprisingly, these libraries had good attendance as noticed by the students when they did their observations.

Now for the rest of the story. Most of the university students were outraged at the condition of the libraries they observed. The bilingual books were located on upper levels, on high shelves, not easily accessible to anyone. One of the future teachers even went in and asked for help in Spanish. She was completely ignored until she "code-switched" to English. She was furious. Others talked about how easy it was to get to the library, *if* you had access to a car. Some of the preservice students decided to make this a "real" experience so they took the bus to the library. After multiple transfers, they decided that they would not do *that* again. It was just too hard to get there and back in any decent amount of time. These university students could find no other public outreach programs at these local centers. The preservice teachers experienced firsthand a glimpse of the frustration that parents and children whose first language is not English feel when they are trying to do something as simple as checking books out of the library.

The availability of the books was an issue; the ease of transport to the libraries was an issue; the way in which the patrons were treated was an issue; lack of outreach was an issue. Bookmobiles would be one way to make the books more accessible, but the *real issue* is how little money is being spent on part of the population who has the least access to any kind of reading materials.

It is not that parents do not value reading and books; rather, it is that the contexts make it hard for them to access the books. This activity in the "real" sociocultural context of the future students caused the preservice teachers to reflect critically on some of their long-held assumptions about literacy of students who are in the process of acquiring an additional language.

Conclusion

In this chapter, we have chosen to ground our theory in authentic classroom experiences. It is one thing to theoretically understand the sociocultural context of teaching and learning, but it is quite another to recognize it when it is taking place in our pedagogical lives. It is one thing to understand *inter*mental and *intra*mental, but it is a far greater challenge to see it taking place. For example, in the case of Manuel, he actively rethought the situation and intramentally understood it. Through his actions of boycotting classes and focusing on home-schooling, he attempted to intermentally mediate the two diverse worlds. However, the administration could not make sense of his actions from his perspective so there was a collision in their intermental functioning. Having interviewed Manuel and viewing his situation from his perspective, we were able to share intermental meaning with him. The point is that he understood the administrators (intramentally and intermentally), they did not understand him.

We chose these real examples to further illustrate the importance of the sociocultural context in relation to our learning and development. Our learning impacts what actions we take. Our learning and development are also seen in relationship to others in our lives. We connect and make connections with others who influence what choices we make.

As educators we have to consider the Pedros of our worlds. One teacher, Kathleen, reached out and took responsible action to include Pedro in a supportive group and encouraged the students to work together. A group of students with Manuel as their spokesperson refused to tolerate discrimination in their world. Sam, a new teacher, journaled his dismay with the deterioration of curriculum in his school district. Was journaling enough? It might be as much as he can do in this space and time. Finding others to help us take further action is key to our success in making changes where we perceive reform needs to happen. Fred's colleague reached out to him to help her make her case for her employment against a potentially hostile administration. Retta found a way to connect with Oscar and, in so doing, found herself to be an advocate, whereas before she had been blaming Oscar for his own sociocultural context being different from hers.

Vygotsky has suggested that teaching means relating to students and relating the curriculum to their lives. From the authentic cases referenced in this chapter, we learned that it may take radical action on the part of students to make visible to others their life experience within the sociocultural context. It may take radical action on the part of teachers to make visible to administrators what curriculum is appropriate. It may take radical action on the part of us all to make visible to policymakers what Vygotsky suggests is pedagogically relevant educational psychology.

E N D N O T E S

1. Many of the names of the teachers and students in this chapter have been changed to protect them from what they consider to be the oppressive environment of their sociocultural context. The original data for Pedro were collected by Kathleen Kennedy and used in her unpublished master's thesis, *The Effects of Complex Instruction on the CTBS Reading Comprehension Scores, and on the Academic and Non-Academic Development of Sixth Grade Students*, California State University, 1993.

2. The Pedro story used in this chapter is adapted from Wink (1997) and Wink, Putney, & Bravo-Lawrence (January/February, 1995). The data for the story of Oscar and Retta were originally collected by Joan Wink for her unpublished dissertation, *The Emergence of the Framework for Intervention in Bilingual Education*, Texas A&M University, 1991.

3. In the process of preparing this manuscript for publication, we discovered that the story of Manuel had taken an unexpected turn for the better. Le was in Joan's office at the University, making final copies of critical parts of the document, when the chair of Joan's department greeted Le with a hearty handshake and hello. Le reminded him of the story of Manuel, a qualitative research project she had completed for his class years before. He remembered the study well because it had been such a heart-wrenching project for the families involved as well as for Le. He told Le that, during the two years following the incident, school board members were elected who were sympathetic to the Latino students in the school. In addition, a Latino superintendent had been hired, along with numerous Latino faculty and staff. Dramatic changes had occurred because these Latino students and families had taken an enormous risk in raising their voices and the consciousness of the surrounding community.

4 The Zone of Proximal Development (ZPD)

What the child can do in cooperation today he can do alone tomorrow. There-fore the only good kind of instruction is that which marches ahead of develop-ment and leads it…. (Vygotsky, 1986, p. 188)

In prior chapters, we have illustrated two of the principal principles that are foundational to understanding Vygotsky's work, especially as it applies to teaching and learning. We have shown that Vygotsky thought in dialectics throughout most of his conceptualizing. He theorized thinking and speech as two essential components of verbal thought that dynamically work together as we make meaning with others and make sense for ourselves through our experiences. He further recognized that using language is both a cognitive function and a cultural tool for advancing our thinking.

At the same time that he theorized how thinking and speech impact our learning and development, he also recognized that our ways of being, our social/cultural/historical selfhood, impacts our learning. Vygotsky worked from the premise that all that we do is inherently social and cultural, even when we are actively internalizing information. Learning does not take place in a vacuum and to understand learning we must also understand the social, cultural, and political context in which learning and development take place.

In this chapter, we will focus on one of Vygotsky's concepts that is perhaps his best known in our Western culture, the zone of proximal development. We will look at the zone in terms of the other two principles we have just discussed in the prior chapters, the inherent connection between thought and language (Chapter 2) and the sociocultural nature of teaching and learning. Our intention is also to further explain, examine, and expand this concept as we view the various ways it has been taken up by others. It is our purpose to share the concept of the zone with visual representations as well as classroom observational data to show that, as students collaborate to construct meaning, they create their own personal zones and move through those zones toward the realization of their potential. This chapter seeks to integrate the theory and the practice of the zone of proximal development.

What is the Zone of Proximal Development?

We have already seen how Vygotsky approached the conceptualization of thinking and speech in a manner that was different from his contemporaries. In the same way, he conceptualized a distinct version of the relationship of learning and development. Rather than viewing learning and development as separate processes in which development takes place before learning can occur, he saw them as an interrelated, dynamic process. During this process students become active participants in their learning through the use of language and interactions with others. In describing such a process, Wells (1994) states that learning takes place in the context of purposeful activity as learner and teacher work together to create a product that has its own intrinsic value (p. 263). This purposeful activity constitutes a social process, with the actors bringing to the process their own lived experiences from their own sociocultural contexts.

Vygotsky viewed this experience as a key factor in impacting the relationship of thought and speech. Students use language to communicate thoughts, and through the social act of verbalizing those thoughts combine their experiences with those of others. Wells (1994) refers to this exchange as "minds-on activity," and indicates that the tool of greatest importance is language, the preeminent joint activity that of discourse, and the purpose of the activity that of creating common knowledge and enhancing individual understanding (p. 263). As we move through this chapter, we will show how this exchange of ideas occurs in classroom activity, and how it relates to the zone of proximal development (ZPD).

Vygotsky (1978, 1986) conceptualized a zone of proximal development as a way of viewing what children are coming to know. In his work as a teacher and as a researcher, he recognized that children were able to solve problems beyond their actual development level if they were given guidance in the form of prompts or leading questions from someone more advanced. This person, the more capable peer, could be another student, a parent, and/or a teacher. Vygotsky (1978) defined the zone as:

> the distance between the actual developmental level as determined by independent problem solving and the level of potential development as determined through problem solving under adult guidance or in collaboration with more capable peers (p. 86).

Vygotsky's framework teaches us that, after a student receives instructional support or tutelage from someone, who happens to be more capable in that particular context, the learner internalizes the new idea and will be more able to perform independently in the next similar problem-solving situation. This notion takes into account individual differences, and focuses on the communicative nature of learning in which the participants come to an understanding of the operations they are performing. Every reader of this book knows the experience of learning a new concept and understanding it while it was being explained, only to leave the context, return home, and not be able to explain it to family and friends. It is only through continual guidance within the zone of proximal development that learners grasp understanding that is more complex and move on to being able to know something well enough to share it with others.

Visualizing the ZPD

In this section, we will demonstrate how conceptualizing is often enhanced by visualizing. Our purpose here is twofold. First, we will share a visual that we have found to be helpful in ours and others' understandings of the construct of the zone of proximal development; secondly, our goal is to encourage readers to enhance their thoughts by generating their own visual portrayals. Quite simply, our wish is that the visuals themselves will become the readers' more capable peer. The words and visual in what follows are meant to initiate learning, which precedes the readers' development.

A Metaphor: A Hot Air Balloon Ride

We begin with the metaphor of a hot air balloon ride as one way of visualizing the ZPD (Figure 4.1). Imagine the concept of Vygotsky's zone of proximal development as a ride in a hot air balloon. The ground represents the child's actual developmental level, which has been determined from independent problem solving. The potential level of a child's development, with assistance from an adult or more capable peer, is illustrated as a cloud in the sky. The sky indicates the unlimited ceiling of one's infinite number of still unexplored levels. As the balloon ascends, it also moves forward at varying rates of speed, depending on shifts of the wind. The altitude is controlled by the pilot's use of occasional blasts from the burner to maintain inflation. There is, however, always an element of risk: An unexpected shift in the wind can cause the balloon to change direction, so that even the pilot cannot be absolutely certain where the balloon is headed and when it will end its flight. Through the vehicle of interactive problem solving, represented by the hot air balloon and passengers, the zone of proximal development is traversed. It is through this interaction that the students arrive at a higher level of development than they would realize alone.

What is Development?

Vygotsky described the changes that characterize development in a lecture he gave in October 1930 (Vygotsky, vol. 1, 1987, p. 24): "In development...what changes is not so much the function...as the relationships and connections between them. In development, groupings of psychological functions emerge that were unknown at preceding stages." His concept of development was complex; it is not that there are predetermined levels of development; rather, it is that experience is often out

FIGURE 4.1   Hot Air Balloon.

in front leading and expanding development in unlimited ways. For Vygotsky, the relationship between development and learning is dynamic, reciprocal, and interrelated. In his view of effective pedagogy, students are called on to be active participants in their own learning and developing. In conceptualizing the zone of proximal development, we always need to be cognizant of this notion of reciprocity and interrelatedness in the Vygotskian notion of a very dynamic process of development (1978).

During this process, children become active participants in their learning by using language in interaction with others. Rather than viewing language as merely a semiotic function of cognition, Vygotsky viewed the use of signs and symbols as mediators of human cognition. In other words, we use language, in our action of speaking, as a tool for developing thought, and, at the same time, we develop language through thought. This reciprocal relationship would then allow us to believe that the social action of using language could lead cognitive development.

This is a major area where Vygotsky differed from his contemporaries. As Zebroski (1994) points out, "...Vygotsky argues that Piaget overemphasizes the intellectual, the biological, the evenness and universality of developmental *stages,* the evolutionary character of development, the centrality of the individual, and the essential independence of thought and language" (p. 195). Knowing that Vygotsky came from a different philosophical orientation than Piaget, it is not surprising that he viewed development in a very different way. Zebroski emphasizes for us the contrast when he states that, "...development itself is in development and is uneven and jerky and context-specific..." (1994, p. 195).

Just as Vygotsky juxtaposed the various theories, which we illustrated in Chapter 1, so has Zebroski (1994) described the contrasting theories of development by narrowing them into three categories. The first category he called "step theory," in which development takes place slowly in a continuous and incremental process that takes the form of a straight line that slants upward and forward (Figure 4.2).

The second category he called "stage theory," in which development occurs at distinct, critical points. In this case, development occurs as a leap from stage to stage in a rapid process from level to level. It is progressive, like the step theory, but it is required that we master one process before leaping to the next one. The movement is progressive not regressive, at any point (Figure 4.2).

In the third category, the most revealing of Vygotskian theory, Zebroski likens development to a tidal wave. In this metaphor, development is both progressive and regressive. However, when the movement is progressive, the wave becomes deeper and higher as it moves forward, exemplifying the cumulative effect of increased development (Figure 4.2).

By looking at the tidal wave, we see that past experiences continually transform themselves as the foundation for the next wave of development. The new wave is qualitatively different from the previous one, yet is connected experientially, which provides an overall continuity to this model. Just as in a tidal wave, development, according to Vygotsky, is a forward and backward movement that is ultimately progressive. The backward movement, while at first appearing to be regressive, is actually a period of risk taking when we are making sense of our world. As Zebroski (1994) wrote, this "...apparent *failure,* and backward development,...nonetheless often foreshadow the reorganization and restructuring of experience and prepare for the developmental leap that follows" (p. 162). Similarly, Newman and Holzman (1993) define this period as one of revolution,

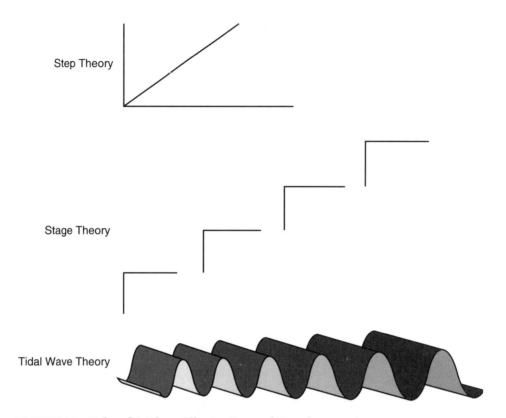

FIGURE 4.2   Zebroski: Three Illustrations of Development.

which prepares us for the next wave of development. Vygotsky saw that the solutions to critical problems arrived at in one level of development then become the source of the next problem to be solved.

It is not lost on us that Zebroski's metaphor of the tidal wave, one that demonstrates the dialectical nature of Vygotsky's work, is easily related to the metaphor of the Vygotskian water drop that we discussed at the beginning of this book. In the case of each metaphor, the dialectical nature of Vygotsky's work is evident. Vygotsky used the metaphor of the water drop to indicate the importance of viewing teaching, learning, and development as reciprocating elements in a process, seemingly opposite elements joined together to make one holistic entity. The new whole contains the property of each element, yet is a qualitatively changed whole. Likewise, in the case of Zebroski's tidal wave, the backward and forward movement of the wave may seem to be opposite and distinct motions. The reality is that these seemingly opposite motions are exactly what make the new whole, which is qualitatively changed. The metaphor signifies the unity of movement as in an actual wave in which the water turns back into itself.

Not only is development itself developmental, but it is also contextually related to our experience with others. As Zebroski (1994) explained: "...Vygotsky contends that the development of the intellect is importantly tied to the development of emotions, that it is the community that leads individual development (which dialectically reconstructs the community)..." (p. 195). As we demonstrated in Chapter 3, learning and development take place within the sociocultural context and in relation with others.

Interpersonal–Intrapersonal Communication

From a Vygotskian perspective, development begins as an interpersonal process of meaning making and then becomes an individualized process of making sense. When we enter into discussion and meaningful interaction with others, we employ the process of moving from inter- to intrapersonal communication (Figure 4.3).

The concepts and language that arise during discussion are at first interpersonal as ideas and words are bounced back and forth between participants. Vygotsky (1978) theorized that every function in the child's cultural development appears twice: first, on the social level, and, later, on the individual level; first, between people (interpsychological), and then inside the child (intrapsychological). This applies equally to voluntary attention, to logical memory, and to the formation of concepts. All the higher functions originate as actual relations between human individuals.

This is what happens in the zone when adults or more capable peers are interacting with each other and offering assistance. Prompts, questions, examples, and explanations exist in the realm of interpersonal communication. Participants are doing today what they are able to do with assistance from others. They will be able to do this problem solving by themselves later when these ideas and words have become internalized. Internalization involves a transfer of responsibility from expert to novice, teacher to pupil; the arena for this transfer is the zone of proximal development (Prawat, 1993, p. 10). At this point concepts are transformed into intrapersonal communication; now, we can have conversation with ourselves about what we know. We can write about our new ideas, talk about them, and converse with others about these concepts that have become actively internalized. Communication about these same ideas will move again into the interpersonal range when we talk with others about what we know.

Scientific and Spontaneous Concepts

Vygotsky (Kozulin, 1990; Wertsch, 1985) believed that instruction leads and supports development through the interaction of two kinds of concepts: scientific or schooled concepts, and spontaneous or everyday concepts. The everyday concepts are those that emerge from the child's own observations and experiences. These generalizations about everyday events are necessary for children to begin acquiring scientific concepts. We begin learning from our interactions with others

Internalization: An
INTERpersonal Process

Transformed into an
INTRApersonal One

Until We Share
Again with Others

FIGURE 4.3   Interpersonal and Intrapersonal Communication.

around us in our sociocultural context through the mediational means of signs, symbols, cultural artifacts, and tools, such as number systems and language.

Spontaneous Concepts in the Community

Vygotsky's concept of mediation "was constantly evolving, including considerations of broader social and cultural processes" that are found in settings such as schools as well as in workplaces and in households (Moll, 2000, p. 257). Extending Vygotsky's work, Moll (1990, 2000) has done extensive work in identifying the kinds of learning that take place through our cultural and social contexts outside of schools. He has worked with classroom teachers doing ethnographic studies of household activities in their students' communities to identify and document the cultural resources abundant in those communities. They refer to the "bodies of knowledge that underlie household activities" as *funds of knowledge* (Moll, 2000, p. 258). Through these studies, teachers come to appreciate the types of resources available to their students on an experiential level in their community contexts outside of school.

Scientific Concepts in the Schools

The other type of concept, scientific concepts, are those that are developed in more formal, schooled settings. We agree with Lee's (2000) questioning of limiting the spontaneous concepts to community settings and the scientific concepts to school settings. The prior example of funds of knowledge suggests that the funds of knowledge that the teachers were observing consisted of both kinds of concepts that had been brought together as ways of knowing.

These concepts can be further differentiated as seen in the box below. In this representation, the spontaneous concepts are defined as being those concepts that we experience in the moment, those that can be observed or known through the senses, and used in an almost unconscious manner. Scientific concepts, on the other hand, are those that are broader and more abstract, and are used in a systematic and purposeful way.

Spontaneous Concepts	Scientific Concepts
Situational	Systematic and generalizable
Empirical	Detached from the concrete
Practical	Used consciously and intentionally

For example, when we were first learning to be teachers, if someone asked us why we put students into small groups to complete an activity, we might give a spontaneous answer based on our experience. We might have said that the students seemed to talk more when they were in small groups, and they produced answers better than if we asked them to solve the problem individually. However, after having studied the scientific concepts of Vygotsky's learning theory, we might provide a more theoretical response based on the zone of proximal development. In many cases with our preservice student teachers and more experienced teachers who have not studied Vygotsky's work, we have heard them say that they knew that kids learned by talking and by working together, but now they have a theoretical language to describe what is going on in facilitated small group interactions.

The Integration of Spontaneous and Scientific Concepts

The more important point is that the two concepts work in harmony with each other; the spontaneous concepts create an experiential path for the development of the scientific. These scientific, or schooled, concepts offer organization to the child's thinking, paving the way for more learning, and ways for the spontaneous concepts to develop and expand into scientific concepts.

The two kinds of concepts work together in a reciprocal relationship and build from and on each other (Figure 4.4). In each realm of concepts, the knowledge is expanding. The spontaneous concepts stem from our sensory experience,

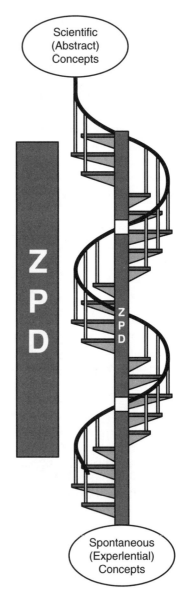

As spontaneous concepts work upward, they clear a path for scientific concepts to become realized.

Where they meet defines the ZPD.

FIGURE 4.4   Integrating Scientific and Spontaneous Concepts.

what we have come to know from observing and doing in our sociocultural context. Through our interactions with others in the academic context, the scientific or schooled concepts lead to generalizations about our world. Thus, the scientific concepts take in the spontaneous concepts, and retool and refine them as we think and learn together.

This process of conceptualizing is a central component of the zone of proximal development. In collaboration with others, the process of constructing schooled concepts merges with our prior experiential concepts through problem-solving activities. The two types of concepts work together in a reciprocal relationship to expand our learning and development.

Performance before Competence

As Vygotsky studied and theorized the zone of proximal development, a parallel construct evolved and became central to his pedagogy and psychology. Vygotsky concluded that the process of development lags behind learning. While the processes of learning and development are interconnected, they do not necessarily advance at the same rate. Educators in his time were especially careful to teach only what the students would be certain to understand based on their actual developmental level. Vygotsky felt that, when educators focus only on the students' actual level, they are orienting the learning to yesterday's development.

This is one of the areas in which Vygotsky differed from Piaget and other contemporaries. Vygotsky believed that some educators were lagging behind students in the process of learning. In his words, "the actual developmental level characterizes mental development retrospectively, while the zone of proximal development characterizes mental development prospectively" (1978, p. 87). This is fundamentally important to teachers now, many of whom come from a tradition that has taught them to assume that a learner *must* be at a certain level developmentally before he or she can learn. Vygotsky would say that learning comes first and leads development. This raises the bar for teachers and makes it possible to assume that good teaching can lead to good learning, which in turn can lead to more development.

Our conceptualization of this idea can be represented by the following table.

Past Learning:	Actual Developmental Level
Present Learning:	Zone of Proximal Development
Future Learning:	Potential Development Level

Cazden (1981) describes the Zone of Proximal Development as "performance before competence" (Moll, 1990, p. 3). The zone allows performance before competence to happen. The collaboration and working together encourages and enhances this; once students have experienced the phenomenon, self-competency and self-concept grow.

Learning Leads Development

The notion of a dynamic development is fundamental to understanding the zone of proximal development. This, in kind, leads to a greater understanding of scientific and spontaneous concepts that are central to the Vygotskian idea of performance before competence.

Recently, Joan was describing for us the context in which she first internalized the concept of performance before competence, although, at that time, she could not have articulated the experience. This internalization occured as she watched her children grow up on a ranch in Arizona. Joan's experience illustrates how authentic, spontaneous concepts from one's community might be used to integrate the scientific concepts of the classroom. Here the two concepts appear initially to be unique and opposite, but later combine and grow to maintain distinct elements of each concept while simultaneously creating a new concept that is qualitatively changed.

> Joan's daughter, Dawn, spent much of her childhood with her Dad working around horses and cattle. When a problem existed, they would talk and think until they found a way to solve it. Problem solving was inherently a part of ranching.
>
> For example, if a calf needed to be found, if a bull was threatening, if a cow were in the creek, Dawn would listen, talk, and think with her Dad until they found a way to solve the problem, much of which took place on horseback. Joan would watch in fascination as Dawn worked on her horse, long before Joan thought Dawn had competence. "How can Dawn do that?" Joan would ask herself. "No one ever taught her to do that! She is not developmentally ready for that." Her performance was always ahead of her competence.
>
> The same was true for Joan's son, Bo, only his zones of proximal development took place on motorbikes, which, each year, seemed to jump higher and go faster. "No one taught him how to do complex stunts—how did he learn to perform those stunts? And, certainly, he isn't old enough to do that yet," Joan thought.

However, learning preceded development; in fact, learning pulled and tugged until greater development evolved. When one is on a horse chasing a bull through the mesquite bush, or when one is high in the air on a motorbike, it is not a question of being at the right developmental level. Learning is a part of the problem-solving process and development rushes to catch up. What Dawn and Bo experienced was a high interest level in authentic problem-solving activities. In both cases, they were not learning about ranching and bike riding, they were living it and developing through the learning experience.

> "I watched in fascination and wondered why we couldn't bring this same performance before competency into the classroom." Joan recalled. "If my

kids, in the context of their real life, were willing to risk and to extend themselves by such a degree, suddenly it became clear that I needed to do something in the classroom that encouraged students to take a risk to reach their next level."

Although Joan did not say that she was seeking to integrate the spontaneous concepts (of the ranch) with the scientific concepts (of her junior class) that is what she realized she needed to do. Nor did she realize that she was attempting to bring the funds of knowledge (rural, in this case) into the classroom. Likewise, Joan could not have said at that time that she was determined to create zones of proximal development where students were safe to take risks in their learning.

As so often happens with good pedagogical practices, teachers learn from children, when they are allowed to listen, and only later come to realize that research supports what students daily are trying to tell us. Students need to operate effectively in the present in order to reach toward their future developmental level.

What Are Funds of Knowledge?

Funds of knowledge are the cultural artifacts and bodies of knowledge that underlie household activities (Moll, 2000). They are the inherent cultural resources found in communities surrounding schools. Funds of knowledge are grounded in the networking that communities do in order to make the best use of those resources. Moll (1990, 2000) and other colleagues have demonstrated the importance of communities of learners within large cultural and familial networks. Within these networks, the zone of proximal development is manifested in different ways. These zones are knowledge-based and authentic.

Funds of knowledge can be situated within a household, in a Vygotskian notion of the individual. For example, in Joan's household when she lived on the ranch in Arizona, the funds of knowledge were evident as her kids performed well beyond their "assumed" developmental level because the context of the ranch encouraged risk taking and problem solving. In addition, each person in the household had individual knowledge that collectively ran the family-centered funds of knowledge.

Funds of knowledge are also situated, in a Vygotskian notion of the collective, from one household to another or to a greater community. For example, Joan realized that the performance before competence that her children displayed on the ranch needed to be extended to enrich the pedagogy of her classroom. It was the connections and interactions from these rural funds of knowledge to the student-centered learning that created the collective.

Another example of the collective nature of the funds of knowledge can be seen in a one-room schoolhouse in rural South Dakota. The following experience is a small sample of data collected in a study of this particular school. As in many qualitative research experiences, the researcher went into the project with one set of questions and came out with answers to surprisingly new questions. In this case, Joan went to study rural and urban education and left the study with data demonstrating a new and unexpected fund of knowledge. Following is one of the stories that happened on an extremely cold day in January. In the following, Tracey is a thirteen-year-old girl who lives in a very isolated area and needs to cross the frozen Cheyenne River daily in order to get to the school, which is several miles from the ranch where she lives. She is sharing her individual funds of knowledge with Joan, and we now share with you to establish the collective funds of knowledge.

"Tracey, how in the world are we going to get across the river?" I asked, looking down at the ice on that cold January day.

"Walk," she replied as she took off with determined thirteen-year-old strides across one-hundred yards of the frozen (I hoped) river. "Come on," she called to me as I hesitated on the bank of snow.

I headed onto the ice; I stood as tall as I could; I swung my arms; I kept my head up; I did all of this to try to hide my terror from Tracey.

Tracey has been crossing this river every day since kindergarten to get to her one-room schoolhouse, which lies two miles south of the river. She is now in the eighth grade, and next year she will have to drive twenty miles on a gravel road and forty miles on blacktop to get to high school.

I had come to visit this little school of seven students as I wanted to articulate the differences and similarities between rural and urban education. I thought I would ask Tracey leading questions like: "So, tell me what you are reading at school? Do you have a school library? What do you get to do during science? Do you and your classmates work together on projects?" Instead, I asked: "What in the world do you do in the spring when the ice starts to melt?"

"Sometimes, we use the four-wheeler. Other times, we take the Argo (a little open vehicle that resembles a tub with six wheels). Or, we use the 4X4 pickup, the tractor, the john-boat (a small oblong boat that resembles a floating block of wood), and sometimes we have to ride horses. But, a lot of the year we can wade across except when we have to use planks to cover the ice and water," she matter-of-factly listed her means of transportation as she scrambled up the bank of snow on the south side of the frozen river.

"What? Planks?" I asked as I hurried to catch up with her.

"Yes, planks to connect the pieces of ice. Don't worry, we have life jackets that we hang on that tree when we get to the other side. Sometimes we have to use a rope to tie my sister and me together. Dad usually goes ahead to check where the river is safest. But, the worst time was when we were on horseback, and my horse fell into a hole in the river, and I had to swim. There was water coming over the saddle," she explained to me.

Tracey, definitely the more capable peer in frozen-river-crossing, was sharing her funds of knowledge as she and Joan made their way to school. Later that afternoon, Joan would experience for herself Vygotsky's concept of performance before competence, as she would be returning alone.

> "the zone of proximal development today will be the actual developmental level tomorrow—that is, what a child can do with assistance today she will be able to do by herself tomorrow…the only 'good learning' is that which is in advance of development" (Vygotsky, 1978, pp. 87–89).

However, in this case, the *child* was Joan, and she didn't have until tomorrow. She had to do this later the same day. Joan spent the morning at school and, at midday, Tracey and her classmates drove twenty miles in another direction for their once-a-week extracurricular activities. This meant two things: First, Joan would have to cross that frozen river alone this time, and, second, that Tracey would be crossing it alone at 10 P.M. in the darkness. Joan wrote:

> I was alone on the riverbank. There was not a person within miles. And, there was the frozen ribbon of ice. I looked at it and thought about the fast-moving currents underneath. I had heard how deceiving ice can be. I thought about Tracey, who has done (or attempted to do it) this every day of her K–8 school experience. I remember thinking that, if the ice should crack or break, there was not a soul who could hear me, much less help me.
>
> I stepped out on the ice, each step forward was a victory in courage for me. I worried that the weight of my fear would make me heavier. It didn't, and the picture in my mind of Tracey, marching boldly ahead earlier in the day, instructing me in how to cross the ice, was what kept me going until I arrived safely on the other side and felt jubilant. Later that night, I thought of Tracey, who would be crossing that frozen river at about 10 P.M. in the bitter cold darkness. (See Endnote 1.)

At first Joan had been concerned for Tracey's safety, given her own terror in accomplishing that feat earlier. For Joan, the fund of knowledge for crossing the river was still new and developing; it was still part of her *potential* development. However, for Tracey, the very same knowledge was her *actual* level of development. She had experienced this problem-solving activity every winter of her life. She had received the assistance of her more capable peers, her dad, and older sister. Her dad had gone to school the same way; her older sister went to school in the same way. This fund of knowledge, crossing the river, had become second nature for Tracey.

As noted by Moll (2000), normative research often does not capture all of the diversity of life, especially how families need to strategize to deal with the concrete and changing conditions of their lives. Vygotsky argued that

> psychology cannot limit itself to direct evidence…. Psychological inquiry is investigation, and like the criminal investigator, the psychologist must take into account indirect evidence and circumstantial clues—which in practice means that works of

art, philosophical arguments and anthropological data are no less important for psychology than direct evidence (Vygotsky, 1986, pp. xv–xvi).

Funds of knowledge include all of the knowledge of families. It is the situatedness of what a family must do to live and even thrive in a particular location. The same is true in classrooms; communities of learners generate their own situated knowledge when they are allowed to.

Models of Parental Involvement

The interchange of funds of knowledge often begins when teachers and families share authentic experiences together. By far, the most meaningful experiences will take place in the community of families, in the neighborhood, in the barrio, in the migrant camp, in the suburbs, in the housing development. We encourage educators to risk the safety of the context of the academic world by seeking authentic experiences in the *real* world of the students. In order to bring the power of the funds of knowledge to the schools, educators need to understand through experience.

One way of initiating a shared experience is by teachers and families joining together to engage in activities (Figure 4.5). By sitting together and reflecting on

FIGURE 4.5 Family Graph (Wink, 2000, p. 134).

My Family				
	My Grandparents	**My Parents**	**Me**	**My Kids**
School				
Work Career				
Religion				
Family				
Travel				
Politics				
Beliefs				
Daily Life				

their individual histories, teachers and families can begin to create a new collective experience that incorporates and values the unique histories of each person, and, simultaneously, creates a new whole, which is qualitatively changed by the act of joining together. This is an activity that brings the dialectics of the water drop and the tidal wave into the reality of one's own community. Our experiences have demonstrated that the process represented in Figure 4.5 is a safe way to begin bringing together diverse groups of people. In this activity, funds of knowledge often begin to emerge, often without the conscious knowledge of the participants.

Another way to critically reflect on experiences of families and schooling is to observe what happens in parent–school activities. If you ask school personnel what happens at functions involving parents, they will likely tell you that they have established relationships with parents in positive, meaningful ways. If you ask the parents what happens at those same functions, you will likely hear a different answer. Our question to you is, how are the educators involving parents in your local schools? Are they asking parents to change to fit the needs of the

FIGURE 4.6 Models for Parental Involvement (Wink, 2000, p. 133).

The We-Are-Going-to-Do-This-*to*-You Model of Parental Involvement	
The We-Are-Going-to-Do-This-*with*-You Model of Parental Involvement	
Doin' It To 'Em	**Doin' It With 'Em**
Goal	
change the parents	change the schools
Objectives	
to melt into the pot	to melt the pot
to discuss building community	to build community
Characteristics of the Meetings	
teachers talk	teachers listen
families listen	families talk
families sit still	families interact
everyone leaves immediately after	people hang around
people leave space between them	people hug
kids go to a room with a sitter	kids work with families
teachers tell objectives	families tell stories
Result	
Dysfunctional School	Functional School

school? Or, are the educators asking what the school can do to fit the needs of the parents and children they serve? The difference in the answers you give to these questions tells you which model of parental involvement the school is using: the We-Are-Going-to-Do-This-*to*-You-Model, or the We-Are-Going-to-Do-This-*with*-You-Model.

As a critically reflective activity, we suggest that you attend a parent involvement meeting at your school. While at the meeting, we want you to activate our critical praxis framework (see Chapter 2) in this way:

1. First, NoteTaking: Describe what you see and hear in the meeting; try to put yourself in the shoes of the parents who are attending.
2. Second, NoteMaking: Interpret what you observed and think of why things are happening in a particular way.
3. Third, NoteRemaking: Transform the areas in which parents are not truly partners with the school so that your school becomes the "Doin' It with 'Em" functional school.

Expanding the ZPD in Schools

In describing the learning process, Wells (1994) states that "learning takes place in the context of purposeful activity, as learner and teacher work together to create a product that has its own intrinsic value" (p. 263). Learning needs to be meaningful, purposeful, relevant, and respectful (Goodman, Bird, & Goodman, 1991). Purposeful activities constitute a social process, with the actors bringing to the process their own lived experiences, from their own sociocultural–historical contexts. Learning in this way becomes transformative as students and teachers construct mutual knowledge through purposeful activities.

A way of further conceptualizing the zone of proximal development as a potentially transformative classroom process is through Vygotsky's constructs of reformulation and internalization (Rieber & Carton, 1987; Vygotsky, 1978, 1986). Vygotsky theorized that, through dialogic and collaborative practices, learners personally reformulate a problem and then formulate a possible solution in their own words. What begins as a collective work is transformed as students take up, or internalize, common language and knowledge of the collective to be used in their personal academic work. From this perspective, participants working together on a problem construct knowledge together that has potential for becoming both collective knowledge and individual knowledge as well as for guiding and transforming subsequent actions (Putney, Green, Dixon, Durán, & Yeager, 2000). Collective learning and development and individual learning and development are integrally tied to each other (Souza Lima, 1995).

As teachers and students work together in a dynamic way, their knowledge of academic content and practices (patterned ways of acting) are transformed as they construct a community of practice (Lave & Wenger, 1991; Rogoff, 1994) or classroom culture (Collins & Green, 1992; Santa Barbara Classroom Discourse

Group, 1992a) with their students. As Moll (1990) argues, for Vygotsky, "the intellectual skills children acquire are directly related to how they interact with others in specific problem-solving environments…[C]hildren internalize and transform the help they receive from others and eventually use these same means of guidance to direct their subsequent problem-solving behaviors" (p. 1). The interactions and activity among members of the class afford students opportunities to learn new ways of accomplishing subsequent tasks of classroom life as well as new content knowledge (Tuyay, Jennings, & Dixon, 1995).

In a similar way, teaching can be viewed as a dialogic and dynamic process through which the teacher learns from observing what students take up and uses this knowledge to formulate and reformulate classroom activity. This dynamic interactive and responsive process supports individual and groups of students in accomplishing current and future tasks that constitute the academic curriculum. Both teachers and students interpret new tasks and draw on past learning to construct knowledge in new events, and both draw on this knowledge to shape subsequent classroom activity. Thus, both teachers and students are learners; only the object of study differs (Floriani, 1997; John-Steiner & Mahn, 1996).

In the next two sections, we will share two examples of the ZPD. In choosing these examples, we have endeavored to demonstrate that the ZPD can be implemented in the most unusual teaching and learning contexts. While both examples took place in the context of international education, the first was planned by the teacher and the second example happened spontaneously.

The Peace Patrol

The zone of proximal development can be implemented in a wide variety of contexts, with any content, on any continent, and under difficult circumstances. That is what we learned from a teacher who teaches in international education. Recently, she had been seeking solutions to violence on campus and decided to try to find ways to make the ZPD increase the development and learning of her students.[2] In what follows, in her own words, is how she found peace through the implementation of the ZPD.

> Conflict resolution is a 'hot topic' among high school counselors. At my intermediate school, I have been interacting with small teams of student peer mediators to work through problem solving. These "more capable peers" have dual functions: First, they have preventive responsibilities, in which they learn role-playing, walking the talk, and wearing the peace uniform; second, they are intervention agents when conflict does arise. The more capable peers have become known as the "Peace Patrol." We believe that these students are modeling a foundation of mediation for the rest of the student body.
>
> I initially introduce the concept of peaceful problem solving, through the use of the ZPD. Next, more capable peers are trained using a variety of methods, including a 'peace' vocabulary giving mediators a framework in

which to expand the concept. They are then ready to interact outside the mediator group with other students as the need arises.

At this point, I have long since moved out of the director position (or more capable peer) and now work with the student more capable peers as they share their abilities to question, to analyze concept growth, and to encourage other students to also become more capable peers. In this way, the peace concept affects ever-widening pools of students who experience successful problem solving outside the classroom, but inside their meaningful social context. Teachers and parents are "in the loop" (or, in a Vygotskian sense, in the zone) through workshops and active participation within and without the school community.

As we knowingly create the zones of proximal development and actively expand the numbers of peer mediators (more capable peers), we've changed a lot from the inside out. We have been experiencing precious peace. Our school atmosphere is more positive; we have far fewer fights; and, more than fifty students—mediators and disputants—have walked away from a scary, frustrating, or hurtful situation feeling better and more confident than they were.

In summarizing the Peace Patrol situation, as the school counselors, teachers, and students utilized the construct of the zone of proximal development to build the peacekeeping strategies in their school, they were also problem posing and problem solving as we saw in the examples in Chapter 2. As the Peace Patrol participants expand their repertoires of dealing with problems on the school grounds, they also mediate problem-solving solutions with their fellow students. In implementing a theoretically-based solution to an initial problem, the entire school has made a transformation from a hurtful place to a nurturing place. They have made school safe for learning.

Mumbo-Jumbo Theory

A vivid example of the ZPD recently happened with Joan and a classroom of adult students in the context of international education. As a way of preparing for a masters' comprehensive final, Joan spent two hours of class time reviewing the ebb and flow of the various theoretical perspectives throughout this century (Figure 1.1). With the test rapidly approaching, the students were focused, drawing their own time lines in preparation for the test, and asking many questions. At the end of this session, the whiteboard in the classroom was completely filled with a long red vertical line that ran the full length of the board. Obviously, it was a time line; dates, people, and ideas were rapidly scrawled above and below the vertical line. In fact, a quick, cursory glance could lead one to believe that it was *mumbo-jumbo*, a mess of scribbles, scrawls, and scratches. However, a closer look by anyone preparing for a master's final would show that the mess contained the big ideas of thought running through this century. At the end of class, Joan recreated in her class journal the exact time line that the students generated (Figure 4.7).

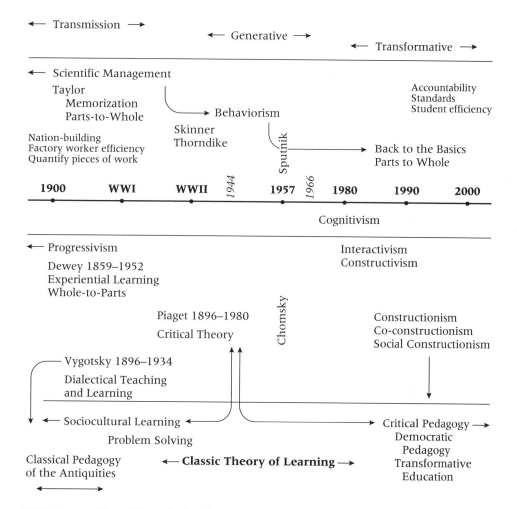

FIGURE 4.7 Time Line of Big Ideas.

On the time line, the students had written *Vygotsky's life* (1896 to 1934); close to his name, they wrote the phrases *dialectical teaching and learning, sociocultural learning,* and *problem solving.* Near his name, and below the time line, they wrote the lifespans of *Dewey* (1859 to 1952) and *Piaget* (1896 to 1980). Below Dewey's name, they scrawled *experiential learning* and *whole-to-parts.* Above Piaget's name, they included the term *generative.* The time line included the simultaneous and conflicting notions of *Progressivism* and *Scientific Management* in the early years of the 1900s.

Above the time line, they wrote *Taylor* under *Scientific Management* with the words *memorization,* and *parts-to-whole.* Not far from Taylor's name, *Skinner, Thorndike,* and *Behaviorism* were followed by *Black Box theory, stimulus–response,* and *quantify–measure.* At the very top of the whiteboard, above *Behaviorism,* they wrote *Transmission.*

In the middle of the horizontal line, *1957* appeared, with *Sputnik* written above the line and with *Chomsky* written below. Both the years *1944* and *1966* were highlighted. Below the late 1970s and moving into the 1980s, the words *cognitivism, interactivism, constructivism, constructionism* (see Table 1.1), *co-constructionism,* and *social constructionism* appeared, followed by arrows to *critical pedagogy, democratic pedagogy,* and *transformative education.*

Critical pedagogy had two arrows beside it, one moving to the right, as an implicated future, and another arrow to the left, pointing directly up to *Critical Theory of the 1940s.* Another arrow from *critical theory* went down to *sociocultural learning.* From *Vygotsky's* name, an arrow indicated the link to *classical pedagogy.*

However, the original questions asked at the beginning of this section were: What is the ZPD? And, who is the more capable peer? What does that time line on a whiteboard have to do with answering those two questions? The answers can be found in what happened next.

At the end of the review session on the time line, Joan grabbed a whiteboard eraser to clean the board. She rapidly drew the eraser across the entire length of the board, but the red marks stayed on the board. She did it again. Nothing. The red marks remained. Joan had obviously used a nonerasable marker for this lesson, not the erasable marker. The students began to chant, "Leave it there, leave it there," because this was the same room where they would soon take their test. However, this international education program leases this classroom from another school. The thought of ruining the whiteboards for a school with a limited budget sent tremors through, at least, Joan's spine.

> "Who knows what to do?" Joan asked the class with panic rising in her voice.
>
> "I know what to do," Chris, who teaches in Kuwait said, as she ran from the room. She soon returned with a bottle of alcohol and lots of wet paper towels. She began to wipe the whiteboard, which soon turned into a smeared bright hot pink, and not so white, board. Steve, who teaches in Turkey, watched what she was doing and went to help her. With continued perseverance and many more wet and then dry towels, the board eventually returned to an almost passable shade of white.
>
> "Now, let's try to refocus our review and remember some of Vygotsky's ideas. Let's start with the ZPD," Joan said to the class at the end of this near-classroom-fiasco.
>
> "Enough of this *mumbo-jumbo* theory," Steve suddenly blurted out. "Just tell us in real language what the ZPD is" More laughter and nervous energy filled the air.

"Okay, Steve," Joan began. "Chris is your more capable peer when it comes to cleaning permanent markers from the whiteboard. You had never learned this and were thoroughly enjoying the possibility that I might have ruined the whiteboard. Chris, as the more capable peer, knew that learners could solve problems beyond their actual developmental level if they receive guidance from a more advanced learner. Thus, Chris pulled us all through our actual developmental level in whiteboard cleaning. What you did in cooperation with Chris today, you can do alone tomorrow. In addition, if this should ever happen again, you could suddenly become the more capable peer in whiteboard cleaning for someone else. And, that is no *mumbo-jumbo* theory."

As Joan was speaking and finally getting the adult learners thinking about their comprehensive final again, the door of the classroom suddenly burst open. Harriet, from the Czech Republic, said, "Dr. Wink, I am sorry to bother you, but do you have anything to clean markers off a whiteboard? I just wrote all over Dr. Titone's whiteboard and can't get it off." A roar of laughter swept through the class again.

"Steve, you are now the more capable peer. Go help her," Joan said.

"And, no mumbo-jumbo theory either, Steve. Just pull her up through the zone to her next developmental level in whiteboard cleaning."

More ZPD in the Classroom

Joan's example of the ZPD is synergetic. It was not a part of the planned curriculum; it simply happened. The trick is to see the pedagogical relevance of many social–cultural events within the classroom culture and to learn from them. It is our contention that the legacy of Vygotsky provides many pedagogical tools that, when implemented, become cognitive coathooks for learning and developing at any given moment.

In the next example of the ZPD, the teacher has assigned roles to the individual students to assure that each student contributes and that all learn. However, as shall be seen, even when the teacher has "planned" to make the ZPD a part of the curriculum, unforeseen events can stall or prevent further learning and developing. Once again, it is the teacher's pedagogical expertise that, when applied appropriately, can assure that the students continue to climb that slippery learning curve

In a sixth-grade classroom, the students were studying a unit on why and how people in societies build various types of structures. For this particular lesson, the teacher assigned student roles to facilitate the learning within each group. For the following small group, the teacher thought that the facilitator, Stephanie, would be the more capable peer. However, the sociocultural context often has an unplanned dynamic of its own that determines the direction of human relationships and learning.

Stephanie's group was working on an activity to build a suspension bridge demonstrating the concepts of tension and compression. As the teacher approached the group to observe their work, she noticed that one student, Jeff, was standing with his arms folded in front of him, scowling somewhat at the attempts of the others in his group to make a satisfactory model. He informed the teacher that he had been excluded from the process by the others. He had given his opinion on how to proceed, and, because they did not agree with him, they ignored his suggestions and continued. Because the roles for group participation had already been constructed by the teacher and students, the teacher attempted to find a way to validate the strengths of this student without breaking down the interaction of the group as a whole.

Turning to the facilitator of the group, the teacher asked if their model truly demonstrated the concepts of tension and compression. The facilitator assured the teacher that their model was fine. However, another group member, the recorder, admitted that their bridge did not follow all of the specifications of a true suspension bridge.

"The strings are wrong," Mario chimed in. "Jeff tried to tell us."

"Jeff, do you have any suggestions for fixing the bridge so that the strings demonstrate the concepts correctly?" the teacher asked. Jeff set about demonstrating how the bridge would have to be reconstructed so that it would comply with the necessary specifications. Turning back to the facilitator of the group, who had done most of the excluding, the teacher asked, "Stephanie, could your group utilize the information offered by Jeff in order to redo the bridge? Ana and Mario seem to be in agreement that something must be done to correct the model as it stands."

"Well, I guess I did ignore Jeff's suggestions earlier," Stephanie admitted. Turning to the others in the group she added, "OK, let's try again. Jeff is the bridge expert, so he can show us how, and we can build it together."

The teacher moved on to another group, and, when she returned to this group, all were collaborating on the new structure. The formerly excluded student was now the more capable peer, happily explaining the concepts of tension and compression with the others. Following his advice, they were able to build a much improved version of their original bridge, which they proudly displayed to the entire class.

In effect, we had an example of students who were attempting to move through the zone of proximal development, but whose progress had been stalled because the student facilitator of the group did not recognize the resource of the more capable peer. The role of the teacher in this case was to facilitate the progress of the group by helping them to refocus trust in each other. Had the teacher insisted that the group members listen to Jeff, who knew what needed to be done, the teacher would have been forcing, not, facilitating. Instead, the teacher asked leading questions to focus the students on the fact that they were not accomplishing the goals of the group work. The group members had been relying on information from a less capable peer, Stephanie, who happened to have been assigned the role of facilitator in their group.

The teacher encouraged the expertise of the more capable peer, Jeff, to emerge in a nonthreatening manner. The other students could then see the advantage of utilizing his knowledge. When the teacher refocused the group, the others became willing to listen to and use Jeff's ideas. With the knowledge of the more capable peer, and the cooperation of the others in the group, they quickly put together an impressive structure that correctly modeled the concepts so that the others in the class could learn from their experience.

As teachers we must be open to the notion of more capable peers. We do not always know in every situation which student will be the more capable. This is important in validating multiple strengths.

Who Really Is the More Capable Peer?

Judy and Juan are classmates with very different economic, social, cultural, and political backgrounds. Judy's family is economically secure; her mother is a teacher and her Dad runs a successful business. They adore their daughter, Judy, and do all they can to assure that she has many positive and varied experiences. Juan, on the other hand, comes from a broken home. His mother is raising five children alone; she works outside the home and simply does not have the time or money to do extra things with her children. Juan's Dad is out of jail, but does not spend time with his family.

Judy is a great reader and knows it. In fact, she is often bossy to the point that her peers don't like to be with her, particularly in a reading group. Juan is the opposite; he is not a good reader, and his peers like to be with him, even in reading groups.

One long, rainy day in class, Olivia, the teacher, went to her closet and pulled out ten giant puzzles for the children to do during their indoor recess time. Although Judy and Juan had not worked together before, Olivia paired them on that rainy day. At that point, none of the students wanted to work with Judy. Olivia was hoping that Juan would model some of his people skills in his innocent and gregarious way. Judy and Juan dumped out the pieces of their puzzle on the floor and began to work.

> "Put all the pieces face up," Judy said, and their fingers went to work. "Now, find the outside pieces. I'll do the top; you do the bottom," she continued.

> "Okay," Juan replied. Juan quickly began connecting the pieces of the bottom of the puzzle.

> "Juan, now do that corner, too," Judy said when she realized that she was not putting the top together as quickly.

> "You are too bossy," Juan replied. "Look, see this piece? Does it look like it goes up there?" he asked her as he showed her a piece for the top of the puzzle.

"Yes," she answered. "Well, get it and put it together with that one," he said to her, still using a friendly tone. She took the two pieces, but could not make them fit together and threw them back into the pile of pieces.

"Give it to me," he responded in a more aggravated tone of voice. She handed it to him with a look that said, sure-like-you're-going-to-make-it-fit.

"Can you see this little loop?" he asked her as his voice began to take on a hint of sarcasm.

"Yeah, Juan, I can see it," she returned his expression.

"Can you see the missing hole on the other piece?" he asked as he pointed to the piece that she had just tossed back into the pile.

"Yes, I can," she pouted.

"Well, grab that piece and put the loop in the hole, and it will fit," he said as he demonstrated each movement of putting the two pieces together.

Reluctantly, Judy began to put the two pieces together and succeeded. "I got it. I got it. I'm so good," she squealed to all in the class. Juan and Judy continued to work on their puzzle and were the first to finish.

"We're done, teacher, we're done," Juan exclaimed.

"Oh, Juan, turkeys are done; people are finished," Judy sighed in exasperation.

This authentic example of the zone of proximal development demonstrates that the more capable peer may not be obvious. In addition, the case-in-point shows that the more capable peer in one context may not be the more capable peer in another.

Cognitively Slipping in the Zone

We have discussed the meaning of the concept of the zone of proximal development and the powerful effect of utilizing that zone in the classroom. However, we recognize that simply grouping students and hoping that they will help each other is not quite enough to ensure positive outcomes and movement toward that potential development level. In our studies of Vygotsky we have found two problems that can thwart even a well-constructed zone of proximal development; the first is safety for the students while in the culture of the classroom, and the second is regression within the zone.

Safety within the ZPD

The Vygotskian legacy encourages students and teachers to take risks in their problem solving. Dialectical thought and language will lead to learning *outside of the box*. This combination of problem solving and dialectical thinking can be risky business. When we create zones of proximal development in the classroom, they must be surrounded by a safe and secure environment. Harste, Woodward, and Burke (1984) refer to risk taking as a strategy. They look to Vygotsky to argue their point as follows: To live within existing rules and predictable patterns is not to grow (p. 136). They advocate a low-risk setting for literacy and language development. They describe this setting as follows: "In such an environment the language user neither guesses wildly, nor does not guess at all; rather, he or she finds himself or herself in a setting where calculated guesses and 'what-I'm-ready-for' are allowed to evolve" (p. 136). In Vygotsky's words,

> what the child can do in cooperation today he/she can do alone tomorrow. Therefore the only good kind of instruction is that which marches ahead of development and leads it; it must be aimed not so much at the ripe as at the ripening functions (1986, p.188).

When we begin to create zones that encourage performance before competence, the teacher is no longer the center of learning. In the zone of proximal development, students using language are central to the learning process. Classrooms need to be organized so that all students continually use their own language to understand the concepts, ideas, and curriculum. It is necessary for students to have time to reflect, to discuss, to organize thoughts, to summarize, and to generate ideas through social interaction.

Regression with the ZPD

Through properly implemented collaboration, students come to trust each other to provide information as learning emerges from the interaction. As students progress through the zone, could it be possible for them to regress during interaction? This was a question raised and researched by Jonathan Tudge (1990), who maintained that, if learners are able to *progress* through the zone, it also could be possible for them to *regress* during peer collaboration. He based this on a study conducted in Ithaca, New York with children who helped each other solve a problem predicting the movement of a balance beam in relation to varying weights placed on it. According to Tudge, the results of the study showed that collaboration with a more capable peer does not guarantee that the joint meaning will be at a higher level, and that the higher level peer could actually regress.

The next day after reading about Tudge's research, Le went to a presentation about bilingual education programs in California and had the opportunity to experience this phenomenon of regression. The presenter, who one could assume was the more capable peer, was attempting to explain the differences in the various types of programs that are associated with bilingual education. Due to the constraints of time, she had tried to give simple definitions of complex program models. As the presenter attempted to explain the various program models, her explanations became intertwined because her knowledge base was not well established. In fact, it became clear that perhaps she was not the more capable peer in the group of colleagues.

As a participant, Le felt compelled to say something because the information being given was incorrect and confusing to everyone else in attendance. However, as Le began to share, she found, much to her surprise, that she simply could not find the words needed to set the situation straight again. The more confusing the discussion became, the more difficult it was to sort through all of the terms and definitions being offered. This happened, in spite of the fact that Le had years of experience with and knowledge of language acquisition and the various models available for diverse student needs.

After the presentation, some of the other participants began to ask Le for clarification as they walked to their cars. Away from the confusion brought on by the other speaker, Le began to share. She was able to clarify the terms that were causing confusion, realizing that the information came to her almost intuitively because she was no longer being influenced by the disorientation of misinformation.

The events had quite an effect on her, and, on arriving home after the session, she phoned a colleague, who had also read the Tudge article, to tell her what had happened. Le told her friend of her confusion and inability to clarify during the presentation, although her confusion vanished after she left the context. Le and her colleague mused on the fact that maybe she had experienced regression within the zone of proximal development, ironically, the day after she learned about it.

The next day, as Le related this story to Joan in her office, Joan suddenly exclaimed, "Le, you were Tudged!" Our apologies to Jonathan Tudge for using his name to explain the phenomenon. However, like our friend, Calvin of the *Calvin and Hobbes* cartoon, we like to *verb words*, and in this case we simply could not resist.

The point we wish to make in the telling of this story is that simply pairing students with more capable peers is not sufficient to insure that increased learning is occurring. The more capable peer or any member of the social learning group can experience regression. However, if we return to Vygostky's take on development with Zebroski's image of the tidal wave, then we can recognize that regression can be a moment of reorganization of thoughts, a moment just before a revolutionary point of understanding (Newman & Holzman, 1993). Zebroski (1994) discussed Vygotsky's model of development as one that is progressive and regressive at the same time. Development in this sense depends on risk taking, which may involve apparent "failure," but that is momentary as the apparent regression may actually prepare the individual for the developmental leap that follows. Given this view of development, Tudge's study showed that the process and the conditions under which the interaction take place are important factors in the movement through the zone. Providing sufficient feedback is one way for teachers to help students confirm their learning.

Children at Play

Vygotsky (1978) stated that "play creates a zone of proximal development of the child. In play a child always behaves beyond his average age, above his daily behavior; in play it is as though he were a head taller than himself" (p. 102).

Play Creates a ZPD.

Play mediates
the learning
of children.

In play,
children become
a head taller
than their
current selves.

Vygotsky, 1978

FIGURE 4.8   A Head Taller than Him- or Herself.

After seeing this graphic, a bilingual teacher shared with us an example of her child at play. This teacher was learning sign language in order to communicate with her four-year-old son, Martín, who is hearing impaired. She and her husband watched in fascination as their son sat on the floor in the family room, signing to himself. Even though he was the only one in the room, he definitely appeared to be conversing with someone else. "When a child's activity consists entirely of play, it is accompanied by extensive soliloquizing" (Vygotsky, 1986, p. 55). The only difference in Martín's case is that he is not soliloquizing by using his voice; he is signing his meaning. In the mother's words, "We watched him with amusement because he appeared to be teaching someone, and he was going a mile a minute, totally in his own little world."

Children at play are in a zone of proximal development. In play, children are acting out real-life situations in which they develop rules that move them beyond their current level. As Vygotsky (1978) stated, "It is incorrect to conceive of play as activity without purpose...creating an imaginary situation can be regarded as a means of developing abstract thought" (p. 103). We have all seen children pretending to be their parents. They act in the manner that the parents would act, sometimes responding with the very words they have heard their parents use.

Play mediates the learning of children, and, through play, children develop abstract thought. *Mediate* means that, in play, children reach beyond their real selves as they take on the roles of the characters they choose to be, and take action appropriate to the behavioral rules that govern those roles. Vygotsky (1978) further compared play to the focus of a magnifying glass, explaining that "play contains all developmental tendencies in a condensed form and is itself a major source of development" (p. 102). During play children are reaching out and extending beyond what they are now, while they are projecting themselves. It is as if when children are in a "let's play" mode, the very act of pretending makes it safe for them to reach beyond their actual level to more advanced levels. The imaginary play world enables kids to reach beyond themselves.

Play creates the zone for children.

Performances of Knowing

The importance of play can be seen in the school setting among older students as well. Shirley Brice Heath (1993) recounted a study of the value of play in the lives of inner-city youth. The research involved ethnographic studies of language use among young people during their extracurricular activities involving various types of youth organizations in three major U.S. cities. These students studied English in ESL classes in secondary school during the day, then participated in a variety of neighborhood youth centers staffed with bilingual adults. The activities in which they were involved at the centers ranged from organized sports to role-playing to actual drama troupes in which the young people wrote, produced, and staged their own productions.

In the study, the young people interviewed felt that at school they were getting by in English, but merely speaking and writing words in their classes did not allow them the opportunity to demonstrate what they really knew. That opportunity arose when they became involved in the work of playing at the youth centers. During their activities, these same students, who felt that their English was just okay, were demonstrating high levels of English competence. In their roles during play, they discovered a level of competence not found in their day-to-day command of language. They were reaching to that higher level of performance before competence. We can imagine Harste, Woodward, and Burke (1984) reading this and saying, "They were scampering to outgrow their current selves" (p. 135).

The significance for educators is evident in the way Heath (1993) described the phenomenon:

> The power of role shifting, of framing themselves in play, and of using the new voices acquired through becoming actors seemed to loosen a host of abilities undiscovered in the ordinary run of classroom requests for displays of knowledge rather than full performances of knowing (p. 181).

Assessment and ZPD

The difference, then, between what children can do with assistance and what they can later do alone is a measure of the developing psychological functions.

This notion takes into account individual differences. It also focuses on the communicative nature of learning in which the participants come to an understanding of the operations they are performing.

It is important to note that Vygotsky conceptualized this notion in reference to two educational problems: how children are assessed and the evaluation of instructional practices (Wertsch, 1985). His concern was that, if we only assess the matured functions, what has been learned, we would miss the possibilities that lie just ahead, in the very next level of performance. This is a notion that even in current times is seen as the distinction between Soviet and U.S. educational research.

Wertsch (1985) cites a discussion in which Leont'ev noted: "American researchers are constantly seeking to discover how the child came to be what he is; we in the USSR are striving to discover not how the child came to be what he is, but how he can become what he not yet is" (p. 67). As Leont'ev describes it, U.S. educators look to the actual development level, while USSR educators look toward children's potential development.

Conclusion

In concluding this chapter, we turn to Vygotsky, the pedagogue, to relate the zone of proximal development to instructional practice. Vygotsky (Wertsch, 1985) noted that "instruction is good only when it proceeds ahead of development. Then it awakens and rouses to life an entire set of functions which are in the stage of maturing, which lie in the zone of proximal development" (p. 71). The notion of studying classroom interaction by analyzing classroom discourse would be a logical extension of the work started by Vygotsky, especially because he was interested in the dynamic changes experienced by children in the learning process. However, Moll (1990) voices an important cautionary note that not all assisted learning (e.g., rote drill and practice, work sheets, and skills-based practice) represents this notion. The zone of proximal development then becomes another case of the individuals' learning and developing within and through their social connections with the collective.

In Vygotsky's view, it was relying on the spontaneous concepts alone to gauge the child's progress that led to the view of development leading instruction. Vygotsky theorized that assessment should focus on what the child is able to do with the assistance of an adult, when the spontaneous concepts encounter the scientific concepts introduced in education.

He took up this work as a way of studying the formation of processes by analyzing the subjects engaging in activities (Moll & Greenberg, 1990) by observing participants who were given tasks to complete that were beyond their present capabilities. By observing what children would do when offered objects to mediate tasks that were initially beyond their present capabilities, Vygotsky emphasized "the child's construction of new means that can help to solve the problem and that restructure the whole task situation" (Valsiner, 1988, p. 137). He could look at the process of the subject's interacting with the environment and the use of tools to mediate the completion of the task.

Moll (1990) further recognized the importance of this work: "The concept of the zone of proximal development integrated social activity into the (previously conceptualized) theory while retaining the significance of sign and tool mediation in understanding human learning and development" (p. 5). This has been our goal in Chapter 4: to integrate the theory with the practice.

E N D N O T E S

1. The data for this story were collected during the academic school year of 1998–1999. In May 1999, Deep Creek School closed its doors for the last time when one family with four children moved. More of this story can be read in J. Wink, (2000), A Day at Deep Creek School. *South Dakota Magazine, 15,* January/February, 26–32.

2. The example of Peace Patrol was shared with us by an international educator, Regina, from Mallorca.

3. Please note the dates, 1944 and 1966, that were written on the whiteboard. These dates were significant because, as the students reviewed for the final, they had included the year of Joan's birth and the year she began teaching. From a Vygotskian perspective, these dates are significant as they reflected the sociocultural context of both the professor's life as well as the sociocultural context of their current classroom experience together. Should you consider such an activity, we highly suggest that you use dates that are personally consequential (see Chapter 5). In this way, students make connections to the time line and their personal dates serve as cognitive coathooks for learning.

4. For more on synergy in the classroom, we refer you to *The Synergetic Classroom: Joyful Teaching and Gentle Discipline,* by C. M. Charles, available from Addison Wesley Longman of New York.

PART THREE

A Construction of Community

[A] public school should not be understood as simply consisting in a crowd of children who have nothing to do with one other (Vygotsky, 1997, p. 237).

Vygotsky's work was grounded in an inclusionist vision of pedagogy. It is our contention that, when we construct communities of learners who are actively engaged in generating new knowledge and seeking to use this knowledge for self- and social transformation, we advocate for a pedagogy that gives hope to all.

In the previous three chapters, we highlighted Vygotsky's thinking by framing our discussion under the umbrella of three general principles of: the dynamic relationship between thought and language, the significance of the sociocultural context, and the importance of the zone of proximal development. Vygotskian principles can be viewed from many perspectives, and in what follows we illustrate two different models of inclusionist practices. Implementing such inclusionist practices can lead to transformative classrooms in which participants construct a respectful and responsible community.

Faltis's Framework

In his work with classroom teachers, Faltis (1993, 1996, 2001), writes that Vygotskian principles turn into four classroom practices: (1) two-way communication, (2) social integration, (3) second-language acquisition, and (4) parental involvement. Faltis applies these principles to what he refers to as "joinfostering" classrooms: classrooms where students speak multiple languages, represent multiple cultures, and are guided by a teacher grounded in the Vygotskian principles and practices. We have found these four constructs to be valuable in describing typical Vygotskian pedagogical processes in classrooms, whether they are heterogeneous or homogenous groupings of students. It is clear, as will be seen in the classroom descriptions that follow, that when students and teachers connect Vygotsky's principles and practices, the result is the construction of community.

In Part 3, our purpose is to present actual experiences that demonstrate this construction of community through Vygotskian principles. In our first example, a very traditional junior high school teacher, Mary, has to rethink her assumptions about language and learning in order to create meaningful two-way communication for all the students. Mary had been teaching the same way she had been taught: Students read the materials and took tests on the content. The students in her class knew they were to be quiet and sit in straight rows. However, this year her class was filled with many levels of language abilities; some knew English well, and some did not. The test scores indicated to her that many were neither learning the content nor English.

At the university, she was studying the ideas of Vygotsky and, with the support of her classmates and the professor, she decided to experiment. She formed small groups; students read to and with each other; and talked about what they were reading, as she circulated to offer assistance as needed. This was a drastic change from the way she had previously been teaching and how students had been expected to learn in her classroom.

These changes in her teaching triggered changes in the students, too. They were more interested, and they felt safe to ask questions of her and of each other. "Teacher, do we have to use English?" asked Maysao. "Hmmm, it doesn't matter what language you use to discuss the questions, as long as everyone participates," she replied, hesitantly at first. Suddenly, two-way communication began. Students who rarely spoke in class previously were now animatedly talking about the reading assignment; some used English, some did not; three different languages were heard from one particularly lively group of students. When they later discussed the questions in a whole-class activity, they answered in English with the knowledge that they had first confirmed the meaning of those questions in the security of their primary language.

From a Vygotskian perspective, encouraging all students to talk to each other in the language they know best helps to generate knowledge. The students made meaning together and made sense personally of the text by talking with each other in a safe environment. What the students did in class with each other's assistance, they will be able to do alone later, and they will be able to do it in English, which is the goal of this class.

What did this teacher do to encourage the principle of two-way communication? She reflected on her own practices; she was courageous enough to give up some control of the class so that the students could use their first language to generate the meaning of the text.

The second example, involving Patrick, who suffers from autism, provides the opportunity to see the power of social integration and its transformative powers. Inclusion refers to the placement of all students into mainstream classes for at least some parts of the day. Many valid reasons support this process, but it also means that teachers without experience and knowledge may be underprepared to meet the needs of all students.

Such was the case of Patrick. When he spoke, he repeated words and phrases loudly in a shrill voice, which is often called "echolalia." On his hand was an imaginary puppet with which he liked to stroke everything in sight. In addition, Patrick's new teacher in the mainstream class had no experience with autism. Her pedagogy was interactive and experiential, and she had many hands-on learning centers where students were free to explore. She was advised that she would need to change to a more structured pedagogical approach to teaching and learning, as Patrick could not succeed in the freedom of her class.

On his first day in this first-grade class, Patrick continued to move around the classroom touching all in sight and talking in his language. His mother followed him to redirect his actions when necessary. The resource teacher came and spoke with the students about the realities of autism; they sat together in a circle with Patrick circling. Eventually, he became physically disruptive and, in spite of repeated attempts by the adults in the room, he would not be still. The students tried modeling for him the way to sit with legs crossed, calling his name and demonstrating how to sit. Eventually, he did exactly as the students showed him. The students clapped and cheered, and Patrick smiled. The teacher explained how fortunate that they were to have Patrick with them, as he would teach them about patience, and they could teach him about being a first grader.

"What do you call someone that shows another person how to do something?" the teacher asked.

"A teacher?" Miguel spoke up first.

"That's right," Mrs. Kelly responded, "And now you are all teachers."

In this brief event, the teacher and students demonstrated the potential power of social integration. Not every day was easy after that, but eventually Patrick began to imitate speech, and he learned to ask questions from another student. He soon joined the small groups in problem-solving activities. Although the teacher had been told that she would have to develop a much more structured approach to accommodate Patrick, she maintained a classroom community that prompted the students to demonstrate for Patrick what it meant to be a successful first grader. Through their explicit modeling and encouragement, the students and teacher together supported his social and academic learning.

What did Mrs. Kelly do to implement social integration? She encouraged students to demonstrate their learning, to question, to be patient, and to generate ideas through social interaction, the path to the construction of community.

The third example demonstrates that a teacher's knowledge of second-language acquisition can completely change students' learning. Many classrooms are filled with students who speak various languages, yet have teachers who speak only English. Once again, teachers are often underprepared for this context. However, there are strategies (Putney & Wink, 1998; Putney, Wu, & Wink,

1999) that can be very helpful when Vygotskian principles and practices move into classrooms. "Speak English, we only speak English in this classroom," the teacher sternly said during an oral review for a social studies exam in a fifth-grade classroom where students represented various language groups. Silence hung in the room.

"Okay, we'll make it a game," the teacher continued. "I'll ask a question, and someone in the first row can give me the answer. If row one can't get it, the next row gets a chance to answer, in English." The teacher did not have enough knowledge of language acquisition to recognize that she was creating a situation in which the English-dominant students had a distinct advantage. With the very next question and answer sequence, only the most outspoken and proficient English-speaking students bothered to take a stab at it. Those who were not as comfortable speaking English simply remained silent.

Even though most students in the classroom had a good command of conversational English, answering questions in academic English about the content from the social studies text was still too difficult. Eventually, the teacher learned from her peers and from her professional development opportunities that, as she came to understand the processes and the time required to achieve in another language, it would mean changing her approaches to teaching and learning. She enrolled not only in second-language acquisition theory and methods classes but also a Spanish class. She soon understood why students didn't readily learn the social studies content from the required text and why it took a long time for them to have enough courage to answer orally in front of their peers.

What did this teacher do to incorporate her emerging knowledge of language acquisition? She adopted many new strategies (Freeman & Freeman, 1994; Putney & Wink, 1998; Putney, Wu, & Wink, 1999) to make social studies comprehensible for students. She learned new ways of grouping students so they had the opportunity to negotiate meaning with their peers. She soon began to adjust her pace of spoken language, to use time lines, graphs, and pictures, and to provide adequate time for access to content.

In the fourth illustration, active parental/family involvement is another example of Vygotskian pedagogy in the classroom. Sandy, the teacher, finally overcame her resistance to family involvement when she learned one way of using cameras in her classroom of first and second graders. To begin this project, she bought five disposable cameras to take to school. She wrote letters to the families explaining that the class would be making a book of the photos they were to take.

On day one, she sent a camera home with each of five students and asked the families to take five pictures of people or things that were important to the child. In her letter, Sharon asked these five families to return the camera on day two. All five cameras were returned successfully, safely, and even proudly.

On day two, she sent the same five cameras home with five other students. This process continued for four days, as she had twenty students in her class. One hundred percent of the cameras were returned that week, despite the many dire predictions Sandy had heard in the teachers' lounge. However, Sandy believed in her students and their families; she had faith in the learners (Freeman & Freeman, 1998). Next, Sandy developed the pictures and pasted them in composite collages on large pieces of paper. Below and around the collages, the students wrote about each picture. For those students who could not yet write, Sandy wrote the sentences as the students dictated. In the book, each student's family was represented as a part of the larger community.

After the book was finished, Sandy noticed more families walking their children to her class in the morning and afternoon. Soon families began to linger in the class before and after school to talk about the books and the pictures. Eventually, the families started staying in the classroom and reading the class books with the students. What did this teacher do to initiate parental involvement? She moved beyond simply inviting families to school, and created a pedagogical process that caused the families to become interested in the activities of the school (Wink & Putney, 2000). The cameras led to active parental involvement; the parental involvement led to the construction of community within the classroom.

Learning and developing takes place within each learner, but it is also grounded in learning as a collective. In this section, we explore a Vygotskian construction of community in two different contexts. First, in Chapter 5 we will focus on the construction of community. We will define and explain the constructs of intersubjectivity, intertextuality, intercontextuality, and consequential progressions. Second, in Chapter 6 we address the construction of communities as defined in a broader community of scholars who are expanding the Vygotskian legacy. We will highlight their contributions as they pursue a vision of Vygotsky. It is our intention to address their unique thought and language by means of a glossary. Our purpose in sharing this growing body of neo-Vygotskian thought is to encourage readers to theorize their own ideas of learning and development to inform their own unique pedagogy.

We come from a historical tradition in which it was assumed that the curriculum focused on basic skills so that the transmission of a general body of knowledge would provide a foundation for economic survival. However, we face a new world in the twenty-first century. There are no guarantees for anyone's economic survival based on a model of education that transmitted what always was assumed to be a neutral and necessary body of knowledge. Citizens of the future need far more. Of course, teachers and families have much to share and pass on to children. However, students of today and citizens of tomorrow will need the ability to transfer and transform their knowledge to challenging, unforeseen problems and complex realities. They will need to solve problems that do not yet exist; they will need to be able to find workable solutions, both individually and with others; and they will need to learn dialectically from oppositional thought. Thus, we turn to Vygotsky, the voice from the past, who leads us to the future.

ENDNOTE

1. The example of Patrick was shared with us by Kris Carle, a fellow of the Southern Nevada Writing Project.

5 Intersubjectivity, Intertextuality, Intercontextuality, and Consequential Progressions

'Whoever enters, leave all hope behind,' should not be written on the school door (Vygotsky, 1993, p. 93).

Too often students are leaving hope behind. It is as if their hope were a backpack that they must leave outside the classroom door. In classrooms, are students encouraged to bring the backpack in, filled with hope, expectations, experiences, and ideas? Or, are they asked to leave those brimming backpacks behind? In a class with a sociocultural context that does not value students and their lived experiences, they are asked to leave the backpacks behind. Given this scenario, how can we ensure that students not only bring the backpack of hope in, but also continue to transform their hope into a new lived reality?

The purpose of this chapter is to discuss new complex constructs that enhance the construction of community across sociocultural, racial, ethnic, and gender lines. Furthermore, our goal is to demonstrate ways in which Vygotsky's legacy of educational psychology leads us to pedagogy. One way of reaching students is for teachers to demonstrate multiple ways, both explicitly and implicitly, for students to link their previous experiences with texts to new learning with new texts. These linkages become Vygotskian tools for solving pedagogical problems.

Thinking, you see, denotes nothing less than the participation of all of our previous experience in the resolution of a current problem…(Vygotsky, 1997, p. 175).

In Chapter 4, we discussed how the Vygotskian notion of the zone of proximal development relates to our teaching and learning. One of the key elements of the zone of proximal development is the connection between what we can do in problem-solving situations with others so that we learn to do those same and similar things independently. That common learning situation results in an intersubjectivity, a space where we connect and create mutual understandings. It is a sociocultural space where thought and language dynamically blend and create knowledge and new understandings. Intersubjectivity can be created in a classroom or community, just as a zone of proximal development can be. We will expand on the previous three chapters as we relate these three principal principles of Vygotsky to concepts from others who have expanded his work.

A Cognitive Coathook: Missing the Plane for New York

We offer the next analogy for readers who perhaps have never previously encountered the terms *intersubjectivity, intertextuality, intercontextuality, historicity,* and *consequential progression*. In what follows, we will not use these specific words, but they are embedded throughout this story, just as they will be throughout this chapter.

Le, Jo, and Amy were scheduled to go to New York together, but Jo missed the plane and had to take a later flight. Le and Amy flew together on the plane, arrived together, checked into the hotel, and left together for their first day of sightseeing, not knowing where Jo was or when she would arrive. Jo arrived later and took a taxi to the hotel, hoping to find her two friends. All three were relieved when they finally found each other in the lobby of the hotel.

"I was lucky to find another flight just a few hours later," Jo told Le and Amy.

"Oh, we wish you would have been with us," Amy responded. "We found the most wonderful little deli with what must certainly have been the world's best sandwich."

"Jo, you would have loved the conversation while we ate there. The owner came over and told us how he had learned about this sandwich as a child from his grandmother. He seemed pleased that we liked it as he said it was his specialty and no one else in the area made that particular sandwich. It was good to see someone take such pride in his family legacy. Apparently, people from all over the world come to *that* deli for *that* sandwich." Le added.

As Amy and Le laughed and shared their news of the deli, the sandwich, and the interesting tidbits about New York, Jo felt a little disconnected and didn't quite understand why it had been such a wonderful time.

The next day all three friends left the hotel early for another day of adventure in New York. First, they walked through Central Park and enjoyed watching all of the families on the ice-skating rink. They even rented skates and enjoyed two invigorating hours on the ice. By midday they were hungry and decided to get their lunch from a sidewalk vendor near the rink. They returned their rented skates and walked over to the food stand. Suddenly, Amy and Le began laughing together as they pointed to the special sandwich featured for the day: Grandma's World Famous Tuna and Sweet Pepper Sandwich. Jo could see nothing funny about the advertised sandwich. Amy and Le explained to her that it was the very same sandwich that they had eaten the day before at the deli. As the three friends ordered this sandwich, Le asked this vendor, "Where did you learn how to make this?"

"Oh, it is very common here; I can't remember when I learned it, but many people sell them," he explained. Le and Amy laughed together and explained to Jo why they thought this was funny. Finally, all three friends ordered this sandwich and sat down to enjoy their meal. However, Jo did not enjoy the lunch as much as her two friends did.

Why not? Jo did not experience it in the same way. She had a sense of what her two friends had experienced the day before, but she was not there so her experience on the second day in New York was different from that of Le and Amy. Jo did not have their reference points; Le and Amy could only tell her; they could not turn the clock back and live it again as a threesome.

Dear Readers, your adventure as you journey through this chapter will be to link this analogy to any new words you find. Throughout this chapter, we will revisit the previous analogy and tie the new language and thoughts to the New York trip. In addition, we will share other examples that demonstrate how intersubjectivity (interS), intertextuality (interT), and intercontextuality (interC) are very closely related to the Vygotskian concepts of the dynamic and reciprocal relationship between thought and language, sociocultural context for learning, and the zone of proximal development.

Throughout this chapter, we are writing about how theory informs practice and practice informs theory. As you read, we invite you to reflect on the ways in which you experience theory informing practice and practice informing theory in your teaching and learning. In the concluding chapter, we will share an authentic and synergetic experience we had with the most abstract and esoteric thought and language.

Demonstrating Complex Constructs

In Chapter 2, we learned that thought and language are interrelated in a dynamic process of development. At times, we have the *thought*, but have never heard of the *word;* at other times, we have the *word,* but the *thought* is still elusive. It is only the union of the two that deepens our understanding of thought and increases our use of language to express even more complex thoughts. In this particular chapter, we anticipate that many readers will not have heard the language, but will have experienced, consciously or unconsciously, the thought at some time in their experiences. As a graduate student (teacher) said to her professor, "You have given me a language to talk about what it is that I do in the classroom."

Based on our understanding of the Vygotskian perspective of thought and language, we will begin this chapter with a definition of each of the new concepts, followed by an example of how they look when experienced by students and teachers in classrooms. However, before sharing those definitions, we must first revisit a fundamental understanding regarding the word *social*, which ties the previous three chapters to the new complex ideas that will be introduced in this chapter.

Social: Two Senses of Meaning

To further understand this chapter, it is important to revisit the Vygotskian notion of two levels of *social*, discussed in Chapter 2. In so doing, we are connecting prior knowledge to future learning. Vygotsky believed that, to understand individual development, he first had to show how the individual interacted with and learned from others.

> One sense of *social*, then, is the interaction with others.

This sense of *social* is similar to what other educational scholars refer to when they talk about the student in interaction with others. However, what was unique in Vygotsky's work, and not always understood by those who read about it, was that his work also defined another sense of *social*.

> Another sense of *social* has to do with the historical and cultural mediation of language used and produced between individuals.

Language is itself a product of the historical, cultural, and social ways of doing and being that have been handed down from those before us. However, language is not static; it changes over time as we interact with new and different individuals. This sense of *social* also connects the action with the language because that is what demonstrates the philosophy underpinning it. As explained by Holzman (1996): "For Vygotsky, the activities of human beings, at all stages of development and organization, are social products and must be seen as historical developments, not merely as interpersonal developments" (p. 87).

Vygotsky viewed speech as having historicity, a way "to textualize one's intent and to situate a locution appropriately in a personal context involving another person with whom one shares a history, however brief" (Bruner, 1987, p. 6). From this perspective, speaking would be viewed as an action one takes to create a text (utterances and nonverbal actions) that another can read and interpret. It is through this interpretation of texts that we come to construct a common text as well as a common context of situation (or way of acting on that text) at a particular point in time.

Theory Is Practice: Amy, Le, and Jo

The first sense of *social* is simply our interactions with others in a social context. Amy and Le experienced this in their shared experience at the deli in New York. The second and deeper sense of *social* carries with it not only our experiences, beliefs, and assumptions, but also those of the people with whom we've had meaningful contact throughout our lives. Jo and Le have shared this over many years in their teaching and learning about Vygotsky. Language carries with it a cultural and historical legacy. The two meanings are different in that the first sense of *social* is in the moment. The second sense of *social* is historical. We don't have to start from square one to create language and knowledge because we benefit from these historical and cultural resources from our past. Those who came before us created a foundation of knowledge from which we draw to enhance our current learning.

However, because we learn by combining our experience through thinking and communicating in the present, we have the potential to move beyond that intertextual past. We are who we are because of where we've been. In a Freirian sense, the first sense is similar to "reading the word," and the second sense is expanded to "reading the word and the world." Just as in the historical continuum, found in Part 1, the second sense of Vygotsky's use of the word *social* is reflective of a more critical perspective.

A Metaphor: A Hall of Mirrors

As a metaphor of the historical and cultural meaning of *social,* we ask that you imagine a long hall of mirrors placed so that you can see your reflection again and again and again. As you see yourself reflected in the mirrors, you imagine that those reflected images that appear smaller and smaller down the long hallway represent all of those in your life who have come before you. Their social and cultural ways of being, the artifacts they created along the way, and who they were historically all add a dimension to who you are today.

Similarly, who you are today, how you interact with others, and the artifacts and legacy that you leave behind as you understand more and deeper perspectives of yourself will become part of those whose lives you have touched in some ways through your life experience. As Vygotsky (1982–84) stated: "We must see ourselves within the context of, and in relation to, what has preceded us; we base ourselves on that even when we deny it" (p. 428). As you come to understand the new terminology in this chapter, you will see more and deeper perspectives on Vygotsky's ideas of learning and development to apply to your own experience of teaching and learning.

InterS: Intersubjectivity

> Intersubjectivity is the collective history and mutual meanings shared by a group of people.

Intersubjectivity is the context of a group of people and the meanings they create through that context. It is that moment within the home when children are learning with their caretakers how to become part of the family. It is that moment within a classroom when personal transformation begins as students take ownership of their shared understandings and experiences. While Vygotsky theorized that adults and children interact to create an intersubjective space, a mutual understanding, he was not able in his short lifetime to further research and explain what occurs in that negotiation and how it takes place.

Theory Is Practice: Amy, Le, and Jo

In our New York analogy, Amy and Le went sightseeing the first day and constructed an intersubjectivity through their mutual experience. They created intersubjectivity with Jo in the lobby of the hotel when they met and shared the story of their day. However, their levels of intersubjectivity are different because Amy and Le shared the experience, while Jo could only imagine it from their retelling.

What Happens When People Talk?

Wertsch (1985) explains intersubjectivity as the point when two speakers create a temporarily shared social world through language or other semiotic mediated negotiations. In his work, Wertsch has studied what constitutes intersubjectivity, the "shared social world…between a child and an adult through the process of the negotiation of meanings" (Kozulin, 1990, p. 170). Simply put, Wertsch has named the process of intersubjectivity as shared definitions that occur in talk. In the following table, we have outlined different definitions of intersubjectivity to help us make sense of the ways in which the term has been used by some of those who have studied Vygotsky's work.

Author	Definition of Intersubjectivity	Key Words
(Wertsch, 1985, p. 159)	exists when interlocutors share some aspect of their situation definitions (ways in which objects and events are represented or defined)	share definitions
(Kosulin, 1990, p. 170)	shared social world between child and adult through the process of negotiation of meanings	process of negotiation of meanings
(Crook, 1994, p. 80)	shared understanding that is mutually recognized	mutually recognized
(Tharp & Gallimore, 1988, p. 89)	in joint activity, the signs and symbols developed through language, the development of common understanding of the purposes and meanings of the activity, the joint engagement in cognitive strategies and problem solving...	joint activity, common understanding of purpose and meanings of activity
(Edwards & Mercer, 1987, p. 84)	the points at which common knowledge is being created	common knowledge

Wertsch (1985) extended Vygotsky's approach to cultural development by further defining *intersubjectivity*. His concern was with the processes taking place between people that make possible internalization of concepts. Wertsch also drew on the work of Rommetviet (1979) to make explicit the notion that, when two speakers come together into a communicative context, they do not necessarily share background knowledge or the same perspectives. "Through semiotically mediated 'negotiation,' however, they create a temporarily shared social world, a state of intersubjectivity" (Wertsch, 1985, p. 161).

Other definitions of *intersubjectivity* range from 'a shared social world' (Kozulin, 1990), to 'a mutual understanding or common knowledge' (Crook, 1994; Edwards & Mercer, 1987; Tharp & Gallimore, 1988), and 'a process of negotiation of meanings' (Kozulin, 1990). Although Edwards and Mercer do not use the term *intersubjectivity*, they discuss the interaction between participants in the zone of proximal development as they construct a common knowledge. Kozulin (1990) also credited Wertsch with broadening and enriching the notion of the zone of proximal development by studying what constituted intersubjectivity, the "shared social world...between a child and an adult through the process of the negotiation of meanings" (p. 170). The work of Wertsch dealt mainly with studies of dyads, typically between mothers and young children.

For our purposes, we will follow the definition of Putney (1996). Intersubjectivity, the sharing of a social world through the process of negotiating meaning, allows us to see what the participants jointly construct in their talk and actions, and thus, how practices associated with being literate in that classroom come into being. (pp. 129–130).

What Can Happen When Students and Teachers Talk

If we move our study of intersubjectivity to the classroom, to the study of language as a resource in the classroom, *intersubjectivity* acquires a broader scope to include the interactions and negotiations of meanings between all participants in the interactional spaces, which shift and move within the instructional activity. Group members, who are interacting through particular organizational patterns for particular purposes, construct interactional spaces (Heras, 1993). Keeping in mind the relationship between thought and language, theoretical constructs continue to evolve and take shape in new ways as members of a group interact in problem-solving activities.

For example, in a classroom setting, students might work in different configurations, such as pairs, for some activities, in small groups at other times, and then as a whole class for other purposes. These interactional spaces can be multiple and co-occurring. Individuals and/or groupings can also be interacting with text, as well as interacting with people and attending to more than one text at a time. They can be moving in and out of multiple spaces as needed to accomplish the interactive discourse in which they are engaged. In their classroom research, Gutierrez and Stone (2000) identify three types of interactional spaces, the *official*, *unofficial*, and *third* spaces. Their naming of these spaces refers to the script or dialogue that may occur within these spaces, and whether students whose voices are not often recognized by others in the classroom are encouraged to participate or develop their own interactional space (see also Dyson, 2000; Smagorinsky & O'Donnell-Allen, 2000).

Classroom teachers, who may never have heard the word *intersubjectivity*, often strive for that elusive moment when students come together around a shared idea and their many common experiences within that context. One problem is that teachers may not explicitly know how to create that intersubjectivity. For this reason, we invite you to think of this word in relationship to your own evolving understanding of the three principal principles of Vygotsky: thought and language, sociocultural learning, and the zone of proximal development.

For your initial understanding, we offered the Amy, Le, and Jo story. What follows is another example of how inquiry within the classroom can also be viewed through the Vygotskian lens as intersubjectivity.

Into the Classroom with the Watermelon Investigation

In the following activity, the Watermelon Investigation, intersubjectivity includes experiences that students bring with them to the classroom. In the following ethnographic case, 85 percent of the twenty-five students are dominant in Spanish, and 15 percent are dominant in English. Both language groups are learning both languages, and learning in both languages.

> On the first day of school in a fifth-grade bilingual classroom, students were seated in table groups of four or five. On a table at the front of the room were six watermelons, each with a number written in felt pen on the side of the melon. The teacher asked students what questions they might generate about the melons. After some discussion, she asked them to determine the cost of the particular watermelon that she had designated for their table group. Because the teacher had given no information about their melons, students first made an individual guess about the cost from just observing their melon. They next collected data about their particular watermelon by carrying it to their table and having each table group member lift the melon to suggest a weight. They made a group estimate of the weight, based on the data they had collected.
>
> Their next suggestion to the teacher was that they needed to know how much it actually weighed, as well as the cost per pound in order to come to a closer estimate of the actual cost. The teacher acknowledged their observation and interpretations by producing a scale for them to use to weigh the melons. However, she still did not give them the cost per pound, asking them instead to think of other ways to collect the data they would need in order to complete the investigation. Students began talking to each other to determine the possible costs.
>
> "Just like when I went to the store with my mom on Saturday. We looked at all the prices and compared them. We can use that cost for our estimate," Marisa said. Her group used her cost per pound as a likely amount for making their estimate. Another group asked permission to call a family friend who worked in a local grocery store. Permission was granted, and they went off with the student teacher to do "field work" in order to get the information they needed. Some groups overheard the costs from other groups and chose to utilize that information for themselves. Toward the end of the activity, the groups reported their revised estimates and compared them with the actual costs reported by the teacher. They discussed as a whole group what their constraints were in completing the activity and why their particular estimates might not have been representative of the actual cost.
>
> Finally, to celebrate what they had learned through their inquiry process, the students ate the watermelon as they reflected on their shared learning. From our perspective, far too seldom do students and teachers creatively and collaboratively celebrate their shared learning. Often these celebrations of inquiry are what connect students to the learning as they later consider how they coconstructed their math inquiry. Not only do these celebrations bring everyone into the process through an authentic experience, later these celebrations will serve as a series of memorable

events in which all participants created a community of learners, and will also be a trigger to remind students of specific prior learning.

In this one activity, multiple interactional spaces were in action. Students as a whole group were participating in the same activity, the Watermelon Investigation. They were also working in table groups consisting of four to five students. Each table group consisted of one English-dominant student, at least one Spanish-dominant student, and at least one bilingual student. The students were responsible for helping each other to understand the math concepts discussed in the two languages in use. This classroom was a vivid example of the reciprocal connection between thought and language discussed in Chapter 2.

Each group discussed the problem at hand to try to determine the cost of their melon. At times they worked in pairs, as in when they weighed the melon. One student weighed the melon while the other partner checked for accuracy, and then they reported to the others at their respective tables. Individual students were also working with their own experiential background, recalling events that helped them bring forth data that would inform the group.

In some cases, individual students overheard the talk of another group and reported to their table group so that they could decide whether to utilize the data from others. Other individual students asked questions of the teacher in order to collect data (the only question the teacher would *not* answer was what the actual cost was). In this one investigation, the students moved through several different interactional spaces in order to make sense of the activity in which they were engaged. We will come back to this activity to see how intertextuality and intercontextuality were an integral part of the sense-making in this investigation.

InterS ≅ InterT + InterC

For us, intersubjectivity is comprised of other concepts that are equally important in making visible what constitutes shared meanings and in examining how they are talked into being through the discursive system, actions and language in use. Two constructs, in particular, are part of intersubjectivity: intertextuality and intercontextuality. We have discovered that it is often easier for those who may be new to these two constructs to grasp them visually as they are negotiating their own initial meanings. Therefore, if this is helpful, think of the following equation as another cognitive coathook.

$$interS \cong interT + interC$$

InterT: Intertextuality

Intertextuality is exactly what the roots of the word imply: 'between' + 'text.' It is that place of learning that makes connections between something we have read or talked about previously and something we are reading or talking about now. We bring the prior text to the present text; we bring our understanding from one text to create a newer and deeper understanding of later text. It is this and more. Intertextuality is also grounded in, not just text, but also all the social world surrounding us and our reading.

Theory Is Practice: Amy, Le, and Jo

For example, in the story of Le, Amy, and Jo, interT took place on the second day of their adventure when they saw the sign on the food stand that advertised the feature sandwich of the day: Grandma's World Famous Tuna and Sweet Pepper Sandwich. Amy and Le saw the sign and laughed, while they explained to Jo the meaning behind their laughter. They recognized that Grandma's recipe was not as unique as the first deli owner had claimed.

This understanding of intertextuality was proposed by Bloome and colleagues (Bloome, 1989; Bloome & Bailey, 1992; Bloome & Egan-Robertson, 1993), who expanded the work of text-based scholars to show how intertextuality is socially constructed through language events. Bloome (1989) first argued that "juxtaposing texts, at whatever level, is not in itself sufficient for intertextuality. Intertextuality is a social construction" (p. 1). Besides being socially constructed and interactionally accomplished, Bloome and Egan-Robertson (1993) established criteria for recognizing an intertextual relationship as one that "is proposed, is recognized, is acknowledged, and has social significance" (p. 311).

In other words, as classroom members interact and interweave their texts, which can be oral, aural, visual, or written (Green, Kantor, & Rogers, 1991; Santa Barbara Classroom Discourse Group, 1992b), they also create a cultural system and attach significance to what they bring forward to compare and contrast. This notion of intertextuality has also been adapted and extended by Jennings (1996). While Bloome and colleagues conceptualized intertextuality in moment-by-moment dialogue, Jennings has expanded the notion to consider the intertextual ties in classroom activities generated by members over an extended length of time, the classroom year.

In the example of the Watermelon Investigation, interT took place several times. The first time was when the students compared the text of their individual thoughts about the cost—their observations based on their prior experiences with watermelons—in order to produce a guess. They next contrasted their individual guesses against the data collected by their table group by lifting their watermelons. They made another intertextual link when the table group members actually weighed the watermelons and compared that weight to their estimates. Finally, in the whole-class setting, they drew a giant chart of the estimated costs from each table group compared to the actual costs of each watermelon from the teacher. In this example, the criteria for recognizing interT become evident when we realize that, through their talk in the varying interactional spaces (individual guesses, table group estimates, and whole-class comparison), these students and their teacher socially constructed interT. They did so by proposing answers, recognizing, and acknowledging each other's thoughts about their data, and drawing conclusions about the project that would be referenced again in future projects.

InterC: Intercontextuality

Building from Bloome's work on intertextuality, Floriani (1993, 1997) introduced *intercontextuality* as part of a larger argument that students and teachers negotiate the nature of everyday life in classrooms. This is a related but separate process that serves particular purposes for members when negotiating meaning and constructing the texts of everyday life. Floriani (1993) further discussed the idea that context is more than environment, setting, or even people in a particular setting. Context is defined here using the classic definition proposed by Erickson and Shultz (1981): "[C]ontexts are constituted by what people are doing and where and when they are doing it..." (p. 148). As a bilingual speaker (Spanish and English), Floriani recognized in Spanish that *contexto* can be read as joining *con* ('with') and *texto* ('text'), thus implying a relationship between an actor and a text. This way of looking at *context* led to conceptualizing it as a way (or ways) of *being with* and having a relationship to/with text.

Theory Is Practice: Amy, Le, and Jo

Reflecting on the story of Le, Amy, and Jo, we last encountered them on the second day of their journey. Let's continue the story to the third day of their adventure when Le, Amy, and Jo entered another New York deli, and the shop owner began to tell them the story of his dear grandmother and her cheesecake, her specialty that no one else in the area could make. Jo laughingly exclaimed, "This sounds familiar, just like in the first deli with Grandma's famous sandwich." In this example, interC takes place when Jo realizes that the actions of this deli owner are the same as the actions of the first deli owner that Amy and Le experienced. Jo is linking the context of one situation with the current context.

Returning to our example of the Watermelon Investigation, we recognize that the teacher first set in place an activity in which students would be able to draw on their past knowledge and experience. She introduced the activity as one in which they would solve a problem together: How much she paid for each of the watermelons. She first asked students to make a guess, and then she led them through more complexity in the activity. The students realized they would need to know both the price and weight to determine the cost. In small groups, they discussed how to estimate the weight of the watermelons. They had to collect data by observing the watermelons, then by weighing them. Then they shared information about possible costs from their own experiences of buying watermelons at the store with their families. They reinvoked the context of figuring costs in the store to use in their current context of figuring the cost of their classroom watermelon.

As the students reflected on the texts and contexts of their own experience with that of their current experience, they began to draw inferences about the problem at hand. This activity set forth an intertextual and intercontextual webbing of ideas and actions from diverse sources as students and teacher worked together to jointly create information that was socially significant to the class in completing their work. Ultimately, they compared and contrasted their estimates with each other in a whole-class activity, then they compared their estimates to the actual costs to see how close they had come with their estimates.

In addition, the Watermelon Investigation became a context for other types of inquiry in this classroom over time. For example, a week later the teacher was explaining that they would soon be doing another type of data collection. She told them to trust their own knowledge because they had done this before, in the context of the first day with the watermelons. One student answered that they would be observing. The teacher acknowledged this, and explained that this time they would take similar actions in observing, except that they would be observing other students on the playground. This is an example of intercontextuality, or referencing and using other contexts for learning as an example of how to learn in a new context (Floriani, 1997; Putney & Floriani, 1999).

It is through this intertextual and intercontextual linking that students learn to *trust their own knowledge*. They were beginning to make connections with their own experience from their home lives and from prior experiences in their classroom lives that promoted sense-making in the moment of their current interactions. From a Vygotskian perspective, it was evident that these students and teacher were working together in a particular communicative context, even though they did not necessarily share background knowledge or the same perspectives. Still, they were able to jointly construct a mutual understanding of what it meant to observe and conduct an investigation through their language in use.

Consequential Progressions

In this section, we will link interS, interT, and interC with consequential progressions. It is building that language (or, learning and experiencing from a Vygotskian perspective) to express the complexity of teaching that is the whole point of consequential progressions.

Theory Is Practice: Amy, Le, and Jo

Returning to our opening story, the trip to New York, we realize that Amy and Le shared an intersubjectivity because of their intertextual and intercontextual connections in their common experience. The fact that they left together on the trip to New York means that they began a history of the trip together that did not include Jo. They began building an intertextual past related to this trip. Whenever we engage in any conversation, no matter how brief, we begin to build historicity.

In the Watermelon Investigation, consequential progression took place when the students and teacher together made interT and InterC links as they conducted the investigation. They began to build historicity on the first day of school, and they continued to use what they learned as they participated in further investigations. Each subsequent inquiry project created their interT and interC paths, and became progressively more complex as their knowledge base expanded.

Text is Talk; Talk is Text

The fact that we start talking already begins a history, and we immediately begin to build an intertextual (text is talk, talk is text) past with each other by talking. We also assume an implicated future in our conversation (Bakhtin, 1981), meaning that our conversation may be revisited in another context, either now or in the future. Therefore, whenever we communicate together, we are working from our own lived experiences, bringing them together, and moving from an intertextual past toward an implicated and negotiated future, which lays the foundation for the next. There is a consequence to participating and how much and in what ways we participate.

Talk as It Relates to Consequential Progressions

Consequential progression (Durán & Szymanski, 1996) was conceptualized to illustrate that as people talk with each other, their conversation builds on what has happened between them in the past. Their interaction is shaping the current talk as a consequence of past texts. Therefore, the interaction is a negotiated production with an implicated future and an intertextual past. That is, as students negotiate the tasks at hand within their peer group, they orient to each other based on their past negotiations and in relation to the eventual progress of their current interaction.

This concept of *negotiated production through activity with an implicated future and an intertextual past* is how this construct was first expanded beyond small group classroom interactions (Putney, 1997; Putney, Green, Dixon, Durán, & Yeager, 2000). Through the discursive system (actions and language in use) of an inquiry-based classroom, the links between academic activities throughout the year are ongoing and are made explicit through intertextual and intercontextual ties. These ties are made both in reference to past activities and in relation to what students will be doing in their current and future work. Thus, the teacher makes explicit the multiple consequential progressions—the intertextual and intercontextual past links to current and implicated future activities. Furthermore, a particular cycle of activity has multiple consequential progressions within it, and cycles of activity across the school year have consequential progressions as well.

That is to say, academic practices that are enacted in the onset of one cycle of activity are elaborated on and expanded within that cycle so that they become a cultural resource to be taken up and utilized by students during the work accomplished in a subsequent cycle of activity. In addition, there is a sequence and a consequence to the ways in which the opportunities for learning the social and academic practices are put into place throughout the school year.

Theory Is Practice: Amy, Le, and Jo

In the story of Amy, Le, and Jo, negotiated production took place on the first day when Amy and Le shared their experience of the deli sandwich. They included Jo when they told her their story. Their negotiated production took on a deeper meaning when all three experienced the deli cheesecake on the third day.

Likewise, in the Watermelon Investigation example, negotiated production took place as the students, in their table groups, discussed and compared the data they collected about their watermelons. Their negotiated production became even more meaningful when they shared in the whole-class discussion and constructed the comparison chart.

The Bill of Rights and Responsibilities

To see consequential progressions at work in a classroom setting, we illustrate the joint creation of a contract that fifth graders agreed on as how they would work together for the school year (see also Yeager, Pattenaude, Fránquiz, & Jennings, 1999). This example demonstrates how this jointly constructed text became a living document as it was reinvoked throughout the year by the teacher, students, and the student teacher who entered midyear.

To better illustrate the contract, we have reproduced an artifact from a fifth grade bilingual classroom: a document entitled the Bill of Rights and Responsibilities (Table 5.1).

The actual classroom artifact had the words neatly written on a large poster, suitable for display. For every right, there was a corresponding responsibility, and they were written in both English and Spanish. At the bottom of the document, under the words "Written and agreed to by the members of the Tower Community," signatures of the students and their teacher lined the bottom of the contract. The teacher displayed the contract in the front of the classroom, in sight of everyone from that day forward. This document was a text that the teacher and students had produced together.

From a cross-case analysis of this teacher's classroom across multiple years, Putney and Floriani (1999) were able to demonstrate how the teacher and students jointly produced such a document each year to serve as part of the governance structure. From year one of the study we have reproduced the ethnographer's field notes from the days in which the document was created. From year two of the study, we have an example from a student's essay to demonstrate similar practices that produced the contract illustrated in Table 5.1. The following excerpts from field notes demonstrate how the teacher initiated the joint construction of the Bill of Rights and Responsibilities.

> On the second day of school, Ms. Y began a discussion of the orienting principles of rights, respect, and responsibility. She indicated that they would coconstruct the meaning of these words over the next two days.

TABLE 5.1   Bill of Rights Contract

Bill of Rights and Responsibilities	Carta de Derechos y Responsabilidades
1. We have the *right* to be safe in our classroom. We have the *responsibility* to walk and to behave safely, without hurting anyone.	**1.** Tenemos el *derecho* a sentirse seguros en nuestra salon de clase. Tenemos la *responsabilidad* a caminar y a comportarse en un modo seguro, sin lastimar a nadie.
2. We have the *right* to study and to learn. We have the *responsibility* to let others learn without bothering them.	**2.** Tenemos el *derecho* a estudiar y a aprender. Tenemos la *responsabilidad* a dejarlos a otros a estudiar, sin molestarlos.
3. We have the *right* to be respected and feel we are all equal in class. We have the *responsibility* to help others and to respect them, without using bad names or laughing at them.	**3.** Tenemos el *derecho* a estar respectado y a sentirse iguales en nuestra clase. Tenemos la *responsabilidad* a ayudar a otras personas y a respectarlos, sin usar nombres malos y sin reirese al una al otro.
4. We have the *right* to be listened to and to be heard. We have the *responsibility* to listen to others.	**4.** Tenemos el *derecho* a estar oído por los otros. Tenemos la *responsabilidad* a escuchar cuando otros hablen.
5. We have the *right* to have our own and our class property respected. We have the *responsibility* to take care of everyone's property.	**5.** Tenemos el *derecho* a tener nuestra propiedad y la de la clase respetada. Tenemos la *responsabilidad* a cuidar de la propiedad de todos.
Written and agreed to by the members of the Tower Community	Según el acuerdo entre los miembros de la Comunidad de la Torre

Together they would generate ways of living, operating, and cooperating in this classroom, and would have to come to an agreement on the meaning of these words. Ms. Y instructed the students to begin by thinking and writing individually what the word *respect* meant and to write what it might look like, indicating that she would do the same. With those instructions she wrote the word *respeto* next to *respect* on the board, and began to write in her notebook. After several minutes of writing she signaled students to stop. She wrote the word *responsible* on the board next to *responsable* and then modeled two ways of using the word. She then asked students to write the word and what they thought of when they heard it.

After this discussion they shared their responses in three ways. First they shared with partners, then the partners joined with another pair to make small groups. After sharing in these small groups, they reconvened as a whole group to share what the classroom would look like if respect and responsibility were what they paid attention to or if those were the classroom rules. As a whole group they then discussed what it meant now to be a member of a new group, and to be part of what Ms. Y named a community. Throughout the day, Ms. Y continued to make visible the relationships of respecting each other and their work, and of taking responsibility for their actions. For homework, she asked each of them to write rules indicating ways to act that showed respect for each other so that, the following day, they could jointly construct their Bill of Rights and Responsibilities.

The next day, they discussed in small groups (table groups) what the rules would be and constructed their Bill of Rights and Responsibilities. The table groups reported to the whole class and Ms. Y wrote the rules on a huge chart to display in the classroom. Once the ideas were recorded in two languages (English and Spanish), she had the community members agree to it and sign their names to the contract. She then distributed a smaller, typed version for students to take home to their parents/guardians.

In this way, Ms. Y began to direct the writing of the classroom norms in the format of the U.S. Bill of Rights, based on the orienting community principles of rights, respect, and responsibilities. In constructing their classroom rules in this way, Ms. Y was again drawing on the collective knowledge that her students brought to the community about what it means to be a responsible citizen. She began formulating the rules from her talk on the first day about what it meant to respect each other and to be responsible. By handing over the construction (Edwards & Mercer, 1987) to the students, Ms. Y invoked the notion of taking responsible actions in constructing their rules to live by. Further, by having the students move from personal response to small group, then to large group, and back to individual, she provided different types of interactional spaces for students to share, contrast, and transform their formulations and understandings.

Thus, the construction of the Bill of Rights and Responsibilities is a curricular point of stability for this teacher because it is a practice that she brings into the classroom at the beginning of each year. The process of how they construct the document remains relatively stable: They brainstorm together in class, they individually produce rights and responsibilities for homework, and then they collectively produce the final document. However, it is precisely this stable process that allows for variability in the actual product, because each year the community members collectively construct the contract together from their individual homework. For example, the analysis of student essays in year two of the study (Putney & Floriani, 1999) produced a description of how the students and their teacher produced this document from the perspective of one student, Janiece:

> We've gotten this community by a contract. That contract is the Bill of
> Rights and Responsibilities. We put this contract together and signed it. We
> made the contract by going home and thinking of rights and responsibilities.
> Then we shared them in class. We picked five rights and five responsibilities
> and put them together. We signed our contract and swore to live by it for
> the rest of the year.

In thinking about their own rights and responsibilities at home, and sharing
those ideas in class, these students intertextually linked their home practice with
what they would be doing in this classroom in terms of dealing with each other in-
terpersonally. They also linked the document to their study of U.S. History as they
studied the construction of the U.S. Bill of Rights. They shared personal meanings
of the importance of rights and responsibilities as they decided which ones were
most appropriate for their classroom. They signed the document, indicating that
they agreed to live by it. Whenever they referred to this document, they were
making intertextual links with the words and meanings they constructed together.

Furthermore, from reading the excerpt of Janiece's essay, we recognize that
these students did more than just write a text. They took particular actions with
their words, both orally and in written form. They thought about it, they brainstormed in class, they decided what was most important to them as a collective, they
constructed the document and then signed it to indicate their acceptance of the ideas
as ways of being members of this community. They created what we are calling *intercontextuality*—particular actions that took place with text under particular conditions.

Therefore, the content of the Bill of Rights and Responsibilities was simultaneously academic content, community building, and instrumental activity, as it
was constructed at the beginning of the year, and established ways in which the
students and teacher would work together throughout the school year (Christie,
1995; Putney et al., 2000). Further, because U.S. history is the academic content
of the fifth-grade social studies curriculum, the construction of this document can
be seen as tying everyday life in the class to academic content that the students
would study later in the year. In this case we have an example of how texts can
be interlinked in multiple ways: text-to-text, the U.S. Bill of Rights with the classroom Bill of Rights and Responsibilities; text-to-life, the connection between
rights and responsibilities at school, at home, and in the larger community; and
life-to-text as the students used this text as a resource in their lives at school
throughout the year (Figure 5.1). (Cochran-Smith, 1984)

We view this type of interactional work as transformative because students
were continually given opportunities to contribute to and draw from the understandings being shaped by the group. Students were asked to draw on their own
knowledge and experiences before sharing ideas with others, which then gave all of
them an equal opportunity to participate in small- and whole-group discussions.
What was shared in pairs, or in small- or whole-class discussions, thus shaped the
basis for the common knowledge or understandings being constructed by the
group. How this knowledge was taken up or internalized by individuals would later
become evident in their work. Students' understandings continued to grow and de-

Intertextual and Intercontextual Elements

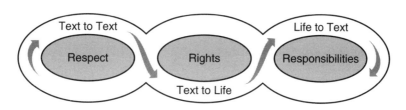

FIGURE 5.1 Text to Life.

velop over time in the context of different projects. Thus, what students learned in one context became consequential for their learning later in another context.

For example, throughout the school year, these participants referred to the document, usually in relation to how they were working together as a community. A particular example happened late in the school year, in May, when they had occasion to reinvoke that context. A student teacher, Ms. M, was completing her "take-over" of the class at this time. She had entered in January, and the students had explained to her then the formulation of their classroom contract, the Bill of Rights and Responsibilities. In May, they were going to work together to build museum exhibits around the theme of the U.S. colonial period, the Americana Museum. Ms. M wanted to insure that they would work well together in groups, because they would be forming new table groups based on the particular theme they wanted to represent. Rather than start all over to build relationships, the student teacher reinvoked that earlier context of the ways they worked together with each other and with text.

To get the students started on their investigations, Ms. M instructed them to create their own personal research folder in which they would keep their notes and any articles or information pertaining to their particular topic. Then, as a group, they needed to decide how they would work together. To help students frame this process, she revisited the Bill of Rights and Responsibilities, reformulating it as a foundation for each groups' contractual agreement.

For example, Ms. M explicitly made connections, intertextual and intercontextual, when she asked the students to recall how they made their Bill of Rights and Responsibilities. She asked that they now repeat that process to construct a new contract of how they would work together in new groups. They would be making a new contract the way they had when they constructed the Bill of Rights and Responsibilities. They brainstormed together what their particular ways of working together would be, then they wrote up a new contract for their table group and signed it to demonstrate their intentions of working together for a successful museum project.

The Bill of Rights and Responsibilities had become more than a mere document hanging on the wall; it had become a dynamic way of working together, with text and with each other. The students and teacher had reached an intersubjective space, a common way of thinking, in realizing what they meant about treating each other with respect. That intersubjectivity, created in part by the linking their past experience with their current thoughts and words (interT) and actions with words (interC), was reinvoked at this particular time to begin a new activity.

In addition, these students did not have to start over from scratch to come to an understanding of how they would work together in these small groups. They had built historicity together; they had created an intertextual and intercontextual past that had become a cultural resource of acting responsibly toward each other. The consequence of having built that past was that they could reinvoke it at any future time and bring all of that historical and cultural meaning together again in a new context. They also created a progression in their understanding of what it meant to work together, built on their past activities. Because of their understandings, they would be able to work well together to create a museum for the rest of the students in the school to enjoy and share on the day of the exhibition.

Classroom teachers may immediately see the relationship of these constructs to classroom teaching and learning. From the very first moment in the classroom, all who are present that day begin to build an intertextual past with each other toward an implicated future. The way in which discourse is constructed in a classroom is highly consequential for teachers and students. Each classroom event/experience becomes progressively more complex and builds on the prior knowledge and experience of the participants. Students and teachers together construct their mutual history of shared experiences, thinking, speaking, and learning.

Viewed in this way, past knowledge and practices become resources for present action, and present activity implicates future actions and knowledge. For example, Putney (1997) found that a student who was absent over an extended period of time (four months) was able to reenter the classroom and use the knowledge of practices she had learned before leaving the classroom. However, she did not have knowledge of the current content being referred to by members and therefore was not able to participate in the same way that she had earlier in the year. Only after she was able to reestablish, or reformulate, a form of common knowledge of the content, was she able to fully participate in the class during the remaining months of the school year (Putney, 1997; Putney et al., 2000). This work demonstrated the importance of the developing community as well as that of the developing individual, and how they intersect. It also raises implications for students who happen to be absent on a particular day as they miss the classroom experiences and learning, which eventually will shape the learning and developing of tomorrow.

Implications for Pull-Out Programs

If, for example, resource students or ESL students are pulled out of class, the consequence is that they will miss part of the intertextual and intercontextual links that others in the classroom have experienced. Another example might be students who want (or have) to miss class for a specific reason. Even if that reason is valid, when the learners return to class, it's like entering an ongoing dialogue. They might be able to catch up with what the others are saying, but those students cannot catch up or make up the context or the series of events that meld into the total experience. The absent students cannot "make up" the turn-taking, the intonation patterns, the gestures, the emotions, the quizzical comments that triggered shared experiences. If a teacher should attempt to take the time to "catch up" for the sake of those who were absent, the learners can acquire a sense of where they were going and what they were doing. However, those students who may have been pulled out or who were absent will have a more difficult time making connections than those who stayed in the classroom.

Brandts (1999), an experienced classroom teacher who researched a classroom environment, discovered that "[p]reparing to leave, leaving, and then re-entering a classroom constitutes a major disruption in a young child's continuity of thought" (p. 10). In one week in November, she documented a series of events that occurred in the classroom that were missed by four students who were in pull-out programs: (1) messages over the intercom for school events and school contests; (2) classroom visits, which included Scott's Golden Retriever, talk about the dog and the visit, the teacher's husband bringing lunch, Farmer Bob reading a poem, an impromptu art lesson from an artist, a grandparent doing storytelling, and a guest reading a book of tales; (3) minilessons for reading and writing, which included connections between authors, connections between subjects and themes, writing letters to grandparents, and mail coming from grandparents.

Following her study, Brandts' recommendations were:

- Remedial reading instruction time can and should be reconfigured so that the learner remains within the community of a classroom.
- It is critical for specialists and classroom teachers to align their approach to teaching reading based on assessment and the child's needs rather than relying solely on a reading series or program.
- Classroom teachers must themselves be competent, vigorous, and rigorous teachers of reading (p. 15).

While this particular study looks specifically at reading pull-out programs, students in many other contexts of specialized instruction have similar experiences (e.g., English as Additional Language, Special Education, Gifted and Talented). From the perspective related here, as the teacher and students interact they construct a common set of expectations, responsibilities, practices, and language that define ways of learning, living, and being in the classroom. These patterns also define what counts as being a teacher and student as well as what counts as knowing and doing in this classroom (Fernie, Davies, Kantor, & McMurray, 1993). The language contexts, practices, and patterns of everyday life formulated and agreed on by members of a class can thus be seen as shaping an interpretive system for a particular class that supports and constrains the opportunities for learning afforded members of particular classrooms (Tuyay, Jennings, & Dixon, 1995). This system is part of the "common knowledge" (Edwards & Mercer, 1987) that members construct as they interact on a moment-by-moment, day-by-day basis.

Earlier we explained the notion of reformulation (Chapter 4) as it related to development and the zone of proximal development. Here we revisit the idea as it relates to the complex ideas of this chapter. To examine the ways in which teachers and students formulate and reformulate the practices and construct common knowledge and explore the consequentiality of actions across time and events, we drew on the interrelated concepts of intersubjectivity, intertextuality, and intercontextuality. These concepts enabled us to examine the interpretive system constructed by teachers and students and to identify the links between texts (intertextual relationships) and contexts (intercontextual relationships) that were socially constructed and interactionally accomplished by members.

As researchers, we can use these constructs to examine what students formulate as knowledge and practices of the community in the spoken texts and written artifacts (e.g., written work and drawings) they construct. We can examine the discourse and written artifacts for formulations of roles (positions that students and teachers can take up), practices, and content knowledge. These formulations and reformulations are made visible in the analysis by highlighting the choices of language used by members, the practices or conventions of language used to construct the written texts, and the ways members interact with, construct, and/or use written and oral texts (Putney & Floriani, 1999).

As teachers, we can use these constructs to evaluate how well our students are taking up the knowledge we construct together. We can also evaluate our teaching as we reflect on whether we explicitly make visible the links between texts and practices that our students interpret and construct. As we construct a language of community and academic development, language and thoughts are intertextually and intercontextually linked to become cultural resources that provide students access to the academic content. These processes and practices are critical to the formulation and construction of a problem-based, inquiry-oriented approach to teaching and learning, one that meets the goal of transformative educational processes advocated by Freire (1970, 1998; Wink, 1997).

Conclusion

Throughout this chapter, we have linked the new language to the extended analogy of the New York adventure of Amy, Le, and Jo so that you could create cognitive coathooks to construct your own meaning for what we assume may be new words. However, in the writing of this chapter we had the unexpected and synergetic experience of living an authentic example. Vygotskian theory informed practice as we wrote of Vygotskian practice informing theory. We share it so that each reader might cocreate historicity with us as we all grow to newer and deeper understandings of abstract and esoteric thought and language.

During the preparation of this chapter, Amy and Le met at a national research conference. Amy had experience in the publishing world; that is, she functioned as a more capable peer. While there, they reviewed and discussed how this chapter would fit into the rest of this book and what the time line would be for completing the book. As a way of revisiting the terms of this chapter, we will share their experiences.

- Intersubjectivity was established as Amy and Le built a common history through shared meanings as they talked about the contents of Chapter 5. Amy and Le created their own intersubjectivity at the point when they temporarily shared their social world through their use of language.
- The interactional spaces were created by Le and Amy as they interacted through these particular organizational patterns of the conference for a particular purpose, the review of this chapter. At times they worked individually as they read, then together as they discussed what they had read.
- The intertextuality ('between' + 'text') of Le and Amy was created as they each brought with them their previous knowledge to the dialogue about this chapter: Amy, who edits other books, brought her knowledge about publishing; Le, who has published other articles about Vygotsky, brought her knowledge of Vygotsky's legacy. Together they socially created (in the rarified air of the conference setting) a shared understanding of the new text they were constructing.
- Intercontextuality (*con*, 'with' + *texto*, 'text') was created as each of them drank their morning coffee and recalled how they had done this once before when Amy and Le had first read the proposal together that Le and Jo had written.
- Consequential progressions were generated by Amy and Le as they each drew on, not only their shared understanding of text and context, but also their historicity, which was begun when they had met at an earlier conference six months ago and relived this conversation over coffee about writing this book.

Jo was not able to attend this national conference, nor did she go to the previous one, where Amy and Le also conferred, and so was not a part of the complex experiences that Le and Amy cocreated. As Jo was not a part of this historicity, she will experience the text and context of this chapter in a different way from Amy and Le.

However, Jo and Le have a grounded implicated future with the entire text/context of this Vygotsky book. For many years, their shared history of talk is text, and text is talk has resulted in the establishment of their own unique creation of community grounded in a pedagogy of hope. Therefore, when the Vygotsky book is finished, Amy will experience it in a unique way from the historicity of shared experiences that Le and Jo bring to this text and context.

Now that we have explained these concepts from our own experience, we turn once again to our distant teacher, Vygotsky, to ground our work in his legacy of educational psychology and pedagogy. This mentor from the past has offered his own advice to the teachers he wrote for in his text on educational psychology

(Vygotsky, 1997). From his study of children's interests, Vygotsky proposed three important pedagogical conclusions:

1. Topics in a course of study must be interconnected. This is the best way to insure a common interest of students around a central theme.

2. Avoid repetition by making instruction focused. Review and relate topics in a more thorough and all-inclusive form, complemented with a wealth of new facts, generalizations, and conclusions. The topics students have already studied are revisited, though unfolded from a new perspective..." (p. 86).

3. Begin with what is familiar to students, and with what arouses their interests naturally.

Now, we imagine that you will experience your own versions of InterT, InterC, and InterS as you interact with the text. As readers, you will link what you are reading now with your own experiences with prior texts and with other people. What we have written may trigger thoughts for you about your own teaching and learning adventures, and those you will experience in the future. At any rate, you now have a way of thinking and talking about your experience through a Vygotskian lens. In Chapter 6, we offer a contextualized glossary of Vygotskian and Neo-Vygotskian terms to further mediate your learning.

6 Beyond Vygotsky

Questions of education will have been resolved when questions of life will have been solved (Vygotsky, 1997, p. 350).

In this chapter, our goal is to share our understandings of the language that has evolved among the community of scholars who study Vygotsky. For some readers, this chapter may serve as a glossary. However, in the Vygotskian sense, this unique language is far more than simply just words: It is a holistic way of thinking. The language surrounding Vygotsky is a reflection of the reciprocal interaction between thought and language. Thought informs language, and language informs thought in a dynamic process.

We will organize this chapter by extending the distinction between *language in* and *language of* as conceptualized by Lin (1993). In her work in classrooms, Lin recognized that students come to the classroom with a language they speak, which they have acquired from their prior experience and schooling. In her research in the classroom, Lin further recognized the particular language that members of the classroom community constructed as *language of* the classroom. She recognized that *language of* is a situated language, one that holds particular meanings for the group that constructed it. This language becomes a sort of shorthand for the group because they share common knowledge, intersubjectivity, of what the words mean. We are applying her distinction to understanding the work of the thought community of scholars who have interpreted and applied Vygotsky's concepts in their research and writing.

Language in: Each of us comes to this book (or to any new context or community) with a language we bring *in*. Each of us brings in a language as we seek to understand the language of the community of scholars seeking to understand Vygotsky.

Language of: Once we begin to explore this book (or any new situation or community) we discover that there is a particular language *of* this new context.

As readers move through this framework and generate their own new understandings, they will become a member of the thought community that looks to Vygotsky for the vision of pedagogy for today and tomorrow. We each have a language we bring in, as we each begin to use the language of Vygotsky. As we grow to understand and use the language of the new community, the new language informs our thinking. The members who seek to accept common meanings for the words of the community mutually construct the language of the new community.

Others might call this phenomenon the use of "golden words." Each group has their own golden words that they use as a type of community shorthand. It is our hope that each reader will enter the Vygotskian thought community and begin to not only use the language of, but also add to the language of the group. As language informs thought and thought informs language, this is the way that ideas are extended, expanded, and implemented in an ever-widening community.

A Definition of Terms Used

For the purpose of furthering the understandings of sociocultural theory, we will define the terms as certain Vygotskian scholars have used them in their work. In this section, we highlight terms used within *A Vision of Vygotsky,* while in the following section we will examine terms from related works. In so doing, we will often use quotations from particular works, rather than offer a "definition," as we feel that this will contextualize the words. While this is not an exhaustive listing of all the words used in sociocultural theory, nor of the works of Neo-Vygotskians that have been published, our intention is to give the readers a sense of the work of many scholars who have extended Vygotsky's own theories. That these scholars continue to add to the knowledge base and inform our practice in terms of teaching and learning is testimony to the enduring work that Vygotsky started so long ago.

Apprenticeship is the passing on of knowledge and skills of the crafts, with an emphasis on application. We demonstrate how mentor and apprentices often shift roles in their work together in Chapter 7.

- Apprenticeship is not just reproducing the past. While the apprentices become independent master crafters, they create new artifacts, adding to cultural resources (Wells, 1999).
- During *apprenticeship,* the individual develops "skills to handle culturally defined problems with available tools, and builds" from these givens to construct new solutions within the context of sociocultural activity" (Rogoff, 1994).

Community of practice is a collaborative term that emphasizes relationships between human action and the social context.

In a community of practice, literacy and language learning are more broadly seen as a set of social practices situated in classroom life. Literacy from this perspective implies capable participation in a given social context where learning takes place. (Lave & Wenger, 1991).

Complementarity is a "mutual internalization, a making into one's own some aspect of one's partner's knowledge" (John-Steiner & Meehan, 2000, p. 45).

Consequential progressions are interactions in activities, signaled by members as a negotiated production that is academically and socially consequential within and across past, current, and implicated future events (Putney et al., 2000).

Construct is an idea or concept theoretically formed from different parts.

Context is a socially constructed setting, which includes the actions of people in the setting. *Context* is defined here using the classic definition proposed by Erickson & Shultz (1981): "Contexts are constituted by what people are *doing* (author's emphasis) and where and when they are doing it..." (p. 148).

Cultural/historical theory is a term coined by Vygotsky to emphasize the historical nature of his research and to contrast his approach to psycholinguistic research from research (phenotypic) that predicts or explains mental functioning. Vygotsky's research offers a way of *understanding* mental processes through disclosure of their emergence and subsequent growth (Vygotsky, 1981).

Development is a revolutionary period of qualitative change (Holzman, 1996).

- Learning and development are in dynamic reciprocal relationship and are thoroughly situated in culture. Development of the individual is "a process in which children grow into the intellectual life of those around them" (Vygotsky, 1978, p. 88).
- It is a dialectic process, a "movement of movement...both continuous and discontinuous, as recursive but not circular" (Zebroski, 1994, p. 161).

Dialectic is a juxtaposition of opposing directions of thought to achieve synthesis. In dialectical synthesis two opposite ideas are united in a continuous whole (Van der Veer & Valsiner, 1991). Vygotsky used the metaphor of a water drop as an example of using a dialectic.

Dialogue is any talk to which two or more people contribute to construct both internal and external meanings.

- Vygotsky argued that "a similar sort of dialogue can take place when one is alone, using the resources appropriated from engaging in dialogue with others" (Wells, 2000, p. 75).
- Vygotsky (1987) stated: "Oral speech is generally dialogic. Dialogue always assumes the interlocutors' knowledge of the crux of the matter. As we have seen, this knowledge allows abbreviations in oral speech" (p. 271). Furthermore, "It is no surprise that written speech is the polar opposite of oral

speech. The situation that is clear to the interlocutors in oral speech, and the potential for expressive intonation, mimic, and gesture, is absent in written speech. The potential for abbreviation is excluded from the outset. Understanding must be produced through words and their proper combination" (p. 272).

- For Freire (1970), *dialogue* is an instrument of liberation. It is the encounter between people mediated by the world, in order to name the world.

Discourse is dialogue that includes certain beliefs, values, and social practices through which members of a speech community constitute their identities (Gee, 1990).

Discursive system is language in use combined with actions (gestures, body language, eye contact, etc.) and the context in which it occurs (Green & Dixon, 1993).

Egocentric speech for Vygotsky is external speech as it turns into internal speech; it is evidence of the point at which knowledge is internalized. For Piaget, in contrast, egocentric speech gives way to inner speech, and is not indicative of internalization of concepts (Vygotsky, 1986).

External speech is language for others. "Inner speech is for oneself. External speech is speech for others" (Vygotsky, 1987, p. 257). "Inner speech is not the exterior aspect of external speech—it is a function in itself" (Vygotsky, 1987, p. 249).

Historicity is the social and cultural past we have coconstructed with others.

Implicated future indicates that, when we interact with others, we construct our conversation under the assumption that the conversational other will construct a future response (Bahktin, 1981).

Inner speech is "a unique form of internal collaboration with oneself" (Vygotsky, 1987, p. 273), which precedes egocentric speech in children. The purpose of inner speech is for oneself, not for others.

Interactional space is an organizational pattern of interactions constructed for particular educational purposes such as small groups, pairs, teams, a whole class, and so on. (Lin, 1993).

Intercontextuality is the linking of cultural practices associated with ways of being or actions taken with text (Floriani, 1993).

Intermental/intramental indicates that all higher mental functions are dependent on semiotic artifacts and practices that are first encountered intermentally in purposeful joint activities in which more expert members of the culture both demonstrate their use and assist the learner in mastering them. Through participation in which his or her performance is assisted, the learner gradually masters the practices in which these artifacts are used so that they also become a resource for intramental activity. As Vygotsky (1981) put it, on its way to becoming an internal mode of activity, "any higher mental function necessarily goes through an external stage in its development because it is initially a social function" (Wells, 1999, p. 136).

Internalization is an active restructuring of knowledge between and among individuals (John-Steiner & Meehan, 2000). It is:

- involvement of individuals in exchanges that are characterized by a sharing of meaning (Rogoff, 1990).
- an inherent developmental relationship between external and internal activity (Wertsch, 1985).
- an active process of co-construction leading to creative contributions (John-Steiner & Meehan, 2000).
- a person's transition from joint collective accomplishment of an activity to individual accomplishment (Davydov & Zinchenko, 1993, p. 102).

Intersubjectivity is the act of constructing common (mutual) meanings between speakers. It is:

- shared understanding that is mutually recognized (Crook, 1994, p. 80).
- the points at which common knowledge is being created (Edwards & Mercer, 1987, p. 84).
- the shared social world between child and adult through the process of negotiation of meanings (Kozulin, 1990, p. 170).
- the mutual understanding that is achieved between people in communication (Rogoff, 1990, p. 67).
- communication that transcends private worlds of participants (Rommetveit, 1979).
- in joint activity, the signs and symbols developed through language, the development of common understanding of the purposes and meanings of the activity, the joint engagement in cognitive strategies and problem solving… (Tharp & Gallimore, 1988, p. 89).
- what exists when interlocutors share some aspect of their situation definitions, which are ways in which objects and events are represented or defined (Wertsch, 1985, p. 159).
- "the sharing of a social world through the process of negotiating meaning [that] allows us to see what the participants jointly construct in their talk and actions, and thus, how practices associated with being literate in that classroom come into being" (Putney, 1996, pp. 129–130).

Interpsychological processes are higher psychological processes unique to humans that can be acquired only through interaction with others, that is, through shared processes that only later will begin to be carried out independently (Leontiev, 1981).

Intertextual past denotes our past interactions with others in which we have created and intertwined texts (verbal, aural, oral, and written) with jointly constructed mutual meanings.

Intertextuality is a socially constructed juxtaposition of texts that is interactionally recognized, acknowledged, and socially significant (Bloome & Egan-Robertson, 1993, pp. 1–2).

Mediation is the transformation of biologically determined processes into higher, mediated, and self-regulated psychological functions (Vygotsky, 1978).

Specifically, Vygotsky believed that the transformation of cognitive processes begins when children start to use language (speech) in order to guide, plan, and monitor their own activities. This use of language for self-regulation can be identified as private speech, which signals the onset of "purely human forms of practical and abstract intelligence" (Vygotsky, 1978, p. 24).

Mediational or cultural tools, such as language, act as bridges to link concrete actions carried out by individuals or groups with "cultural, institutional, and historical settings" (Wertsch, 1985, p. 21).

Negotiated production is the result of joint knowledge construction in interaction with others.

Praxis is the union of reflection and action.

Psychological tool and function of language indicates a dual purpose in that speech takes on a function of social contact and organization, and, at the same time, becomes a tool for structuring thought (Vygotsky, 1986). It includes signs and symbol systems such as language, mathematical symbols, and scientific diagrams (John-Steiner & Meehan, 2000).

Scaffolding is the support a teacher or tutor provides in helping children move from joint to independent problem solving (Wood, Bruner, & Ross, 1976). "As the analogy implies, *scaffolding* is the gradual withdrawal of adult control and support as a function of children's increasing mastery of a given task" (Moll & Greenberg, 1990, p. 139).

Semiotic mediation is the use of signs and/or symbols to augment our actions. Through semiotic mediation, we create linkages that turn the sign into a symbol. Mediation is a part of semiotics; it is what the signs do to make meaning; it is the use and function of signs or the process of transforming signs into symbols that are meaningful (Lee & Smagorinsky, 2000).

Semiotic tools are words used to affect our external environment. They are words that trigger action, or language that works to make meaning. For Vygotsky, semiotic tools differed from semiotic signs, which are words used to sustain one's thinking. The use of tools and signs shares the property of involving mediated activity (Vygotsky, 1978). The study of semiotics indicates how we continually use language and thought to generate more meaning, to grow and develop our mental abilities.

Signs and symbols are forms of language in the general sense. In a Vygotskian sense, signs and symbols do more than simply link a word to a thing. The word at first serves as a sign, but eventually it becomes a symbol for the thing. In a Vygotskian sense, it is the use of signs to solve problems, mental instruments that help us construct more knowledge. The sign influences the symbol, and the symbol influences the sign.

Sociocultural theory emphasizes social activity and cultural practice as sources of thinking, the importance of mediation in human psychological functioning, the centrality of pedagogy in development, and the inseparability of the individual from the social context (Vygotsky, 1981).

Verbal thought is the linkage of the multiple layers of language and thought as they transform themselves into greater mental abilities, the joining of thought and language to make meaning. It is the action, the process of language and thought coming together, to expand and enrich both.

Word meaning is the product of verbal thought. It is the smallest element of thought and language. Meaning is always evolving, growing, changing. Word meaning is to *denotation* as word sense is to *connotation*. Vygotsky's use of the word *znachenie* was tied more to the social, historical, and cultural public world (Wertsch, 2000).

Word sense is the more personal interpretation of a word. Again, Vygotsky's use of the word *smysl*, expressed the individual's emotional and motivational experiences (Yaroshevsky, 1989).

Zone of proximal development is the distance between the actual developmental level, as determined by independent problem solving, and the level of potential development as determined through problem solving under adult guidance or in collaboration with more capable peers (Vygotsky, 1978, p. 86).

- The zone makes possible performance before competence (Cazden, 1981).
- A theory of intellectual development that acknowledges that children undergo quite profound changes in their understanding by engaging in joint activity and conversation with other people (Edwards & Mercer, 1987).
- A *zoped* is a dialogue between the child and his or her future, rather than a dialogue between the child and an adult's past (Griffen & Cole, 1984).
- ZPD is the transformation of an interpersonal process to an intrapersonal one (John-Steiner & Souberman, 1978).
- A true advance in the child's reasoning resulting from the collaborative forms of thinking in which the child's everyday concepts come into contact with the scientific concepts introduced by adults (Kozulin, 1990).
- It is a key theoretical construct, capturing the individual within the concrete social situation of learning and development (Moll, 1990).
- ZPD identifies the social dynamics of change (Moll, 1990).
- The ZPD is a proper unit of study for understanding unique human activity, especially learning and development and their relationship (Newman & Holzman, 1993).
- The ZPD is not a place at all; it is an activity, an historical unity, the essential socialness of human beings expressed as revolutionary activity (Newman & Holzman, 1993).
- It reveals the contrast between assisted performance and unassisted performance (Tharp & Gallimore, 1988).
- ZPD specifies the interdependence of the process of child development and the socially provided resources for that development (Valsiner, 1988).
- ZPD defines those functions that have not yet matured…buds or flowers of development, and characterizes mental development prospectively (Vygotsky, 1978).
- It is the dynamic region of sensitivity in which the transition from interpsychological to intrapsychological functioning can be made (Wertsch, 1985).
- It is a possible transition, not a fixed state of consciousness (Shepel, 1995).

Related Terms

Activity theory provides a unified account of Vygotsky's original proposals on the nature and development of human behavior.

- It is the concept that human behavior results from the integration of socially and culturally constructed forms of mediation into human activity (Lantolf, 2000).
- It is also currently in use as *cultural-historical-activity theory* that combines the two strands of sociocultural theory and activity theory (Cole, 1996; Cole & Engestrom, 1993).
- "[H]uman behavior and mind must be considered in terms of purposive and culturally meaningful actions rather than as biological, adaptive reactions" (Kozulin, 1986, p. 266).

Appropriation is the acquisition and use of cultural tools that result from being involved in organized activities. This term was coined by Vygotsky's associate, Leont'ev (1981), to replace Piaget's notion of assimilation (denoting a biological metaphor), with a term that is sociocultural in nature (Newman, Griffen, & Cole, 1989).

Dialogism is found in the works of Mikhail Bakhtin, thought by many scholars to complement the work of Vygotsky. A "dialogic encounter" is one in which one speaker's concrete utterances come into contact with…the utterances of another (Wertsch, 1991). With respect to application of dialogism to teacher professional development, Ball (2000) notes that teacher philosophies are dialogic in nature, shaped by their interactions around the theory, concepts, and ideas that they focus on inside and outside class.

Distributed cognition specifies that "human thinking is not reducible to individual properties or traits. Instead, it is always mediated, distributed among persons, artifacts, activities, and settings" (Moll, 2000, p. 265).

Legitimate peripheral participation, one of the essential premises of the community of practice framework, identifies learning as occurring while newcomers participate in various peripheral roles alongside more experienced or competent members in community practice (Lave & Wenger, 1991).

Conclusion

In the Chapters 4 and 5, we assume that readers will bring their own language, thoughts, and experiences to this text; each reader will bring a **language in** to this text; after finishing this chapter, each reader will also have a **language of** the text. This new language reflects the knowledge that has been cocreated as we each engaged with text. Construction of community is not simply collaboration; it is also the process of becoming a part of all that we have experienced and all that we read. We close with Vera John-Steiner, who captures the essence of a Vygotskian notion of construction of community.

> Central to his approach is a view of the mind which extends beyond the 'skull,' which does not situate thinking in the confined spaces of the individual brain or mind. Instead, he proposes a sustained dynamic between other humans both present and past, book, the rest of our material and nonmaterial culture, and the individual engaged in symbolic activity. For Vygotsky, interaction with caregivers, peers, teachers, and the material world is the basis of intellectual development" (John-Steiner, 1997, p. xviii).

In Chapter 7, we will continue with Vera John-Steiner as we move from the construction of community to apprenticing and, finally, to mentoring.

E N D N O T E

The authors wish to thank Chris Iddings for her assistance on assembling and defining the terms in this chapter.

7 Mentoring: Vygotsky's Vision Extended

These processes of internalization do not take place in isolation. They are embedded in apprenticeships with parents, mentors, and distant teachers....
When these collaborations are successful, novices develop fluency, and learn how experienced artists and scientists think. At the same time, such collaborations offer renewal for the experienced individual and the use of shared knowledge for the novice's development of self. From a Vygotskian point of view, these interactions are central to the transformation of the novice into an experienced thinker (John-Steiner, 1997, p. xxiii).

The journey of writing this book has been an authentic Vygotskian experience of transformative mentoring. We have used our thought and language to cocreate new knowledge. Our learning together has been influenced by our ever-evolving social, cultural, historical, and political context. We have written, read, and reflected in our zone of proximal development. Walking this road has generated another question: What is new about Vygotsky? Apprenticeship is at the center of Vygotsky's idea of learning and developing. The construct of apprenticeship has led us to mentoring as a natural extension of Vygotskian theory.

Not only have we lived this in our relationship with each other and others, but in relationships with schools and universities. Partnerships, collaboration, interdisciplinary studies, school and community connections, and problem solving are central to pedagogy today. It is timely to visit the idea of mentoring through the Vygotskian lens to seek answers posed by these collaborative processes. We come from a tradition that often valued individual learning in schools. Yet, in life, it is often one's ability to work with others that leads to success. In addition, our path to success may be a rocky one or a smooth one, depending on circumstances along the way, our interactions with others who either help or hinder our efforts, and the opportunities that are afforded us as we make our way. A part of being successful also has to do with being open to what comes our way, maintaining perspective, and being persistent and resilient in working toward our goal of life-long learning.

In what follows, we introduce a model that illustrates these ideas in terms of both teaching and mentoring. This model integrates and extends the Vygotskian vision of learning and developing. Our own journey of mentoring, from the first moment that we met has followed this model, even though we were not aware of it initially.

Cultural Competency for Transformative Education

Olivia was a twenty-two-year-old African American woman attempting to earn her undergraduate degree in Elementary Education at a large university attended by primarily Anglo-American students. More than anything else in the world, Olivia wanted to become a teacher. No one in her family had been a teacher; in fact, no one in her family had ever attended or graduated from college. But Olivia's second-grade teacher had captured her attention many years earlier, assuring Olivia that she was a smart student and could accomplish any goal. Mrs. Givehand was an insightful and charming African American woman who skillfully instilled such a sense of confidence in Olivia that she decided in second grade to become a teacher just like Mrs. Givehand.

Olivia's academic journey at the university had been fairly successful. She earned the grades necessary to gain entrance to the College of Education. However, she failed the entrance exam that she was required to pass prior to enrolling in the advanced teacher education courses. Olivia could not continue her program, and her goal of becoming a teacher seemed beyond her grasp. She gave herself one more semester to pass the test, or she would have to leave the university and seek other paths through life.

Olivia was sitting on the bench in the College of Education, discouraged by her plight, and trying to absorb the enormity of her immediate situation, when a professor passed by. Dr. Kindersley, a forty-five-year-old Anglo-American woman, was taking a short break from working her way through another seemingly never-ending pile of papers on her desk. Noticing Olivia's disheartened appearance, Dr. Kindersley stopped, gently asked Olivia if everything was all right, and inquired what could she do to help. Olivia explained her dilemma. Dr. Kindersley invited Olivia to her office where they set up tutorial sessions to help Olivia pass her entrance exam.

Olivia and Dr. Kindersley met several times during the following weeks. However, Olivia was not successful in her next attempt to pass the exam, but she returned to Dr. Kindersley, who encouraged her to try again. The next time Olivia passed the exam. Her journey to becoming a teacher continued.

Dr. Kindersley and Olivia formed a friendship as Olivia successfully completed her teacher preparation and breezed through her student teaching. Olivia was offered a teaching position during her student teaching experience, and she began her new profession enthusiastically.

Dr. Kindersley maintained a supportive relationship with Olivia, especially during the first few years of her teaching career. One of their favorite topics of conversation focused on the importance of Olivia's mentoring all of *her* students to pursue their future goals.

This poignant personal experience demonstrates the presence of cultural competency, which encompasses the beliefs and actions displayed by individuals who respond authentically and interact with people from other experiences and cultures. A Cultural Competencies Model, developed by Nancy P. Gallavan, follows as a way of conceptualizing inclusive and transformative education (Figure 7.1). This model has the potential to move us beyond the classroom walls and into the social spaces we encounter throughout our journey.

Gallavan Cultural Competencies Model

The Cultural Competencies Model consists of three elements: components, sources, and outcomes. In Figure 7.1 we relate them to the Vygotskian principles of thought, language, and experience, the sociocultural context, and the zone of proximal development respectively. In what follows, we explain the model, then tie it to our own mentoring experience. The three components of the Gallavan Cultural Competencies Model include: **Information (I), Access (A),** and **Opportunity (O)** (Figure 7.1). People need **information** to know and to understand themselves and others in the past, present, and future. Everyone needs **access** or the ability to go places: physically, mentally, emotionally, academically, socially, professionally, financially, and so forth. Getting or being given access to gain information or to use information is vital to our growth and success. Likewise, each of

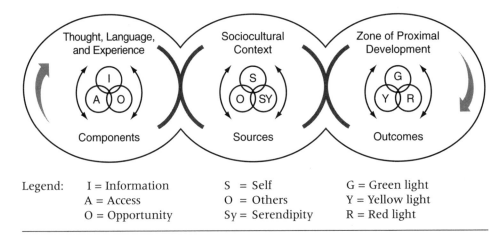

FIGURE 7.1   **Gallavan Cultural Competencies Model in a Vygotskian Context.**

us benefits from the **opportunity** or chance to do what we choose to do with our lives personally and professionally. Opportunity enables us to gain and use information while allowing us access to desired spaces.

All three components must exist for the Cultural Competencies Model to be effective, although each of the three components generally does not exist in the same strength simultaneously. Each of the three components dynamically expands and contracts to support the other two components as necessary with changes over time. Additionally, no one component of the Cultural Competencies Model must precede the other two components. Each of the three components plays a significant but ever-adjusting role to maintain a holistic balance.

Information, Access, and Opportunity

In a Vygotskian sense, mentors often initiate the cycle of information, access, and opportunity. They open the door for novices/apprentices to know, to go, to do. What makes Vygotsky's notion of mentoring unique is that the process is not one-way. Just as Vygotsky emphasized the reciprocity and dynamic relationship between thought, language, and experience, so too is information, access, and opportunity reciprocal between mentors and novices. For example, ten years ago, Joan, as a mentor, initiated a cycle of information, access, and opportunity to the world of Vygotsky for Le. However, now the information, access, and opportunity often flow from Le to Joan.

In the Cultural Competencies Model, not unlike Vygotsky's notion of development, the movement is not linear; one particular component of information, access, and opportunity does not precede another. The three components overlap; they dynamically expand and contract in strength. They interact with one another simultaneously, and events are initiated within any one component.

Opportunity may be an occasion that an individual seeks, that another individual provides, or simply seems to occur serendipitously. During any given opportunity, we may become aware of the need for additional information and/or the application of previously gained information. Similarly, during any given opportunity, we may realize that we need access or that we are being provided access to new and different opportunities. Each of the three components work collaboratively and in conjunction with one another.

Potential Sources and Consequential Outcomes

In the Cultural Competencies Model potential sources of information, access, and opportunity are represented as three overlapping circles that dynamically expand and contract in balance with one another. The potential sources include: (1) the individual **self** (**S**), (2) one or many **others** (**O**), and (3) **serendipity** (**Sy**), or that which seems to happen outside of our control or imagination (Figure 7.1). These potential sources are related to the Vygotskian principle of sociocultural context in that the information, access, and opportunity we gain depends on the interrelationships among self, others, and serendipitous experiences.

We can realize how self and others become potential sources in the Cultural Competencies Model. Perhaps the most elusive potential source centers on the existence of serendipity—chance, good fortune, coincidence, accident, our seeming to be in the right place at the right time with the right people and the right preparation. Without warning, we are provided the needed or wanted information, easy access, and/or the perfect opportunity when often we were not even aware that we needed it or wanted it. Each of our lives seems to reflect the joyful importance of serendipitous activities that support our paths, remove the barriers, provide appropriate interventions, and so on, while prompting new information, access, and opportunities causing us to grow, learn, and change.

Regardless of the potential source (self, others, or serendipity), an individual may find positive support for achieving the goal related to needed or wanted information, access, and/or opportunity: the green light. The individual continues the same journey with additional information, access, and opportunity.

A second consequence, the yellow light, occurs when an individual encounters a situation in which information, access, and/or opportunity are not provided, are not provided fully, are not provided in a way that the individual can understand and/or use, or the individual is not fully supported. This consequence requires the individual to try new approaches to achieve the original goal.

When the individual encounters total resistance and comes to a complete stop, the third consequence, the red light, occurs. Regardless of the source, the individual must stop, change directions, and take a totally new road. At this point, the individual may abandon the journey altogether and return to previously known pathways. Our goal in presenting this model was to encourage us as teachers, mentors, and learners to focus on the potential of each in the sociocultural context.

In summary, as seen in the graphic display of the model, we first experience the three components (information, access, opportunity) through the Vygotskian notion of thought, language, and experience. Second, the sociocultural context is experienced through the potential sources of self, others, and serendipity in a dynamic relationship. Third, the consequential outcomes illustrate movement through the zone of proximal development. Just as Vygotsky (1997) intertwined the dynamic and reciprocal actions of teachers, learners, and the social environment as crucial to the educational process, here we envision the confluence of information, access, and opportunity with the potential sources relating the self, others, and serendipity. To further examine the process of mentoring in light of the cultural competencies model in a Vygotskian context, we stop to reflect on how this model has connected our experience directly to the Vygotskian legacy.

Serendipitous Meeting of Minds:
LeAnn Reflects

We have become increasingly aware of the importance of mentoring as an important aspect of mediating learning and development. The educational process doesn't end; it shifts as we continue to encounter more experienced others. As we have already demonstrated, the notion of the more experienced or capable other can alternate depending on the situations and settings. Our own journey has been one of a reciprocal mentoring, although we could not have known that at the outset.

At the beginning of our personal journey, in August of 1991, Joan was a newly hired assistant professor, fresh from finishing her dissertation. She had arrived in town several weeks before classes began to get her new home settled. I was a returnee to graduate school, seeking a change in career, coming back to my roots in education. However, this had not been a smooth transition at all. Having a thirteen-year lapse from teaching Spanish made the prospect of returning to secondary education rather daunting. I had already taken one graduate course with an advisor who cautioned me to "figure out what I wanted to do before continuing for a master's degree." She sent me to the department chair in hopes of finding what program would fit my needs.

I could not understand at that time what was happening. Instead of mentoring me, this advisor was tossing me to someone else. I made an appointment with the secretary to meet with the chair of the department the next day. I went home feeling like I should just drop the whole idea of going back to teaching. My husband wisely reminded me that she was not the only advisor, nor was this the only university accessible to me. I decided to try one more time.

The next day I went back to the department office, and, still feeling like I had been reprimanded, I approached the chair's office for our meeting. As I introduced myself and sat across from his desk, those old memories of being sent to the principal's office began to surface in my psyche. The chair must have detected my unease because he listened to my story carefully, then smiled a wry smile.

> "I know just what you need to do," he said. "We hired a new professor, and she just arrived in town. She will be coordinating a new program for us in multilingual/multicultural education. Why don't you give her a call?" he queried as he wrote down her telephone number and handed it to me.
>
> "Call her at home?" I asked in astonishment.
>
> "Sure, she said if any student needed her, just give her a call," he replied.
>
> "Well, that's a novelty," I murmured under my breath as I left his office. I thanked him for his help and headed for home. I called as soon as I walked in the door, and the voice on the other end spoke with such enthusiasm that I just *knew* that this professor was going to be different from all the others I had encountered.

Joan quickly outlined for me a program of study that fit exactly what I wanted to do. The program wasn't official yet, but they were working on getting it established, and it would likely be done by the time I would graduate two years later. I switched advisors, of course, and could not wait to take my first class with my new mentor.

On the first night of class, Joan breezed in and set the pace for the class. We were constructing our own knowledge together. Her syllabus did not look like any others I had seen. It was full of questions, and the list of readings was extensive, but interesting. We had to keep a journal, and she was going to read it! What had I gotten myself into?

In this context, Joan was the teacher, and LeAnn was a confused student in Joan's first graduate class, one that focused on Vygotsky. Joan was the mentor, LeAnn the apprentice.

September 15, 1991

LeAnn wrote in her journal for Joan's class.

Confusion—I read the requirements for this class and realize that I am not familiar with any of the terminology or concepts. Vygotsky who? The zone of what? Talk about a learning experience—this will be one!

Joan responded in the journal.

Be patient with yourself, with me, and with Vygotsky. Together we will make this okay.

October 15, 1991

LeAnn wrote again in her journal for Joan's class.

I left education because I felt that I did not belong. I came back because I knew that kids are not learning what they need to know. In this class we are learning that there are three principal principles which, when applied in schools, might help kids learn. However, the assignments sound foreign to me. We're supposed to do a portfolio evaluation of two students—this is not clear to me.

Joan wrote back to LeAnn.

You are making good progress. Watch the students carefully. Think of the three principal principles as you watch them. Write in your journal everything you observe: Do they get to collaborate? What is the evidence? Do they problem-solve in meaningful ways? How is their thinking and their speaking related?

November 15, 1991

LeAnn wrote to Joan.

I came back to education because I wanted to make a difference. This class is just beginning to show me how to do that. I still have much to learn, but when I first heard you talking in class, I felt that I was in a foreign language classroom. Now I am beginning to understand the concepts for myself. Thought and language: As I learn these new words from the text, it's true that it does affect my thinking. Sociocultural context: I can see how the context of this class has played a major role in my own learning. Zone of proximal development: We do that in class every week.

Joan wrote back.

You really should write an article about Vygotsky.

That was the beginning of our mentor–apprentice relationship. I took many other classes from Joan and soon I became a *more capable peer* for other graduate students in her class. I watched the faces of students new to Joan's style of teaching on the first night of class. I knew what they were thinking as they perused the syllabus. I had experienced that moment of panic, realizing that I would be far more responsible for my learning than I had ever thought possible. It's a little bit scary to be turned loose to learn as much as one can, especially for those of us who come from a traditional, recitation background. Joan would leave the room for a few minutes to get some books from her office, and the first question from a nervous group of students would always be, "Okay, who's had this professor before? Is she serious about the work we are going to do?" I would talk excitedly about the previous classes I had taken, reassuring them that not only would they *get it*, but that they would actually *like* this course in the end. I told them to stay with it for five weeks, and then decide if they really wanted to drop the course. Only one student ever did.

Often, assumptions about mentoring are narrowly defined. Traditionally, we might have thought that a mentor was a teacher. In addition, we might have thought that an apprentice was a student. We might have thought of those roles as fixed. However, that was before we met the works of Vygotsky, and before we met each other. The three principal principles of Vygotsky have redefined and expanded our roles multiple times since then.

LeAnn's Journal Reflection Continues

A year later, LeAnn was taking another graduate course from Joan. In the following journal entry for that class, it is easy to see that LeAnn's learning is starting to go in new directions.

March, 1992

LeAnn is reflecting on a journal article.

This article says that a student who turns in exactly what the teacher expects is not critically thinking. They are not questioning why; they are just parroting what the teacher has taught and what the teacher expects to hear back from the student. Well, I was thunderstruck! I thought that I was doing so well, and all this time I was skimming the surface? I was getting good grades, but I was not learning to question what was being put in front of me? How could I go this far in my educational process, and not be considered a good student?

I had put this on the back burner for some time, but it suddenly came leaping out at me when you said that I was doing wonderful things, just not what you had assigned! In your classes I have really been able to go out on a limb to discover what is important and relevant to me.

Joan wrote back.

Stay out there on that limb! By the way, have you ever thought about getting a Ph.D.?

That was the spark that initiated the rest of the story. Two years earlier, my first academic advisor told me I was not structured enough to ever finish a master's program. In terms of the Cultural Competencies Model, her discouraging remarks had almost been enough to shut down both access and opportunity for me to finish. However, because I had support from a spouse who thought I could do anything, and a personal resolve to carry on, I was open to the serendipity of meeting the one person who willingly and joyfully agreed to open the door of access, and provide the opportunity I was seeking.

Serendipity was at work as information, access, and opportunity continued to flow in that context. Now my mentor was advising me to go on for a doctorate. I entered the doctoral program at the University of California, Santa Barbara, where I happened on another pair of mentors who were to take me on a different route to Vygotsky. Judith Green and Carol Dixon had been constructing a research collective of professors, graduate students, and local classroom teachers who were also fellows of the South Coast Writing Project. By joining the Santa Barbara Classroom Discourse Group, I encountered a research methodology that both fit and greatly enriched my philosophical perspective. I also found a research collective in which the mentors and novices learned from and supported each other continually throughout their work together. I was doing ethnographic classroom research with the best, and I used my knowledge and experience with Vygotsky's theories to explain what was going on in the classrooms where we researched with teachers and students. While I was working on my dissertation, the mentoring relationship evolved as I would E-mail Joan. By "talking it out" over E-mail, I was making sense of Vygotsky's work while Joan was also encountering different interpretations of Vygotsky. Vygotsky's principle of thinking and speaking was prevailing through the electronic medium.

Years Later: The Mentoring Continues

So here we are together, years later, still out on that limb. Our roles are changing, our experiences have varied, and our sociocultural context has evolved; the world has changed. By reflecting on our journaling with each other over the past ten years, it is clear to us that our roles have often been fluid and flexible, depending on the context in which we were working. As there were no set boundaries constraining the roles within our mentoring relationship, we were both able to grow in our collaborative efforts, resulting in richer understandings of mentoring. Because our assumptions allowed our roles to change and grow, the zones of possibilities for each of us were and continue to be unlimited.

The mentor in one context is not assured of that role in another context. In any mentoring relationship, there is a dialectical relationship between a mentor and an apprentice or novice, just as there is between a teacher and a learner. This dynamic relationship is reciprocal, depending on the sociocultural context. As we were thinking through this concluding chapter, we realized how a Vygotskian relationship of mentor–novice can be likened to a spark plug, as suggested by John-Steiner

(1997). The teacher–mentor brings the spark; where it goes with the learner/apprentice is unknown, unlimited, and uncontrollable. In return, the novice offers a spark for the mentor as the collaboration prompts the mentor to reenvision the issue at hand.

In our own way, we have continued to build on the collaborative effort we started back in that graduate class. However, our discussions and collaborations have changed considerably. Over the past four years, we have shared syllabi with each other. Over E-mail, we have brainstormed ways to use contract grades in our respective courses. We have written some articles together and huddled over one computer in Turlock. We have written other articles together, using dueling laptop computers as we took over the dining room table in Las Vegas. We have worked in hotel rooms at conferences, and we even wrote a book chapter together one summer month via E-mail, LeAnn in Las Vegas and Joan in South Dakota. Our mentoring journey has been eventful, successfully collaborative, mostly joyful, and never boring. The only serious battles we've had, were with our computers. We've even managed to bridge the communication gap between Mac and PC most of the time!

While our mentoring relationship with each other continues, in our own respective educational spaces we have taken up the mentoring process with others. The relationships and networking with students, classroom teachers, and colleagues continually add to our learning process. The work of Vygotsky continues to be a basis for our work. As we were writing this book, LeAnn's discussions with her colleague, Nancy Gallavan, led to the serendipity of the inclusion of the Cultural Competencies Model. In their conversations together at the university, Nancy was working through her extensive background on cultural diversity, making sense of the Vygotskian theories as LeAnn explained them. Vygotsky's work resonated with Nancy's own classroom observations and experiences from which she derived the model. In explaining the model, LeAnn was making sense of it through her own experiences of working with Joan.

We recognized that Nancy's process of coming to understand Vygotsky was an example of how John-Steiner and Meehan (2000) expressed interdependence and social construction as complementarity, or the creative convergence of thought from different disciplines or perspectives. Through our discussions, we recognized the complementarity of our perspectives. Thus, we presented the Gallavan Cultural Competencies Model through a Vygotskian context in this way: First, the components of information, access, and opportunity fit Vygotsky's pedagogical principle of thought, language, and experience providing information to know. Second, the sources that influence those components are participants in our sociocultural context, offering access to go. Third, in the zone of proximal development we can envision the outcomes made available through opportunity to do problem solving with others so that we move from what we cannot do today (red light) to what we can, with help from others (yellow light), into independent problem solving (green light) as we reformulate and transform our learning. Combining these constructs extends our thinking and helps us apply the ideas in different settings and under different conditions.

New Directions: Our Mentoring Grows and Changes

Reflecting on the quotation (John-Steiner, 1997) at the beginning of this chapter, we see that a Vygotskian mentoring experience indeed can transform a *novice* into an *experienced thinker*. Years ago LeAnn wrote, "Vygotsky who?" in her journal. Recently, she wrote to Joan in an E-mail:

> *Learning and development are reciprocally and dynamically interwoven processes, which occur formally, and informally across many settings, one of which is the classroom. To understand what is available to be known and how it is constructed, we must examine what is occurring within the intersubjective spaces as participants interact with each other. To further understand the notion of intersubjectivity, I have outlined a set of constructs that, taken together, offer a complex look at classroom discursive practices and processes: intertextuality, intercontextuality, and consequential progressions.*

Joan replied on E-mail:

> *You've come a long way since Vygotsky who? What is the difference between intertextuality and intercontextuality, and how will the readers remember it?*

LeAnn's reply began:

> *Well Joan, imagine that we were taking a trip together to New York City. You missed the plane, but I continued on the journey and met up with you the next day....*

Summary

We hope that, for our readers, it is now obvious that the Vygotskian legacy is not only a theory for us. It is exactly what we have lived. The mentor, Joan, of ten years ago has consistently been led to reexamine, rethink, and regenerate her principles and practices as the assumed novice, LeAnn, invigorated, expanded, and transformed pedagogical insights. Vygotsky's concept of mentoring is reciprocal; so was ours.

From Vygotsky we have come to know that our experience has primacy in our learning, and that experience is reflected in our language and our thoughts. The sociocultural, historical context of the teacher and the learner becomes a zone of proximal development that informs both active participants through this dialectical experience.

We suggest that the dialectic of the mentor–apprentice relationship is the same as that of teacher–learner. It is through the original metaphor of the water drop that these seeming opposites are unified. As the relationships between teaching–learning develop, inquiry is the unifying principle.

This has been a book about the importance of *teaching, learning*, and *developing* from a Vygotskian perspective. We have *developed* in new and surprising ways through our sociocultural context. Our development brings us to a place where we are partners in our learning and teaching. Sometimes we are teachers, learners, professors, practitioners, inquirers, but we are always teaching, learning, and developing.

For some this book may be about new thoughts and new language. However, we remind you that these ideas are grounded in the antiquities of dialectical learning. The ideas of Vygotsky have a long tradition that we are simply revisiting as we listen to the voice of the past who leads us to the future. Vygotsky's notions of mentoring can also be illustrated by an excerpt from the Talmud (Yeager, 1999) that two bilingual teacher–researchers in our community share with students in their classes.

> To look is one thing.
> To see what you look at is another.
> To understand what you see is a third.
> To learn from what you understand is still something else.
> But to act on what you learn is
> All that really matters.

REFERENCES

Bakhtin, M. M. (1981). *The dialogic imagination: Four essays by M. M. Bakhtin* (M. Holquist, Trans.). Austin: University of Texas Press.

Ball, A. F. (2000). Teachers' developing philosophies on literacy and their use in urban schools: A Vygotskian perspective. In C. D. Lee & P. Smagorinsky (Eds.), *Vygotskian perspectives on literacy research: Constructing meaning through collaborative inquiry* (pp. 226–255). New York: Cambridge University Press.

Bandura, A. (1977). *Social learning theory.* Upper Saddle River, NJ: Prentice Hall.

Bialystok, E., & Hakuta, K. (1994). *In other words.* New York: Basic Books.

Blanck, G. (1990). The man and his cause. In L. C. Moll (Ed.), *Vygotsky and education: Instructional implications of sociohistorical psychology* (pp. 31–58). New York: Cambridge University Press.

Bloome, D. (1989). *The social construction of intertextuality in classroom literacy learning.* Paper presented at the American Educational Research Association, San Francisco.

Bloome, D., & Bailey, F. M. (1992). Studying language and literacy through events, particularity, and intertextuality. In R. Beach, J. L. Green, M. L. Kamil, & T. Shanahan (Eds.), *Multidisciplinary perspectives on literacy research* (pp. 181–210). Urbana, IL: National Council of Teachers of English.

Bloome, D., & Egan-Robertson, A. (1993). The social construction of intertextuality in classroom reading and writing lessons. *Reading Research Quarterly, 28*(4), 305–333.

Brandts, L. (1999). Are pullout programs sabotaging classroom community in our elementary schools? *Primary Voices K–6, 7*(3), 9–15.

Bruner, J. (1987). Prologue to the English edition. In R. W. Rieber & A. S. Carton (Eds.), *The collected works of L. S. Vygotsky* (Vol. 1, pp. 1–16). New York: Plenum.

Bruner, J. (1996, September 15). *Celebrating diversity: Piaget and Vygotsky.* Paper presented at the Vygotsky–Piaget Conference of the Second Congress of Sociocultural Research, Geneva.

Cazden, C. (1981). Performance before competence: Assistance to child discourse in the zone of proximal development. *Quarterly Newsletter of the Laboratory of Comparative Human Cognition, 3*(1), 5–8.

Charles, C. M. *The synergetic classroom: Joyful teaching and gentle discipline.* New York: Addison Wesley Longman.

Christie, F. (1995). Pedagogic discourse in the primary school. *Linguistics and Education, 7,* 221–242.

Cochran-Smith, M. (1984). *The making of a reader.* Norwood, NJ: Ablex.

Cole, M. (1996). *Cultural psychology: A once and future discipline.* Cambridge, MA: Harvard University Press.

Cole, M., & Engestrom, Y. (1993). A cultural-historical approach to distributed cognition. In G. Saolomon (Ed.), *Distributed cognitions: Psychological and educational considerations* (pp. 1–46). New York: Cambridge University Press.

Collins, E., & Green, J. (1992). Learning in classroom settings: Making or breaking a culture. In H. Marshall (Ed.), *Redefining student learning: Roots of educational change* (pp. 59–86). Norwood, NJ: Ablex.

Crook, C. (1994). *Computers and the collaborative experience of learning.* London: Routledge.

Cummins, J. (1989). *Empowering minority students.* Sacramento: California Association of Bilingual Education.

Cummins, J. (1996). *Negotiating identities: Education for empowerment in a diverse society.* Ontario, California: California Association for Bilingual Education.

Cummins, J. (1999). Alternative paradigms in bilingual education research: Does theory have a place? *Educational Researcher, 28*(7), 26–32.

Davydov, V. V. (1997). Introduction: Lev Vygotsky and educational psychology, *Educational psychology* (pp. xxi–xxxix). Boca Raton, FL: St. Lucie.

Davydov, V. V., & Zinchenko, V. P. (1993). Vygotsky's contribution to the development of psychology. In H. Daniels (Ed.), *Charting the agenda: Educational activity after Vygotsky* (pp. 93–106). New York: Routledge.

del Río, P., & Álvarez, A. (1995). Directivity: The cultural and educational construction of morality and agency. Some questions arising from the legacy of Vygotsky. *Anthropology and Education Quarterly, 26*(4), 384–409.

Dewey, J. (1954). *The public and its problems.* Athens, OH: The Swallow Press.

Dewey, J. (1991). *The school and society and the child and the curriculum (A centennial publication).* Chicago: University of Chicago Press.

Dixon, C., & Horn, H. (1995). Writing across the curriculum. In J. H. Block, S. T. Everson, & T. G. Guskey (Eds.), *School improvement programs* (pp. 247–64). New York: Scholastic.

Durán, R. P., & Szymanski, M. H. (1995). Cooperative learning interaction and construction of activity. *Discourse Processes, 10*(1), 149–164.

Durán, R. P., & Szymanski, M. H. (1996). *Assessing framing of literacy activity among bilingual students.* Santa Barbara: University of California, Santa Barbara.

Dyson, A. H. (2000). Linking writing and community development through Children's Forum. In C. D. Lee & P. Smagorinsky (Eds.), *Vygotskian perspectives on literacy research: Constructing meaning through collaborative inquiry* (pp. 127–149). New York: Cambridge University Press.

Edwards, D., & Mercer, N. (1987). *Common knowledge: The development of understanding in the classroom.* Cambridge, MA: Routledge.

Emihovich, C., & Souza Lima, E. (1995). The many facets of Vygotsky: A cultural–historical voice from the future. *Anthropology and Education Quarterly, 26*(4), 375–383.

Erickson, F., & Shultz, J. (1981). When is the context. In J. Green & C. Wallat (Eds.), *Ethnography and language in educational settings.* Norwood, NJ: Ablex.

Faltis, C. (1993). *Joinfostering: Adapting teaching strategies for the multilingual classroom.* New York: Macmillan.

Faltis, C. J. (1996). *Joinfostering: Adapting teaching for the multilingual classroom.* (2nd ed.). New York: Merrill.

Faltis, C. J. (2001). *Joinfostering: Adapting teaching for the multilingual classroom.* (3rd ed.). New York: Merrill.

Fernie, D., Davies, B., Kantor, R., & McMurray, P. (1993). Becoming a person: Creating integrated gender, peer and student positionings in a preschool classroom. *International Journal of Qualitative Research in Education, 6*(2), 95–110.

Fleck, L. (1979). *Genesis and development of a scientific fact.* Chicago: Chicago University Press.

Floriani, A. (1993). Negotiating what counts: Roles and relationships, texts and contexts, content and meaning. *Linguistics and Education, 5,* 241–273.

Floriani, A. (1997). *Creating a community of learners: Opportunities for learning and negotiating meaning in a bilingual classroom.* Unpublished dissertation, University of California, Santa Barbara.

Frank, C. (1999). *Ethnographic eyes: A teacher's guide to classroom observation.* Portsmouth, NH: Heinemann.

Freeman, Y., & Freeman, D. (1994). *Between worlds: Access to second language acquisition.* Portsmouth, NH: Heinemann.

Freeman, Y., & Freeman, D. (1998). *ESL/EFL teaching principles for success.* Portsmouth, NH: Heinemann.

Freire, P. (1970). *Pedagogy of the oppressed.* New York: Seabury.

Freire, P. (1998). *Pedagogy of freedom: Ethics, democracy, and civic courage* (P. Clarke, Trans.). Lanham, MD: Rowman & Littlefield.

Gagne, R. M. (1985). *The conditions of learning* (4th ed.). New York: Holt, Reinhart, & Winston.

Gee, J. (1990). *Social linguistics and literacies: Ideology in discourse.* London: Falmer.

Goodman, K. S., Bird, L. B., & Goodman, Y. M. (1991). *The whole language catalog.* Santa Rosa, CA: American School Publishers.

Gredler, M. E. (1997). *Learning and instruction: Theory into practice.* Upper Saddle River, NJ: Prentice-Hall.

Green, J., & Dixon, C. (1993). Talking knowledge into being: Discursive and social practices in classrooms. *Linguistics and Education, 5,* 231–240.

Green, J., Kantor, R., & Rogers, T. (1991). Exploring the complexity of language and learning in the classroom. In B. Jones & L. Idol (Eds.), *Educational values and cognitive instruction: Implications for reform* (Vol. 2, pp. 333–364). Hillsdale, NJ: Erlbaum.

Green, J. L., & Meyer, L. A. (1991). The embeddedness of reading in classroom life: Reading as a situated process. In C. Baker & A. Luke (Eds.), *Towards a critical sociology of reading pedagogy* (pp. 141–160). Philadelphia: John Benjamins.

Griffen, P., & Cole, M. (Eds.). (1984). *Current activity for the future: The Zo-ped* (Vol. 23). San Francisco: Jossey-Bass.

Gutierrez, K. D., & Stone, L. D. (2000). Synchronic and diachronic dimensions of social practice: An emerging methodology for cultural-historical perpectives on literacy learning. In C. D. Lee & P. Smagorinsky (Eds.), *Vygotskian perspectives on literacy research: Constructing meaning through collaborative inquiry* (pp. 150–164). New York: Cambridge University Press.

Harste, J. C., Woodward, V. A., & Burke, C. L. (1984). *Language stories and literacy lessons.* Portsmouth, NH: Heinemann.

Heard, A. (May 25,1970). Academic ambassador. *Newsweek,* 69.

Heath, S. B. (1993). Inner city life through drama: Imagining the language classroom. *TESOL Quarterly, 27*(2), 177–192.

Heras, A. I. (1993). The construction of understanding in a sixth grade bilingual classroom. *Linguistics and Education, 5,* 275–299.

Holzman, L. H. (1996). Pragmatism and dialectical materialism. In H. Daniels (Ed.), *An introduction to Vygotsky* (pp. 75–98). New York: Routledge.

Horton, M., & Freire, P. (1990). *We make the road by walking.* Philadelphia: Temple University Press.

Hruby, G. G. (2001). Sociological, postmodern, and new realism perspectives in social constructionism: Implications for literacy research. *Reading Research Quarterly, 36*(1), 48–62.

Jennings, L. (1996). *Multiple contexts for learning social justice: An ethnographic and sociolinguistic study of a fifth grade bilingual classroom.* Unpublished dissertation, University of California, Santa Barbara.

John-Steiner, V. (1996). *Knowledge construction in creativity.* Paper presented at the NCTE Research Conference.

John-Steiner, V. (1997). *Notebooks of the mind: Explorations of thinking.* Oxford: Oxford University Press.

John-Steiner, V., & Mahn, H. (1996). Sociocultural approaches to learning and development: A Vygotskian framework. *Educational Psychologist, 31.*

John-Steiner, V., & Meehan, T. M. (2000). Creativity and collaboration in knowledge construction. In C. D. Lee & P. Smagorinsky (Eds.), *Vygotskian perspectives on literacy research: Constructing meaning through collaborative inquiry* (pp. 31–50). New York: Cambridge University Press.

John-Steiner, V., Panofsky, C. P., & Smith, L. W. (1994). *Sociocultural approaches to language and literacy: An interactionist perspective.* Cambridge, UK; Cambridge University Press.

John-Steiner, V., & Souberman, E. (1978). Afterword in L. S. Vygotsky, *Mind in society: The development of higher psychological processes.* Cambridge: Harvard University Press.

Kennedy, Kathleen (1993). *The effects of complex instruction on the ctbs reading comprehension scores, and on the academic and non-academic development of sixth grade students.* Unpublished thesis, California State University, Turlock.

Kohl, H. (1994). *I won't learn from you: And other thoughts on creative maladjustment.* New York: The New Press.

Kohn, A. (2000). *The case against standardized testing: Raising the scores, ruining the schools.* Portsmouth, NH: Heinemann.

Kozulin, A. (1986). The concept of activity in Soviet psychology: Vygotsky, his disciples and critics. *American Psychologist, March,* 264–274.

Kozulin, A. (1990). *Vygotsky's psychology: A biography of ideas.* Cambridge, MA: Harvard University Press.

Krashen, S. D. (1990). *How reading and writing make you smarter, or, how smart people read and write.* Paper presented at the Georgetown Round Table on Languages and Linguistics, Washington, DC.

Krashen, S. D. (1996). *Under attack: The case against bilingual education.* Culver City, CA: Language Education Associates.

Kuhn, T. S. (1970). *The structure of scientific revolutions* (2nd ed.). Chicago: University of Chicago Press.

Lankshear, C., & McLaren, P. L. (1993). Introduction. In C. Lankshear & P. L. McLaren (Eds.), *Critical literacy: Politics, praxis, and the postmodern* (pp. 1–56). Albany, NY: State University of New York Press.

Lantolf, J. (2000). *Sociocultural theory and second language learning.* New York: Oxford University Press.

Lave, J., & Wenger, E. (1991). *Situated learning: Legitimate peripheral participation.* Cambridge, UK: Cambridge University Press.

Lee, C. D. (2000). Signifying in the zone of proximal development. In C. D. Lee & P. Smagorinsky (Eds.), *Vygotskian perspectives on literacy research: Constructing meaning through collaborative inquiry* (pp. 191–225). New York: Cambridge University Press.

Lee, C. D., & Smagorinsky, P. (Eds.). (2000). *Vygotskian perspectives on literacy research: Constructing meaning through collaborative inquiry.* New York: Cambridge University Press.

Leontiev, A. N. (1981). *Problems in development of mind.* Moscow: Progress.

Lin, L. (1993). Language of and in the classroom: Constructing the patterns of social life. *Linguistics and Education, 5,* 367–409.

Luria, A. R. (1979). *The making of mind.* Cambridge, MA: Harvard University Press.

Marshall, H. (1988). Work or learning: Implications of classroom metaphors. *Educational Researcher, 17,* 9–16.

Marshall, H. (Ed.). (1992a). *Redefining student learning: Roots of educational change.* Norwood, NJ: Ablex.

Marshall, H. (1992b). *Reconceptualizing learning for restructured schools.* Paper presented at the American Educational Research Association Meeting, San Francisco.

Marshall, H. (1992c). Seeing, redefining, and supporting student learning. In H. Marshall (Ed.), *Redefining student learning: Roots of educational change.* (pp. 1–32). Norwood, NJ: Ablex.

Minick, N. (1987). The development of Vygotsky's thought: An introduction. In R. W. Rieber & A. S. Carton (Eds.), *The collected works of L. S. Vygotsky.* New York: Plenum.

Moll, L. (1990). *Vygotsky and education.* New York: Cambridge University Press.

Moll, L. (2000). Inspired by Vygotsky: Ethnographic experiments in education. In C. D. Lee & P. Smagorinsky (Eds.), *Vygotskian perspectives on literacy research: Constructing meaning through collaborative inquiry* (pp. 256–268). New York: Cambridge University Press.

Moll, L., & Greenberg, J. B. (1990). Creating zones of possibilities: Combining social contexts for instruction. In L. C. Moll (Ed.), *Vygotsky and education: Instructional implications of sociohistorical psychology* (pp. 319–348). New York: Cambridge University Press.

Mumsford, L. (1956). *The transformations of man.* New York: Harper.

Newman, D., Griffen, P., & Cole, M. (1989). *The construction zone: Working for cognitive change in school.* Cambridge, UK: Cambridge University Press.

Newman, F., & Holzman, L. (1993). *Lev Vygotsky: Revolutionary scientist.* London: Routledge.

Newman, J. W. (1998). *America's teachers: An introduction to education.* New York: Addison Wesley Longman.

Nieto, S. (1996). *Affirming diversity: The sociopolitical context of multicultural education.* White Plains, NY: Longman.

Oakes, J., & Lipton, M. (1999). *Teaching to change the world.* New York: McGraw Hill College.

Palincsar, A. S., & Brown, A. L. (1986). Interactive teaching to promote independent learning from text. *Reading Teacher, 39*(8), 771–777.

Phillips, J. (1975). *The origins of intellect: Piaget's theory.* San Francisco: W. H. Freeman.

Piaget, J. (1971). *The construction of reality in the child.* New York: Ballantine.

Popham, W. J. (1998). *Your school should not be evaluated by standardized test scores.* [Online essay], 8–26. Available at: http://www.aasa.org/issues_and_insights/assessment/8_26_98_Popham_standardized.htm, American Association of School Administrators.

Prawat, R. (1993). The value of ideas: Problems versus possibilities in learning. *Educational Researcher, 22*(6), 5–16.

Putney, L. G. (1996). You are it: Meaning making as a collective and historical process. *Australian Journal of Language and Literacy, 19*(2), 129–143.

Putney, L. G. (1997). *Collective–individual development in a fifth grade bilingual classroom: An interactional ethnographic analysis of historicity and consequentiality.* Unpublished Dissertation, University of California, Santa Barbara.

Putney, L. G., & Floriani, A. (1999). Examining transformative processes and practices: A cross-case analysis of life in two bilingual classrooms. *Journal of Classroom Interaction, 34*(2), 17–29.

Putney, L. G., Green, J. L., Dixon, C. N., Durán, R., & Yeager, B. (2000). Consequential progressions: Exploring collective–individual development in a bilingual classroom. In C. D. Lee & P. Smagorinsky (Eds.), *Vygotskian perspectives on literacy research: Constructing meaning through collaborative inquiry* (pp. 86–126). New York: Cambridge University Press.

Putney, L. G., Green, J. L., Dixon, C. N., & Kelly, G. (1999). Evolution of qualitative research methodology: Looking beyond defense to possibilities. *Reading Research Quarterly, 34*(3), 368–377.

Putney, L. G., & Wink, J. (1998). Breaking rules: Constructing avenues of access in multilingual classrooms. *TESOL Journal, 7*(3), 29–34.

Putney, L., Wu, Y., & Wink, J. (1999). What can English-dominant teachers do in a multilingual context? Stop, think, and proceed with care. *California Reader, 32*(2), 10–15.

Rieber, R. W., & Carton, A. S. (1987). *The collected works of L. S. Vygotsky.* New York: Plenum.

Rogoff, B. (1990). *Apprenticeship in thinking: Cognitive development in social context.* Oxford: Oxford University Press.

Rogoff, B. (1994). Developing understanding of the idea of communities of learners. *Mind, Culture, and Activity, 1,* 209–229.

Rommetveit, R. (1979). Deep structure of sentence versus message structure: Some critical remarks on current paradigms, and suggestions for an alternative approach. In R. Rommetveit & R. Blakar (Eds.), *Studies of language, thought and verbal communication.* London: Academic.

Ryan, W. (1976). *Blaming the victim.* New York: Vintage.

Santa Barbara Classroom Discourse Group. (1992a). Constructing literacy in classrooms: Literate actions as social accomplishments. In H. Marshall (Ed.), *Redefining student learning: Roots of educational change* (pp. 119–150). Norwood, NJ: Ablex.

Santa Barbara Classroom Discourse Group. (1992b). Do you see what we see? The referential and intertextual nature of classroom life. *Journal of Classroom Interaction, 27*(2), 29–36.

Sarason, S. B. (1990). *The predictable failure of educational reform: Can we change course before it's too late?* San Francisco: Jossey-Bass.

Shepel, E. N. L. (1995). Teacher self-identification in culture from Vygotsky's developmental perspective. *Anthropology and Education Quarterly, 26*(4), 425–442.

Shor, I. (1999). What is critical literacy? In I. Shor & C. Pari (Eds.), *Critical literacy in action: Writing words, changing worlds* (pp. 1–30). Portsmouth, NH: Boynton/Cook.

Skinner, B. F. (1969). *Contingencies of reinforcement.* New York: Appleton-Century-Crofts.

Smagorinsky, P., & O'Donnell-Allen, C. (2000). Idiocultural diversity in small groups: The role of the relational framework in collaborative learning. In C. D. Lee & P. Smagorinsky (Eds.), *Vygotskian perspectives on literacy research: Constructing meaning through collaborative inquiry* (pp. 165–190). New York: Cambridge University Press.

Smith, F. (1998). *The book of learning and forgetting.* New York: Teacher's College Press.

Souza Lima, E. (1995). Culture revisited: Vygotsky's ideas in Brazil. *Anthropology and Education Quarterly, 26*(4), 443–457.

Tharp, R. G., & Gallimore, R. (1988). *Rousing minds to life.* New York: Cambridge University Press.

Thorndike, E. L. (1905). *The elements of psychology.* New York: A. G. Seiler.

Tolstoy, L. (1903). *Pedagogicheskie stat'e (Pedagogical writings).* Moscow: Kusherev.

Tudge, J. (1990). Vygotsky, the zone of proximal development, and peer collaboration: Implications for classroom practice. In L. C. Moll (Ed.), *Vygotsky and education: Instructional implications and applications of sociohistorical psychology* (pp. 155–174). Cambridge, UK: Cambridge University Press.

Tuyay, S., Jennings, L., & Dixon, C. (1995). Classroom discourse and opportunities to learn: An ethnographic study of knowledge construction in a bilingual third-grade classroom. *Discourse Processes, 10*(1), 75–110.

Valsiner, J. (1988). *Developmental psychology in the Soviet Union.* Bloomington, IN: Indiana University Press.

Van der Veer, R., & Valsiner, J. (1991). *Understanding Vygotsky: A quest for synthesis.* Cambridge, MA: Basil Blackwell.

Vygodskaya, G. L. (1995). His life. *School Psychology International, 16*(2), 105–116.

Vygotsky, L. S. (1962). *Thought and language* (E. H. G. Vakar, Trans.). Cambridge, MA: MIT Press.

Vygotsky, L. S. (1978). *Mind in society: The development of higher psychological processes.* Cambridge, MA: Harvard University Press.

Vygotsky, L. S. (1981). The genesis of higher mental functions. In J. V. Wertsch (Ed.), *The concept of activity in Soviet psychology* (pp. 144–188). Armonk, NY: Sharpe.

Vygotsky, L. S. (1982–84). *Collected works,* (2 vols.). Moscow: Progress.

Vygotsky, L. S. (1986). *Thought and language.* Cambridge, MA: MIT Press.

Vygotsky, L. S. (1987). *The collected works of L. S. Vygotsky* (N. Minick, Trans. Vol. 1). New York: Plenum.

Vygotsky, L. S. (1993). *The collected works of L. S. Vygotsky* (Vol. 2). New York: Plenum.

Vygotsky, L. S. (1997). *Educational psychology* (R. Silverman, Trans.). Boca Raton, FL: St. Lucie.

Wadsworth, B. J. (1996). *Piaget's theory of cognitive and affective development: Foundations of constructivism* (5th ed.). White Plains, NY: Longman.

Watson, J. B. (1913). Psychology as the behaviorist sees it. *Psychological Bulletin, 20,* 158–177.

Wells, G. (Ed.). (1994). *Changing schools from within: Creating communities of inquiry.* Toronto, Canada: The Ontario Institute for Studies in Education.

Wells, G. (1999). *Dialogic inquiry: Toward a sociocultural practice and theory of education.* Cambridge, UK: Cambridge University Press.

Wells, G. (2000). Dialogic inquiry in education: Building on the legacy of Vygotsky. In C. D. Lee & P. Smagorinsky (Eds.), *Vygotskian perspectives on literacy research: Constructing meaning through collaborative inquiry* (pp. 51–85). New York: Cambridge University Press.

Wells, G., & Chang-Wells, G. J. (1992). *Constructing knowledge together: Classrooms as centers of inquiry and literacy.* Portsmouth, NH: Heinemann.

Wertsch, J. (1985). *Vygotsky and the social formation of mind.* Cambridge, MA: Harvard University Press.

Wertsch, J. (1991). *Voices of the mind.* Cambridge, MA: Harvard University Press.

Wertsch, J. (2000). Vygotsky's two minds on the nature of meaning. In C. D. Lee & P. Smagorinsky (Eds.), *Vygotskian perspectives on literacy research: Constructing meaning through collaborative inquiry* (pp. 19–30). New York: Cambridge University Press.

Wertsch, J., & Tulviste, P. (1996). L. S. Vygotsky and contemporary developmental psychology. In H. Daniels (Ed.), *An introduction to Vygotsky* (pp. 53–74). New York: Routledge.

Wink, J. (1991). *The emergence of the framework for intervention in bilingual education.* Unpublished Dissertation, Texas A&M University.

Wink, J. (1997). *Critical pedagogy: Notes from the real world.* White Plains, NY: Addison Wesley Longman.

Wink, J. (2000). *Critical pedagogy: Notes from the real world* (2nd ed.). White Plains, NY: Addison Wesley Longman.

Wink, J., & Putney, L. G. (2000). Turning transformative principles into practice: Strategies for English dominant teachers in a multilingual context. In R. D. J. Tinajero (Ed.), *The power of two languages: Effective dual language use across the curriculum for academic success* (revised ed.) New York: Macmillan.

Wink, J., Putney, L., & Bravo-Lawrence, I. (1995, January/February). Socioculturally learning:

What in the world does it mean? *CABE Newsletter, 17,* 8–9, 22.

Wood, D., Bruner, J., & Ross, S. (1976). The role of tutoring in problem-solving. *Journal of Child Psychology and Psychiatry, 17,* 89–100.

Woolfolk, A. E. (1998). *Educational psychology* (7th ed.). Boston, MA: Allyn & Bacon.

Yaroshevsky, M. (1989). *Lev Vygotsky: Outstanding Soviet psychologists* (S. Syrovatkin, Trans.). Moscow: Progress.

Yeager, B. (1999). Constructing a community of inquirers. *Primary Voices K–6, 7*(3), 37–52.

Yeager, B., Pattenaude, I., Fránquiz, M., & Jennings, L. (1999). Rights, respect, and responsibility: Toward a theory of action in two bilingual classrooms. In J. Robertson (Ed.), *Elementary voices: Teaching for a tolerant world K–6* (pp. 196–218). Urbana, IL: National Council of Teachers of English.

Zebroski, J. T. (1994). *Thinking through theory: Vygotskian perspectives on the teaching of writing.* Portsmouth, NH: Boynton/Cook.

INDEX